Reshaping Your INVESTMENT STRATEGIES for the 1980s

Henry B. Zimmer
V. Jeanne Kaufman

Reshaping Your INVESTMENT STRATEGIES for the 1980s

A TOTEM BOOK
Toronto

First published 1982
by Collins Publishers
100 Lesmill Road, Don Mills, Ontario

This new edition published 1983
by TOTEM BOOKS
a division of Collins Publishers
100 Lesmill Road, Don Mills, Ontario

Canadian Cataloguing in Publication Data
Zimmer, Henry B., 1944–
  Reshaping your investment strategies for the 1980s

  ISBN 0-00-217120-1

  1. Investments. 2. Finance, Personal. I. Kaufman,
V. Jeanne. II. Title.

HG5421.Z45 1983   332.6'78   C83-098826-2

Composed by Attic Typesetting Inc.
Designed by David Shaw & Associates Ltd.

Contents

Acknowledgements

We wish to dedicate this book to Prime Minister Pierre Elliott Trudeau, former Finance Minister Allan J. MacEachen and U.S. President Ronald Reagan, whose budgets and policies have made it necessary for all of us to reshape our investment strategies for today.

We would also like to thank Doug Henderson of Dominion Securities Ames and Peter Ohler of Masters Gallery in Calgary for their advice on specialized areas of investment and art, respectively.

Special thanks go to our editors, Margaret Paull of Collins Publishers and Ingrid Philipp Cook, for their direction in organizing our material.

Our sincere appreciation to Shana Zimmer who once again provided long hours of painstaking work and technical assistance.

CHAPTER ONE

Financial Perspectives for the 1980s

If you have taken the trouble to pick this book up off the shelf—even if you haven't bought it yet—you probably already realize that the 1980s are just not going to be the same for most Canadians as the 1970s. If the 1970s had to be summarized in one word, that word would be "inflation". At the end of the decade, we all understood that inflation eroded away at our capital and decreased the purchasing power of our money. If we kept our savings in interest-bearing deposits, a combination of inflation and taxes created actual monetary losses. We came to realize that there was no longer any sense in saving money slowly towards eventual security. Instead, large numbers of often inexperienced investors were attracted to new areas for investment. Hence, we experienced the gold rush of the 1970s, an enormous boom in real estate, and a massive movement of funds into the stock market in the quest for a hedge against inflation. The experts' unanimous advice was to invest for capital growth and not immediate income.

The 1970s saw the emergence of new corporate giants and the decline and fall of others as businesses struggled to come to grips with the reduction in the real purchasing power of their earned profits. Investors and analysts began to disregard corporate balance sheets, which now bore no relationship to the real value of business assets. Debt commitments of large companies rose dramatically as they too joined in the mad scramble to borrow funds not only to maintain their levels of operations, but also to produce growth for their shareholders.

At the end of the decade, in spite of rising interest costs, most Canadians were still eager to borrow for investment purposes, in order to take advantage of the high inflation. Fortunes were made as a result of changes in monetary conditions and not necessarily changes in the values of the investments themselves.

Then, perhaps when least expected, circumstances suddenly changed. Probably the one man who will have the greatest impact on history over the next few decades is U.S. President Ronald Reagan. Certainly, any politician who ran for high office in the 1970s vowed in his campaign to wage war against inflation. However, only Mr. Reagan was actually serious! Mr. Reagan promised that he would end the inflation of the 1970s by instituting cutbacks in spending and limiting incentives for speculation. Specifically, we have seen the United States impose a very substantial upward adjustment of interest rates, which has filtered through to other countries, including Canada. The increased costs of borrowing money slowed economic growth dramatically as business owners and investors began to see that the change was more than just temporary. The abrupt reversal in government policies has created its own unique set of problems. Efforts to "lick" inflation have resulted in recession and unemployment levels in North America have gradually become intolerable. Although interest rates have moderated somewhat in the fall of 1982, there is no guarantee that this trend won't be reversed. If high rates of interest persist, an imminent economic recovery becomes very unlikely indeed.

Ironically, the "little guy" is always the person who draws the short straw. During highly inflationary times, it is the pensioner on a fixed income who suffers the most. On the other hand, during a recession, the pensioner finds that his dollars will buy more goods and services. But then someone else suffers—the wage earner who is the first one laid off when his employer cuts back in spending. Massive layoffs decrease production and compound the downward spiral.

This book will help you restructure your investment strategies in order to survive during hard times and prosper when the economic situation eventually turns around. It should be of great benefit to anyone with a family income of $30,000 a year or more. You will see that in order to survive the turbulent 1980s, you will have to invest. Otherwise, for reasons discussed in Chapter Four, if you stand still you will continue to lose ground financially. You will see that the suggestions in this book cover a wide range of topics, and will appeal to all investors—from the most conservative to the most aggressive. A major emphasis is that *any investment policy must be tailored to the comfort level and lifestyle of the individual*. You will see that the principles or basics of any investments can be easily understood if you just take a little time and make some effort. Then you can decide what avenues are suitable for your circumstances. During the 1970s, books by people explaining how *they* made millions of dollars were popular. Today, these are of little value since so much has changed.

The purpose of *this* book is not to debate economic issues or policies but to accept facts as they are and try to provide suggestions so that you may better adapt to the investment climate of the 1980s. In our opinion, there is no single ironclad investment pattern into which anyone must unwillingly force himself. There is also no single secure long-term investment. In other words, there is nothing that we are aware of into which you can place your investment capital today, forget about for a period of ten or fifteen years, and suddenly find yourself exceptionally wealthy at the end. The key to investing in the 1980s is flexibility.

Perhaps the most important point is that with a proper investment strategy, you can make large profits both in good times and in bad. There are always opportunities. On October 29, 1929, when the stock market crashed, more than sixteen million shares were traded. The history books report that everyone wanted to sell out. However, we all overlook the fact that in order for these sales to take place, *someone* had to *buy* sixteen million shares, too. Perhaps the purchasers, in retrospect, did not make good investments although they certainly felt that there was an opportunity to make money. There are always so many differences of opinion that in almost all economic situations there are opportunities to capitalize by either buying or selling.

At this point, we have come to a major crossroads. The recession that began in 1981 may be our last chance to mend our ways and reform our national spending habits before it is too late. However, if interest rates continue high in times of recession, the current "hard times" could easily develop into the next depression. On the other hand, if interest rates moderate substantially and the government begins to print money to cover its ever-increasing deficit, we could have hyperinflation. At the time this is being written, the future is certainly uncertain. It is conceivable that U.S. President Reagan will be forced to back down permanently from his tight monetary policies. Many governments are trying to persuade the United States to retain lower interest rates. Mr. Reagan may have no choice if one of the underdeveloped countries that owes the U.S. Government and American banks untold millions of dollars defaults on its obligations. Then, the United States may be forced to "reinflate" in order to prevent American lending institutions from going bankrupt.

Alternatively, Canadians could decide to try to become masters of their own destiny. It is possible (but not likely) that we could have a "made in Canada" interest rate of around 12%. This approach would create its own set of problems. There would have to be currency export restrictions, the Canadian dollar would drop even further and imports would become much more expensive. To make the program work—at least for a while—would probably also require not just voluntary, but mandatory, wage and price controls. In spite of these precautions, inflation in excess of those limits with which we struggled in the past would quite probably result.

In the long run, a depression may be inevitable—whether as a result of increasing unemployment and its snowball effect on economic conditions or as a result of hyperinflation, which would render our dollar completely worthless.

It is quite likely that our government (if not that of the United States) will crank up the clattering monetary calliope for one last fling. If they do, it will literally be a dollar-junkie's dream. If we do get another blast out of this system, it will probably be on an unprecedented level. It will be a whopper—

reasonably short-lived, but a real boomer. We have no reason to believe that the government would intentionally throw its people headlong into a depression. This certainly would not bode well for re-election and Mr. Trudeau is a masterful politician. Then again, if our government persists in its policies, unemployment may get worse, more businesses may close their doors and it may soon be too late for a speedy recovery.

Where Do We Go From Here?

Many years ago, an American author by the name of Frank R. Stockton wrote a story called "The Lady, or the Tiger?" The plot was quite simple. A poor servant in the employ of the king had the audacity to fall in love with the king's daughter. When the king found out and was made to realize that the servant's love was reciprocated, he was faced with a dilemma: should he permit a marriage or not? To decide, he took a rather novel approach. The poor peasant was placed into an arena in front of a sell-out crowd one fine sunny afternoon and pointed in the direction of two closed doors. Behind one was the king's daughter and behind the other, a vicious tiger. The poor hero was asked to point towards the door that he wished to be opened and the king promised him that whatever he picked, he could "keep." Either way, the crowd was sure to get an afternoon's entertainment. While the plot of this story may be somewhat trite, Stockton took an interesting approach when it came to answering the central question posed by the story. At the very end, he left it up to the reader to surmise whether the peasant chose the lady or the tiger.

This story has its parallels in today's economic climate. The lady, of course, is inflation, which given proper investment strategy, could make all of us millionaires for a day (before we realize that our dollar has no value). The tiger, on the other hand, is a depression in which only the hardiest survive. Like Mr. Stockton, we do not choose to predict whether we will soon experience an economic revival or a complete "bust." Our economic crystal ball is as cloudy as everyone else's. Nevertheless, we can assure you that our ideas on investment strategies will prove useful no matter what "ending" our economy eventually experiences. For in real life, even in a depression, there are always opportunities to attain wealth. The key is flexibility in your investment policies and the agility to shift directions as circumstances change. This book is geared towards helping you achieve that objective.

Investment Planning for Hard Times

If the recession deepens, we suggest that you concentrate specifically on the chapters in this book dealing with investing in a principal residence, registered retirement savings plans, life insurance, and bonds and other interest-bearing investments. You will see that if you are able to hang onto your job or business, the registered retirement savings plan is a very important aspect of your personal well-being. Also, you will need to maintain as much life insurance as you can possibly afford, perhaps not to protect a large estate but to provide an ongoing income to your dependants if you should happen to die prematurely.

While buying a house may not be a good idea until you feel that the housing market has bottomed, if you already own a residence, Chapter Six will show you how important it is to pay for it. In fact, a fully-paid home is, in our opinion, your best investment whether times are good or bad. If your goal is simply to preserve your capital, Chapter Four dealing with bonds and other interest-producing investments is important. You will see that you can have your cake and eat it, too. Specifically, you can earn the prevailing rate of interest while still setting the stage for a capital-gains bonus if interest rates change. All this requires is for you to be a little bit more adventurous than simply being content with standard bank accounts or pure term deposits.

If you are more aggressive, Chapter Eight on investing in the stock market should have some appeal as well. You will see that not only is it possible to make money by buying stock at a low price and selling it at a higher price later on but that the reverse is also true. You can sell a stock which you do not own in anticipation of buying it back at a cheaper price to cover your "short" position.

Investment Planning During an Inflationary Cycle

If things turn around, as we have every reason to believe they will (sooner or later), the emphasis with which you should be reading this book becomes somewhat different. If inflation increases and the dollar declines more and more in value, it may again make good sense to become a borrower. Inflation will cause your investments to appreciate while you will be able to pay off your debt in dollars that are worth less and less. Thus, Chapter Three, To Borrow or Not to Borrow, becomes of paramount importance. You will see that you do not necessarily need large accumulations of savings to make investments. All that you require is the ability to handle debt out of excess cash flow from your job, business or profession. If your interest expense is tax-deductible, the government will subsidize this program.

Renewed inflation could signal another real estate boom, especially if interest rates drop substantially and stay down. Hence, the importance of Chapter Seven on investing in real estate. You will probably be more cautious than you might have been in the 1970s. Your objective may no longer be to acquire a piece of property as a fifteen- or twenty-year investment. Perhaps holding periods of two or three years may be more appropriate. If interest rates continue to decline and people begin to move their savings out of interest-bearing investments, the demand for gold, silver and collectibles will also start to pick up. We may not see the gold fever of the late 1970s that quickly, but bear in mind that many experts still feel that if inflation runs out of control, gold could easily reach $3,000 an ounce by the end of the decade.

Changing Your Plans

It is our hope that, unlike a popular novel, you will read this book several times over the next few years as economic conditions change and as you adjust your own goals and objectives. Of course, the chapters on financial privacy, choosing a professional, and awareness and discipline will be important no matter what happens. We may have to become used to a perpetual cycle of recessions and recoveries. It is conceivable that these cycles will become more and more exaggerated as time goes by. Each recession may be greater than the last and each recovery more inflated. However, we all owe it to ourselves to learn from past mistakes. Most people keep hoping that booms will continue regardless of signs that they will end. If by the end of 1983, you pick up your morning newspaper and see pictures of people lined up around the block in front of banks and jewellery stores to buy all available stocks of gold, then perhaps *you* should be thinking of selling.

Remember as you go through this book that regardless of the economic situation or the time in history, there is always money to be made if you are able to assess the situation and grasp an immediate advantage. You must be adaptable and you must maintain your perspective. You will read about many investment alternatives which have not ordinarily been seriously considered by most investors for significant portions of their investment portfolios in the past. These approaches should now be examined for their usefulness during a chaotic decade. We will show you how in many instances, the risks in these areas can be significantly reduced by building in "investment insurance."

This book is designed to include suggestions which are as important and useful for the small investor as they are to the person who is looking to protect and maintain several million dollars' worth of assets. Having scanned the topics, you will see that most of these are not new and they are not likely to be totally unfamiliar. However, all are being presented for reconsideration because investing in the 1980s must be approached differently than in the 1970s. You will see that if you take some initiative you can do much better than by merely reacting to what others tell you and going along with the herd. Timing is now the most crucial issue in every person's life. Many of us felt that if we missed one boom during the seventies, we would have ample opportunity to recoup during another. On the other hand, the next inflationary run-up (whenever it occurs) may be the last one in this decade.

You should also realize that although Canada and the United States are intimately involved both economically and culturally, investment attitudes in the two countries are considerably different. The investment suggestions which we have made in this book are based on a knowledge of the Canadian income tax system. This system has a much varied thrust from that of the United States. That difference is in large part the basis for the creation of this book and the emphasis of our approach. Many suggestions made in U.S. publications are simply not as applicable to Canadian investors because of differences in our tax regulations. Canadians have also never been, and are not likely to be, in the near future, as aggressive investors as their American counterparts. However, this fact in itself can make Canada a particularly interesting financial arena for those people who are able to develop an attitude which condones "guarded" risk-taking. By guarded, we mean that it is possible to take advantage of what might otherwise be a risky situation, yet by utilizing various means, limiting your loss potential.

The ups and downs of our economy over the next few years will *eventually* call for increasing security and withdrawal from risky financial situations. Financial agility, which presumes a high measure of liquidity and control on the part of an investor, is now one of the most important aspects of any investment strategy. Again, *a single approach or any single investment is not a reliable choice for an extended period of time*. People often have a tendency to realize small gains and then fail to recognize losses. As their losses become larger and larger, the gains are quickly eliminated, or worse. You will come to realize that the length of time during which any investment does represent an optimal holding may stretch from perhaps only a few weeks to over a year. You must set your own realistic objectives and make your own choices however difficult this may be. We promise that this book will help you to meet that challenge.

Today, we are at an economic juncture. Will the recession worsen or will the economy turn around and move upwards? We used the analogy of "the lady or the tiger". However, there is one basic difference. The poor peasant in the story was permitted to make *one choice only*, which would affect the rest of his life (and even his actual life span). But in your case, if you find that a particular investment strategy isn't working in the way you projected, you can always count on a second chance.

ISIPs & RHOSPs in 1983

Readers of the 1983 paperback edition of this book will, of course, be asking whether the events of the last eight or nine months are of any significance in their own attempts to reshape their investment strategies.

Actually, not much has happened. While interest rates have, in fact, moderated, the fear that this is only temporary is enough to keep most people on the sidelines away from any aggressive borrowing. We have suffered through yet another federal Budget, this time with only a few income tax changes. Our government finished the 1982/83 fiscal year with a deficit over $25-billion, and the expectation for the year now in progress is even worse—a deficit of over $30-billion. The spring Budget makes very few concrete proposals designed to turn the economy around. The major exceptions are the important new incentives offered by the Registered Home Ownership Plan and the new Indexed Security Investment Plan, which are both discussed in Chapter Fifteen. This new chapter in the book also contains our thoughts on prospects for the coming year in more detail.

CHAPTER TWO

Specific Investment Strategies

The last chapter should have convinced you to reshape your investment strategies for the 1980s, recognizing the importance of both flexibility and appropriate timing as you move from one type of investment into another. The purpose of this chapter is to help you determine where you stand in terms of investment philosophy. No matter what you choose to do, you must be comfortable with your choices. We do not mean to imply that every single person must be stereotyped. However, before going into the specifics of investing in bonds, the stock market, real estate, or anything else, for that matter, it is important that you first clearly understand your own goals and objectives.

In this chapter, we will examine the positions of five different individuals in various income categories. These are the executive, the employee or novice investor, the professional, the owner-manager of his own business and the single career woman. We will make various investment and tax planning suggestions that are appropriate for these individuals and their situations. Obviously, there is no single plan that is suitable for all executives or all professionals. A good deal depends on the living requirements of the individuals involved and the degree of aggressiveness with which each is comfortable. However, you will see that many of our suggestions are quite adaptable to people in various income brackets and with different goals and objectives.

Once we have dealt with the five profiles, we will examine a few variations. For example what strategies might be appropriate for a young professional couple who have no children and are renting a city apartment? How should an employee who is fifty-five years old and is concerned that an unwise investment may cost him his life savings protect himself? What about the widow or divorcee in her forties or fifties whose life insurance policy or property settlement has left her $50,000 to $100,000 to invest for her future?

Then, in the chapters which follow, we will examine the specifics of various types of investments and fill in all the details. When you have finished reading this book, you may want to come back to this particular chapter and reread it. You will then be in a position to fully comprehend the implications of different types of investments and how these strategies fit into *your* personal investment program.

The Executive

Profile: Extremely conservative

Age 49

Marital status: Spouse with no income; two dependent children—one in college and a second in high school

Salary: Earns $125,000 a year as president of a chocolate bar manufacturing company

Disposable income over and above living requirements: $1,500/month

Contributes $3,500 a year to his employer's pension plan

Assets:

Home—fair market value $300,000; cost $180,000

Term deposits—$180,000 at 15%

Stocks in employer's company—fair market value $20,000; cost $5,000

Liabilities: Mortgage—$75,000 at 13%, due in 3 years

Strategy

This man is typical of many executives who have few investments other than their homes and perhaps a small amount of stock in the companies they work for. His income has been substantial but he has not aggressively pursued other types of investments. In addition, his wife has no income and one of the children is now of college age. In this instance, we would first attempt to find some way to minimize his tax burden because he receives a large salary and has minimal tax exemptions. He does not qualify for a registered retirement savings program, since he contributes the maximum amount to the corporate pension plan.

To begin with, we would consider income splitting. Specifically, a promissory note should be drawn up through which he would lend $100,000 out of his present term deposits to his wife, in cash (see Chapter Four). The loan would be non-interest-bearing. She could then invest the full $100,000 in a combination of term deposits and retractable preferred shares (Chapter Eight, Investing in the Stock Market, pages 138–39). In this manner, she should be able to earn approximately $15,000 a year. If the bulk of her investment were in shares, there would be no tax payable because of the dividend tax credit (pages 135–38). However, the executive would lose his personal exemption for his wife and this would cost him about $1,500 annually. After taxes, however, the wife's investment income would be approximately $13,500. If and when there is a capital gain on these preferred shares, it would be taxed at a very low rate in the hands of the wife. A $13,500 net return on $100,000 is considerably higher than the after-tax rate of return which this executive is presently earning on his term deposits.

Since the mortgage is due in three years, the annual after-tax investment income retained by the wife should be set aside to be put down against the mortgage. Since mortgage interest on a home is not tax-deductible (see Chapter Six), one of the family's short-term goals should be to completely discharge the mortgage when it comes due in three years. This can be done by making additional annual payments (up to 10% of the original mortgage balance, in most cases) from the excess disposable income and by saving some $40,000 out of the wife's after-tax income over that same three-year period.

We then suggest that the executive lend, using a similar

promissory note, $30,000 to his child enrolled in university. This child is presently being supported in his studies by his father with after-tax dollars. Such a loan is permissible as long as the child is over the age of eighteen. Since the child has no other income, the yield on a $30,000 investment would not be taxed at all, and (at 15%) interest of $4,500 per annum could easily cover the child's living requirements. When the child graduates from university, father can simply call the loan and again lend the funds to the second child, thereby extending this entire procedure. As explained on page 55, the father should protect his investment by making specific arrangements with the bank so that the child would not be able to draw on the original capital without his father's written permission.

With $130,000 out of the family's $180,000 in term deposits now utilized, we would then recommend that the executive continue to maintain approximately $7,000 to $10,000 in term deposits in his own name. The purpose here would be to earn $1,000 of interest income each year which would be tax-free (see pages 46–47). We suggest that the remaining $40,000 be invested in gold or silver through a Swiss bank account (Chapter Thirteen), as a hedge against potential disaster. This would allow the executive to diversify his interests and spread his risks outside North America. In this particular case, the executive should not be too concerned about the short-term movements in gold or silver.

Next, the executive should examine the stock which he is presently holding. These are shares of the corporation by which he is employed. He has received these shares at a very low cost and their present value is considerably higher. However, it is not always good planning for an executive to be "married" to the shares of his corporation. He must not only review the past performance of this investment but he must consider the future potential of these shares and whether they represent a sound investment. If the executive anticipates little future growth, we suggest that he sell them, absorb the tax on the capital gain, and use the balance to make other investments. Since the executive is president of a company which manufactures chocolate bars, there is a good chance that he has some knowledge of the components that go into the manufacturing process. If he is familiar with the markets in sugar and/or cocoa beans, for example, he might consider investing the proceeds from the sale of stock in the commodities market. Of course (as described in Chapter Nine) the commodities market is risky. On the other hand, even if the executive in this case were to lose, for example, up to half of his $20,000 capital, he would still be in reasonable financial shape. He can afford to speculate — as long as he is comfortable in doing so.

If the executive finds he enjoys a slightly more aggressive approach, he could consider his equity in his house as an investment pool. If he remortgages the home or takes a further mortgage on it, and uses the funds for investment purposes, the interest expense will now be tax-deductible. The executive should therefore consider the possibility of borrowing approximately $50,000 some time in the next year either for the purchase of a real estate investment (as outlined in Chapters Two and Seven) or for an investment in Canadian public securities. Even if interest on the borrowed funds is not covered by income earned on a current basis, he can offset this interest against his taxable income from employment. He would only do this if he feels that the potential for capital gains on the sale of these investments would ultimately repay him for the after-tax interest cost which he must absorb out of his excess cash-flow from employment. Bear in mind that interest expense (when deductible) gives an individual the opportunity to earn half-taxable capital gains at a future date. This is explained fully in Chapter Seven.

Certainly, with part of the $1,500 a month disposable income over and above his living expenses, the executive should also consider a life insurance policy. One of the objectives of this policy would be to secure the debt incurred on money borrowed for investments. The second purpose would be to provide capital so that if the executive were to die, his wife and family would not be forced to take a reduction in their standard of living. As explained on pages 80 and 81, employer-sponsored pension programs and group life policies alone are not generally adequate to meet the requirements of a family.

Finally, if either the executive or his wife is interested in art, they might choose an area in which they could become more knowledgeable. Then, perhaps once a year, three or four thousand dollars out of excess disposable income could be marked for an investment in collectibles. As explained in Chapter Twelve, it is generally advantageous to buy one expensive piece rather than several cheaper works which are less likely to appreciate over a period of time.

The Employee

Profile: A novice investor; uninformed, too willing to take risks; has no specific goals or objectives except getting rich quickly

Age 32

Marital status: Married — wife has recently begun working and earns $12,000 per year; two children — both in grade school

Salary: $30,000 per annum

Combined disposable income over and above living requirements: $500/month

Assets:
   Home — fair market value $100,000; cost $80,000
   Term deposits — $4,000 at 15%
   Stocks — fair market value $3,000; cost $5,000
   RRSP — $5,000

Liabilities:
   Mortgage — $60,000 at 18%
   Charge accounts — $2,000 at 24%, payments of $150/month
   Bank loan for stock — $4,000 at 19%
   Automobile payments — $180/month

Strategy

In this situation, we are dealing with a young family which is trying to get on its feet financially. The major objective should be to establish equity in the home. So far, the family has no defined investment pattern and our first recommendation is that it should keep a certain amount of money in reserve to meet any emergencies. Until now, personal requirements such as gifts, vacations, or major appliances have been financed through borrowings. Now that the wife has begun to work, it will be easier to get the family's financial affairs on the right track.

Our hypothetical novice investor should begin by examining his holdings in stocks. These have not been profitable to this point and he must decide whether there is a real justification in keeping them any longer. While stock market investments make for good cocktail party conversations, they are not something in which the unsophisticated investor should dabble. Unless there is an excellent chance for a quick turnaround, our employee should sell out and pay down his bank loan. This would leave him owing a balance of only $1,000. One-half of the capital loss of $2,000 would be tax-deductible. Presumably, the tax saving of $400 to $500, which would be received as a refund at the end of the year, could be used to pay down half of the remaining balance of the bank loan. At 19% interest, there is little justification for retaining the loan, especially since the investment is a "loser".

Every effort should also be made to pay off the charge account balances out of excess family disposable income over the following three or four months. This would require putting down approximately $500 to $600 each month on these bills instead of the present $150. It should be borne in mind that the 24% interest rate is excessive in comparison to the value which these charge accounts represent. The interest is not tax-deductible, and in order to support a 24% interest burden, the employee would have to earn 40% to 45% on his invested capital. Whatever sacrifices are necessary to meet this objective should be considered as only short-term inconveniences. Again, the charge account balances should be paid off without hesitation. The family does have the option of using its $4,000 term deposit to do so. However, this would leave them with no short-term emergency funds and therefore a pay-out period of about three to four months is not unreasonable.

As a medium-term goal, husband and wife should then try

to save up another $10,000 for term deposit investments. In addition to the existing deposits, $3,000 should be saved up by Mr. Employee so that he may earn 15% on $7,000 annually. This would give him $1,000 a year of tax-free interest income. Then, if his wife can save $7,000, as well, she too can earn $1,000 a year without any taxation.

The future efforts of this family should, however, be directed mainly towards paying down as much as they can on their mortgage each year on the anniversary date. If Mrs. Employee gets a substantial raise and her income jumps from $12,000 to $15,000 or $16,000, instead of this family increasing their standard of living, the excess after-tax funds should be used towards paying down the mortgage. Remember that an 18% non-deductible mortgage interest rate is extremely expensive. Possibly, if either husband or wife has parents who are reasonably well off and have investments in term deposits, they may consider approaching them for a non-interest-bearing loan towards the mortgage payment. This procedure will be explained in Chapter Six.

It would also be a good idea for Mr. Employee to invest part of his extra disposable income in some life insurance. Certainly, at a bare minimum, the mortgage balance owing should be covered by life insurance so that if he does die prematurely, his wife and family are not left destitute. At this stage, term insurance might be most appropriate because Mr. Employee may not feel that he can afford a more permanent type of coverage. Of course, any term policy that is taken out should be easily convertible into permanent coverage at some future time. (See Chapter Five.)

The family should also try to save a few thousand dollars a year for investment in RRSPs. Perhaps, after the charge account debts have been settled, husband and wife could earmark $300 a month out of their extra disposable income of $500 a month towards the establishment of an RRSP. Then, as either of them gets a raise in pay, additional funds could be appropriated for that purpose. It might be difficult to save in conjunction with accumulating the necessary funds to pay down the mortgage. Thus, if required, funds for contribution to an RRSP should be borrowed and paid out over the year—even though the interest on this kind of loan is no longer tax deductible. As explained on pages 65 to 67, the actual interest cost on an RRSP borrowing is small and does not warrant ignoring the opportunities to use this type of tax-deferred vehicle. Of course, when an income tax refund is received as a result of the RRSP contribution, that amount should be immediately applied towards a reduction of the RRSP debt.

Other major investment plans should probably be postponed for several years until the family is in more stable financial condition and the incomes have risen to higher levels. The employee and his family may also have to consider curtailing their standard of living for the next few years to make the suggested medium-term financial goals possible. This means taking inexpensive vacations and postponing, wherever possible, the purchase of personal luxury items. For this family, borrowing money to buy gold, silver or to make stock market investments is not recommended at this time.

The Professional

Profile: A high flyer—still caught up in the inflationary psychology of the 1970s
Age 45
Marital status: Wife is active in his practice—income $15,000; two children both in high school
Net income from his practice: $80,000
Disposable income over and above living requirements: $1,000/month
Assets:
    Home—fair market value $225,000; cost $150,000
    Stocks—fair market value $25,000; cost $45,000
    Commodity contracts—fair market value $20,000; cost $35,000
    Automobiles—cost $45,000
    RRSP—$15,000
    Term deposit—$2,000 at 15%

Liabilities:
   First mortgage — $130,000 at 15%
   Second mortgage — $45,000 at 19%
   Bank loan for RRSP — $5,500
   Car loan — $40,000

Strategy

This man is in the position of many successful self-employed professionals who earn significant amounts of income but have not been able to manage their money well. Our professional has expensive tastes and enjoys taking risks. He realizes that he is young and can earn back whatever losses he may incur on his investments.

This man needs to do more than review his investment portfolio. He needs to examine his entire methodology of investing. He is typical of many high-income earners who invest rashly or without discipline and lose significant amounts of money.

If he has previously picked his own investments, he should try to determine the cause of his consistent losses. His instincts may be correct, but perhaps he does not cut his losses and take advantage of winning streaks. Certainly, if he wants to continue to invest in commodities, he should protect his positions through the use of stop-loss orders. (These are discussed in Chapter Nine, Commodities and Options, pages 162–63.)

If he is not investing his funds himself, but has turned them over to a broker who is investing on his behalf, then he should certainly look around for a better source of information and service. He has suffered a great penalty for the privilege of having someone else assume his investment responsibilities. If he cannot learn from the mistakes which he has made either personally or in choosing an adviser, then he ought to get out of the market entirely and find some other type of investment better suited to his temperament.

At the moment, the professional is doing all of his investing in his own name, and the losses he has accumulated are so large that if he were to realize all of them at one time, he would not be able to deduct the full amount for income tax purposes in one year. Perhaps, if he decides that he will no longer be involved in futures or commodities, he may decide to report his loss of $15,000 as a trading transaction. In this case, it would become fully deductible (see page 170). However, if he ever goes back into commodities, the professional would then have to be prepared to report all profits as fully taxable income.

Even if he doesn't get any significant tax benefits, the professional should still close out his loss positions. For the time being, perhaps he might consider simply using the funds to eliminate his second mortgage. A 19% interest rate is quite expensive. If he is prepared either to get better investment counselling or spend more time on his own affairs, our professional could consider remortgaging at a later date either for a real estate investment or for the stock market — especially if interest rates are low at the time.

If he does not wish to borrow, his savings should then be used in two areas. First, these funds should be deployed towards paying down the first mortgage on the home. Second, any investments that the family might make out of surplus earnings should be structured in the name of Mrs. Professional. She is in a low tax bracket and would be able to earn investment income and capital gains at a relatively low cost.

When the smoke clears, we can see that the professional's major asset is the equity that he has in his home. Increased growth here is highly dependent on an inflationary economy and could be severely affected by a deflationary situation. Therefore, as his practice expands, he should be willing to commit a portion of his portfolio to gold or silver. If, for example, he finds a few hundred dollars "lying around" from time to time after all other commitments have been met, he might consider visiting his bank once in a while between the hours of 10:00 a.m. and 1:15 p.m. for the purpose of picking up a Krugerrand or two. Finally, the professional should think twice about whether he really needs expensive cars to impress his clients. Once he has gotten this luxury out of his system, the next time around, he might make a more conservative choice. As in the cases of the executive and employee, the professional should also maintain adequate life insurance as well as an ongoing RRSP program.

The Owner-Manager

Profile: Conservative; devotes all his energy to his own small business

Age 55

Marital status: Wife active in business, receives $20,000 per year; three children—two married, one in college (self-supporting)

Corporation pays the small business tax rate and earns a net income of $100,000 per year after salaries are paid

Excess cash generated (not required for business expansion) is $25,000 a year or about 25% of net income

Corporation owes shareholder $20,000 on a non-interest-bearing demand basis and has a relatively low debt load

Personal income: The owner-manager receives a salary of $75,000 annually

Assets:
   Home—fair market value $200,000; cost $75,000
   Term deposits—$50,000; $25,000 in the name of each spouse
   RRSPs—husband $35,000; wife $30,000
   Art collection—fair market value $30,000
   Canada Savings Bonds—$40,000 in wife's name at 16%
Liabilities: Mortgage on home—$20,000 at 8¾% due 1997

Strategy

In order to maintain the small business tax rate for the corporation, this couple may be looking at significantly higher personal incomes in the future. In other words, the corporation may be forced to pay out large salaries in order to create corporate deductions. In this case, the business owner, who is already in a financially secure position, may also be facing a large influx of income which requires intelligent consideration before any investment decision is made. This profile is indicative of a successful but conservative couple who have spent their lives building up a business but without creating a large investment portfolio. It has likely only been within the last few years that they have received substantial amounts of income from their corporation.

Although they are carrying a low mortgage in comparison to the value of their assets, they should consider that the interest on this debt is still non-deductible. If general interest rates drop low enough, they may consider paying off their mortgage in order to create a debt-free asset which could then be remortgaged for investment purposes. In this way, future mortgage interest would be available as a deduction against taxable income. They could pay off their mortgage by drawing against their present term deposits or by extracting the funds owing to them by their corporation. On the other hand, if interest rates stay high, the non-deductibility of the mortgage interest does not pose any serious problem and there is little point in repaying it.

In all probability, the owner-manager in this example is not interested in taking risks involving commodities or options. He would also think twice about making a real estate investment because of the time and attention that such an investment often requires. Although he has the wherewithal to get involved in these markets, we must bear in mind that a potential investment is as much a factor of one's comfort level as it is anything else. And yet, keeping money in term deposits does not provide a good hedge for inflation — especially when the resulting interest income is heavily taxed. Since Mrs. Owner-Manager already receives $20,000 a year from the business, her 16% Canada Savings Bond interest represents a net yield of only around 9% after tax. She might therefore consider cashing in the bonds and buying some retractable preferred shares (see pages 138–39). The dividend income will be taxed at a lower overall rate than interest and her after-tax yield will be significantly higher.

As an alternative, the couple should consider cashing the Canada Savings Bonds and transferring some funds into a Swiss bank account (as described in Chapter Thirteen) in order to diversify some of their assets out of North America. The amount in that account could be maintained either in Swiss francs or in gold and silver. As they continue to receive income from the corporation over and above dollars needed for living expenses, they should consider transferring a substantial portion of that amount to a Swiss bank account as well. In addition, if their children require funds for *their* homes, non-interest-bearing loans could be made to the children for that purpose. Of course, it would be nice for the children to show their gratitude by making annual gifts equal to what might otherwise be the after-tax interest incomes that their parents could earn. This procedure is described in Chapter Six.

As the corporation accumulates excess cash out of profits, it should begin to maintain a cash reserve for emergencies. However, it should also be kept in mind that the corporation could make investments in gold, silver or collectibles in the same way as an individual. In addition, there is nothing to prevent the corporation from making some of its investments overseas. A private corporation is simply an extension of its owners and can make the same investments as they can. However, if the small business tax rate applies, the corporation is capable of investing (approximately) seventy-five cents on the dollar instead of paying out larger salaries to the shareholders, who would then only retain fifty cents on the dollar.

Since this couple is in their fifties, they should take maximum advantage of the contributions which they are permitted to make to personal RRSPs. Fortunately, they will be able to do this out of cash earnings and will not have to borrow the necessary funds.

They should also have their wills reviewed and updated if necessary. They appear to have been receiving reasonably good (although somewhat conservative) advice in that they already both have RRSPs and the term deposits have been split. One of the points they should consider in their personal estate planning is whether or not they wish to specify the disposition of their art collection in their wills or whether it is more practical to pass these works on to their children now, while retaining a life interest for themselves. In this way, the art could remain in their home for their personal enjoyment, but it would be effectively owned by the children so that future growth in values would not be taxable at the time of the parents' deaths.

Some thought should also be given towards establishing the continuity of the business. Are there key employees who should be made shareholders so that the business could continue to run effectively if Mr. and/or Mrs. Shareholder-Manager are unable to participate? Is it advisable to wait for the next boom and sell the business outright? If so, do the shareholder-managers wish to retire or perhaps stay on as employees? In doing this sample assessment, we have not considered the value of the business as a family asset because each case is different. Even though the business is extremely profitable, it may be that its goodwill is related to the owners themselves and the business by itself may not be particularly saleable. This certainly is a major factor in the overall planning picture.

The Career Woman

Profile: Conservative; so far has taken no interest in learning about investment alternatives.
Age 38
Marital status: Single
Salary: $40,000 per annum
Disposable income over and above living requirements: $800/month
Contributes $2,400 a year to her employer's pension plan
Assets:
    Term deposits—$24,000 at 15%
    Jewellery—$14,000 original cost
    Antiques and artwork—$40,000 original cost
Liabilities: None

Strategy

This woman lives in a luxury apartment and is typical of the single person with no dependants who is earning a good living and has extra disposable income. She has conservatively put aside more than a half-year's income, which is invested in term deposits. Her post-retirement program is looked after through participation in her employer's pension plan. She has, over the years, indulged herself in "the finer things in life" such as jewellery, antiques and collectibles. Because this woman has a salary income of $40,000, she is in approximately a 45% income tax bracket. Accordingly, she should first consider putting aside $1,100 over the course of the year towards an RRSP. As described in Chapter Five, an individual who is a member of an employer-sponsored pension plan can contribute a total of $3,500 between the pension plan and an RRSP. In this case, since the contribution to the pension is $2,400, there is a balance of $1,100 available for the RRSP.

While the investment in term deposits is certainly conservative, it should be recognized that interest income over $1,000 a year is fully taxable. Thus, we would recommend that our career woman limit her term deposits to approximately $7,000 instead of $24,000. This would leave $17,000 available for other investments, such as "deep discount" bonds (see pages 57–61), where there is the opportunity to combine interest and capital gains. She might also consider investments in the stock market — if she is willing to try a less conservative approach. Even then part of the funds could perhaps be placed into retractable preferred shares with a high dividend yield.

While her collection of jewellery has a cost of $14,000, it should be recognized that this is not really an investment. Jewellery may be attractive and may have sentimental value, but for the reasons described in Chapter Ten, it is one of the poorest ways to invest in precious metals or stones. If our career woman wants to take part of her excess disposable income and purchase gold or silver from time to time, there are better ways of accomplishing this objective.

One of the most important decisions that the career woman has to make is whether to invest in a home or a condominium. In all probability, the acquisition of a bungalow or cottage would not be particularly attractive because of the maintenance involved. What then would be a proper investment decision with respect to a condominium apartment or townhouse?

Actually, there is no single right answer on what to do. Certainly, the downpayment requirements would necessitate cashing in virtually all the term deposits and eliminating any liquid security that our career woman has. A good deal therefore would depend on her health, job stability and the potential for being transferred. Certainly, in a poor market, the acquisition of real estate is not advised. In fact, we do not generally recommend any real estate acquisitions until interest rates moderate by a few percentage points. This is discussed more fully in Chapter Seven. On the other hand, if interest rates do continue to drop and we experience another boom in the real estate market, the purchase of a home could become an excellent investment. A principal residence presents the only opportunity to make a profit without being forced to pay income taxes. On the other hand, the purchase of a home by a single person involves a tremendous commitment. On balance, a final decision must be a personal one, and any assistance rendered by a professional investment counsellor is only of minor value.

Other Models

If we were to examine the position of a young professional couple who are renting a city apartment we would probably find that their profile is very similar to that of the career woman. In terms of shaping their investment strategies, a good deal depends on whether or not they intend to have children. If they do, their profile might then resemble a cross between the employee or novice investor and the professional, who were dealt with earlier in this chapter.

A fifty-five-year-old married employee several years away from retirement, who is perhaps somewhat concerned about the possibility of making a serious mistake in any investments, would probably be best served by the most conservative approaches illustrated in our profiles. This individual, being close to retirement, may not get a second chance. We hope that this type of person will see, as he reads through the remainder of this book, that he can combine a conservative investment approach with one that is also profitable. In other words, investing only in term deposits is not the answer! The same considerations would hold true if we were to profile an older couple who do not own their own business, are not involved in professional practice, but have some $10,000 or $20,000 to invest. Similarly, the widow or divorcee who has perhaps somewhere between $50,000 and $100,000 to invest should find that several of the options presented in this book suit both her needs and temperament.

Summary

You should be able to identify with at least one or two of the specific examples which have been outlined here. Many of the suggestions which have been made in each instance are equally applicable to people in a variety of situations and income brackets. They can be modified to fit almost any set of circumstances. Our approach is to emphasize tax minimization without incurring extraordinary risk. We recommend that you stabilize and balance your financial portfolio through a diversification of investments. In all cases, realize that planning must suit the temperament and desires of the individuals involved while still providing them with the maximum opportunity for after-tax capital retention.

Remember flexibility and timing. If you make a mistake, do not hesitate to sell out, cut your losses and go on to something else. Reshaping your investment strategies is certainly a challenge but it can be very rewarding at the end.

CHAPTER THREE

To Borrow or Not to Borrow — That Is the Question

Before 1981, *not* to borrow money was almost the equivalent of criminal negligence. In the latter part of the 1970s, the annual cost of borrowing was approximately only 13%. If borrowed funds were used for investment purposes, this 13% "gross" cost was then reduced to only 6½% (or even less) for individuals with taxable incomes over $30,000. This is because for tax purposes there were no restrictions against deducting interest on funds used for investments. In fact, in the United States, even if money was borrowed for the purpose of buying a home, the interest was (and still is) tax-deductible. Given an after-tax cost of borrowing of only 6½% and an inflation rate several percentage points higher, it was almost impossible to lose money! Of course, you would not borrow money at 13% from a lending institution for the purpose of investing in term deposits yielding 11%. However, if your investments were geared towards the stock market, real estate, collectibles, or commodities such as gold and silver, you were almost certain to come out ahead.

By the end of the 1970s, most people in middle- or upper-income brackets realized the advantages of borrowing, and the high demand for suitable investments contributed to ever-escalating prices. The rate of inflation was pushed even higher by the guarantee of almost certain capital appreciation, and vice versa. In order to prolong the economic boom, the U.S. and Canadian governments did nothing to control inflation.

Finally, the newly elected administration of U.S. President Ronald Reagan decided that the situation was becoming critical, with hyperinflation being just around the corner. Mr. Reagan concluded that the artificially low interest rate of the 1970s was one of the major factors creating this unhealthy situation. The U.S. then took drastic steps to rectify this problem and, all at once, the interest rate jumped dramatically. With great political astuteness, Mr. Reagan succeeded in raising the interest rate while successfully placing the entire blame for all problems confronting his administration squarely on the shoulders of former president Jimmy Carter.

Meanwhile, in Canada, our Mr. Trudeau was suddenly caught in a terrible squeeze. For the past fourteen years, the Trudeau government has preached Canadian autonomy. A major plank in the Liberal government platform has been Canadian nationalism. Only Canadian-controlled private companies enjoy favourable tax rates. We have experienced the effects of the Foreign Investment Review Act and the Canadianization of the oil industry. Recently, a major effort was made to repatriate the Canadian Constitution. Yet, our economy is, of necessity, tied in to that of the United States, so when the U.S. "asked" us to raise our interest rates, the Canadian government simply answered, "How high?" Generally, the Canadian interest rate has closely paralleled that of the United States. However, Pierre Trudeau (unlike Ronald Reagan) has no previous administration on which to place the blame. In retrospect, Mr. Trudeau's largest mistake may have been in only allowing the Conservative government to function for a few short months back in 1979—not enough time for Mr. Clark to have gotten into really serious trouble!

1981 was, therefore, a year of adjustment. In a very short span of time North Americans paid for the excesses of the last decade. Looking back, we could all have lived quite comfortably during the 1970s had the interest rate gone up by a little less than 1% each year. We could all have adjusted our business programs and our lifestyles to accommodate this situation. However, when an interest rate jumps as much as 10% in one year, this creates financial havoc.

What is a "Proper" Interest Rate?

In the summer of 1981, when interest rates in Canada peaked at around 23%, the newspapers, magazines and other media were full of stories and articles dealing with the "poor" people who were losing their homes. One couldn't help but sympathize when confronted with pictures of young families standing outside their heavily mortgaged homes with moving vans in the driveways and "For Sale" signs decorating the front lawns.

And yet few people stopped to examine a *lender's* position. Most lenders tend to be either individuals in high tax brackets or large corporations. Any individual whose taxable income exceeds $30,000 a year is approaching a 50% income tax bracket. Moreover, public companies pay a 50% tax rate on all profits (as do private corporations on their investment income). Given an inflation rate which reached 12% in 1981, a lender would have had to place money at a 24% rate of interest just to break even! Anything short of that rate resulted in a *loss of purchasing power*.

Many people erroneously blamed the chartered banks for the jump in rates. And yet, the Canadian banks really don't particularly care if the Bank of Canada charges them interest at 12% while they in turn lend funds at 15%, or whether the Bank of Canada charges 20%, requiring the banks to extend loans at 23%. In either case, a bank makes a profit on the same 3% "spread". Similarly, a chartered bank will profit from the same type of spread on funds received from depositors. If the going rate of interest paid to depositors is high, the banks simply adjust their lending rates on funds advanced to borrowers for the mark-up required. It should be noted, however, that in addition to borrowing funds from the Bank of Canada and depositors, the chartered banks also obtain funds from a third source—their own retained earnings. Many of the banks have been in business for long periods of time, and have accumulated substantial retained profits. If a chartered bank does not lend out its own retained earnings at twice the prevailing inflation rate, the shareholders lose money! *A pre-tax return equal to double the rate of inflation is required just to break even.*

While it would therefore appear that interest rates should always be pegged at twice the prevailing rate of inflation, this is not quite so. To some extent, each of us can afford to receive interest income at a lesser rate and still come out with a positive return on investment. For example, under Canadian law, the first $1,000 of investment income received from unrelated parties by any individual each year is tax-free. Thus, as a starting point for *anyone's* investment program, we recommend that the first several thousand dollars of one's accumulated savings be put aside to earn a safe, conservative interest yield. For example, if the going rate of interest is 14%, you would require approximately $7,000 of capital to earn the "magic" $1,000 each year. Where an investment yield is not taxable, the gross yield and the net yield are the same, so you can afford to earn less than twice the inflation factor without losing. For the same reason, it would not be unreasonable (given an inflation factor of 12%) to earn somewhere around 15% or 16% interest in a tax-sheltered investment.

Specifically, you should examine the registered retirement savings plan (discussed in detail in Chapter Five) or an employer-sponsored pension plan program where funds are invested at this rate. These deferred income plans are not subject to immediate taxation. Thus, a gross yield only a few per cent higher than the inflation rate produces a net positive return. In the United States (but not in Canada) it is also possible for an investor who is otherwise taxed in a high bracket to place funds into tax-free municipal bonds. There are also charitable foundations and non-profit organizations who can afford to earn a more conservative yield than twice the inflation rate. Again, as long as interest income is not eroded by taxation, these institutions can afford to earn that much less. Thus, taking both taxable and non-taxable interest incomes into account, a good rule of thumb is that a realistic interest rate should be a few per cent less than twice the inflation factor. Given an inflation rate of say 10%, a realistic interest rate would then be in the order of 16% to 18%.

You might now ask why, with an inflation rate between 10% and 12%, was it in fact necessary for interest rates to peak at around 23% in mid-1981? The answer to that is simple. The only way that the North American governments could succeed in raising rates from 13% to 18% without risking a voters' revolt was to first bring the rate up to 23% and then allow it to *slip back*. Having seen the damage that a 23% interest rate will cause, the public then welcomes a stabilization of the rate at around 18%, with the knowledge and understanding that, as bad as things are, *they could have been worse*. Think about it. If, for example, you were given the option to remortgage your house for a five-year period at a fixed interest rate of 15% – 18%, would you accept? If you are like most people you probably would. You would recognize that there is little chance of a substantial and extended *permanent* decline in rates (assuming no major change in government monetary policies). Furthermore, you would welcome the opportunity to protect yourself against the extraordinarily high rates of the summer of 1981. And yet, if in 1979 you had been approached with an offer of mortgage financing at even 15%, it would have been rejected immediately.

Of Floating Rates . . .

All of us have been forced to swallow the bitter medicine of the much higher interest rates created by the war against inflation. At the present time, barring significant policy changes, we do not really see any reason for the interest rate to fluctuate dramatically. Of course, if inflation abates, we might expect at least a small decline in the interest rate. On the other hand, if inflation persists and the Canadian dollar starts to fall once more, we may, in fact, again see rates in excess of 20%.

In 1981, the Canadian government made a significant move designed to ensure that we would never again be faced with such a dramatic change in rates virtually overnight. Specifically, legislation was introduced to allow the interest rate to "float" weekly. On the surface, such a change makes great sense. As the government monitors the pace of inflation, it can adjust interest rates almost instantly. And yet, it appears that the "good intentions" have backfired. A floating rate of interest does not encourage the kind of *stability* and *confidence* which both business owners and investors require. The inability to predict what the interest rate will be six months, a year, or even two years down the road, makes it very difficult for anyone to commit himself to a long-term investment or business project. How does one build a plant for business expansion—or an office building or shopping centre—if one does not know what the prevailing rate of interest will be when the time comes to put the final financing into place? Will the production from that plant or the rents generated by the office building or shopping centre produce sufficient revenues to meet the carrying costs?

As another example, take a manufacturing company which manufactures different types of widgets. Let us assume that we are dealing with a solid business with $1-million of inventory backed up by shareholders' equity of $200,000 and a bank loan of $800,000. Each year assume that this hypothetical company produces a catalogue for its products that furnishes potential buyers with a price list for the following twelve months. Certainly, whatever price the company charges for its products must be sufficient to absorb all operating costs and return a profit. Since operating costs include interest on the bank loan, the unit price would depend largely on whether the interest rate on the loan averages, say, 16% at one extreme or 25% on the other. In many cases, failure to account for the potential cost on the high side can result in eventual bankruptcy. Then again, if the manufacturer overcompensates for his risk and prices his product too high, this just adds to the problem of inflation. Moreover, if customers refuse to pay the higher price, the business can easily slide downhill.

Lack of stability is another of the major causes of the current recession. In our opinion, what is needed now is a stable interest rate for periods of at least one year at a time. In this way, businesses and investors would be better able to plan their affairs. Before making a debt commitment, we could all calculate the exact rate of return on investment required to at least break even or show a profit.

A "Made in Canada" Interest Rate?

At the time this is being written, and as mentioned in Chapter One, there is much speculation as to whether or not Canada can afford to go its own way in establishing an interest rate. The recession which started in summer 1981 has been getting steadily worse and most people feel that a substantial decline in interest rates is needed as an incentive to get the economy moving again. Several provinces have already introduced programs to subsidize borrowers, in order to precipitate a recovery. And yet, if *Canada* were to establish an interest rate of only 12% while the U.S. imposes rates at 18%, the Canadian dollar would plummet like a stone. The reason for this is very simple to understand. If you were an investor who could only earn a 12% return on a particular investment in Canada while a comparable yield outside the country is 50% higher, where would you turn? A "made in Canada" interest rate would therefore not be viable unless it were accompanied by stringent foreign exchange controls. Specifically, currency export restrictions would have to be imposed at that point.

A "made in Canada" interest rate would also have other implications. In the short-term, it would probably turn the Canadian economy around, since low interest rates encourage everyone to borrow money for investment purposes. However, the medium-term effect could be highly inflationary. Moreover, if the Canadian dollar dropped substantially in relation to other currencies, imported goods would become much more expensive. Since Canada imports more than it exports, again the effect would be to fuel inflation. Perhaps, the province of Alberta could benefit in the short run, since exports of gas and oil are priced in U.S. currency. However, for the country as a whole, a low interest rate could spell disaster — unless Canadians exercise voluntary restraint in their spending and wage demands or support a program of income and price controls. Strikes would have to be made illegal and we would be forced to emphasize productivity so that we could rely less heavily on imported goods.

Where Is the Interest Rate Headed?

If you ask two economists whether the interest rate is headed up or down you are likely to receive three answers. In fact, no one knows for certain. Clearly, in times of recession, the interest rate should drop to some extent. Unfortunately, both the Canadian and U.S. governments are experiencing large deficits and they are going to the marketplace to borrow enormous sums of money. Whenever a government places heavy demands on a country's money supply, private borrowers must then pay premium rates in order to obtain funds for themselves. *This serves to keep the interest rate high.* As the recession grows, government revenues tend to decrease. This creates even greater deficits and an increased need to borrow. It is a vicious circle. An alternative solution to government monetary problems is for Canada and the United States to simply crank up their printing presses to supply themselves with funds. Of course, this would tend to devalue the respective currencies and would again result in another round of heavy inflation.

In short, there does not appear to be any satisfactory solution, and while some economists predict increases in interest rates while others predict decreases, the chances remain fairly good that the interest rate will remain more or less stable for the time being. Most of the examples in this book will assume a borrowing cost to investors and businesses of 18% to 20%. On the other hand, a 14%–16% interest *income* rate will also be assumed. The difference, of course, is the accommodation fee which is charged by lenders to put funds into place. Certainly, if at the time you are reading this, the rates vary by one or two percentage points, these differences should not adversely affect your investment decisions. You will see that we recommend certain investment approaches when interest rates are high and others when interest rates are low.

When Are You Ready to Invest?

Most people operate under the misconception that they require substantial capital or savings for the purpose of making an investment. Actually, you don't need a substantial initial "stake" as long as you have the personal "earning power" to carry debt. In addition, an investment does not necessarily have to carry itself as long as the cost of maintaining it is more than offset by the potential for capital appreciation. The amount of debt which you can support depends, of course, on your income and spending commitments. Ask yourself, however, whether or not you could save $375 a month if you had to. If you are capable of saving say $4,500 a year, you could carry a *minimum* debt load of $25,000 at 18%. This, of course, assumes that for tax purposes your interest expense is non-deductible. On the other hand, if your interest is deductible and your taxable income is otherwise in excess of about $30,000 a year, you could carry a debt load of double, or $50,000, at the same net after-tax cost. This is illustrated in the example following:

$50,000 × 18% =	$9,000
Less: Tax saving from interest deductibility	4,500
Net after-tax cost of borrowing	$4,500

In other words, surplus earnings from your job, business, or profession could be used for the purpose of making investments. Of course, you have many different choices in terms of where to invest. Obviously, even if interest costs were fully deductible in all cases, you would still not borrow at 18% in order to invest in guaranteed income certificates which yield 16%. On the other hand, you might be willing to borrow money for an investment in stocks, commodities, real estate, gold, silver, antiques or works of art. All of these share one common denominator—the potential for capital appreciation. *As long as the after-tax cost of borrowing is more than offset by the after-tax capital appreciation, you wind up ahead of the game.* Certainly, the lower the interest rate is before taxes, the cheaper the cost becomes on an after-tax basis, as well.

There are two key points which must always be kept in mind. First, you must always think in terms of after-tax dollars. In other words, is your interest on borrowed money deductible or is the interest non-deductible? Second, when you evaluate the return on a potential investment, it is the *after-tax* and *not* the yield before taxes which is important.

We do not mean to suggest that everyone should be willing to borrow money. Some people are just not comfortable with any debt whatsoever. If you want to, you can therefore accumulate your initial investment capital the hard way by saving a few hundred dollars a month. Unfortunately, the frustration of knowing how long it takes to save a meaningful sum of money generally serves to increase a natural inclination to *spend* surplus earning power rather than adopt a savings program. The amount borrowed in the previous examples ranged between $25,000 and $50,000 at a cost of approximately $375 a month for the privilege. (The actual limit depends on whether or not the interest is deductible.) Note, however, that $50,000 is neither a "magic" number nor a realistic borrowing for everyone reading this book. Each one of us has a personal "comfort level", which determines the maximum debt load which that individual can handle. If your borrowings exceed this comfort level, serious psychological disadvantages can result—especially if your investments decline in value. It is certainly not our intention to suggest that you become overloaded with debt.

On occasion, we have defined a millionaire as an individual who *owes* a million dollars. While the definition is certainly somewhat facetious, it does have merit. Presumably, if one owes a million dollars, he also has a million dollars in assets. If (over time) the assets double in value while the cost of the debt shrinks with inflation, the borrower does eventually become a bona fide millionaire. Some people are in fact able to accumulate substantial investment capital without going to the marketplace for borrowed funds. This is certainly the case if you are a top-notch athlete or entertainer and have a much higher than average annual income. Even in spite of high taxes, it may be possible for you to set aside substantial capital within a short time. And yet, for most of us, life is not that easy. Without taking some risk there is no reward.

For several years, both in seminars and in other books, we

have dealt with the concept of a "forced savings plan" for the executive. Such a plan simply consists of borrowing money for investment purposes — within the personal comfort level of the individual — where the debt is carried by the individual's monthly earnings from his employment, profession or business and not necessarily by the investments themselves. The borrowed funds are then placed into property which will, it is hoped, appreciate in value. Of course, the investor should also be comfortable with the investments themselves. A good portion of this book will explore the various investment alternatives that you do, in fact, have. In some cases, you will find that you can use substantial leverage. A great deal depends on whether your choice in investments yields income on an ongoing basis. In other words, do your stocks pay dividends or do your real estate holdings pay you rent? Another major factor is always the question of interest *deductibility*. As you will see in Chapter Ten, you cannot deduct interest on funds borrowed to acquire gold, silver, art or antiques *unless* you are prepared to report eventual profits on sale as fully taxable ordinary income. Of course, when the interest rate is 18%, there is substantially more risk in borrowing than there was several years ago when the rates were only around 13%. On the other hand, investing for capital growth may soon prove advantageous again. *If interest costs do in fact decline (temporarily) over the next few years, you will probably realize that you actually have no choice but to borrow — if you wish to accumulate wealth.*

For the moment, forget about borrowing money. Assume, for example, that you have $50,000 of capital available for investment. Perhaps you have sold other properties which you owned, or perhaps this $50,000 represents a lifetime of savings or winnings from a lottery or an inheritance. What can you do with your money? As you will see more clearly in the next chapter, if you simply take your cash and place the funds into a bank account at 16%, your *after-tax* yield in most cases is only around 8% and yet your dollars are being eroded by inflation at a rate which is considerably higher. In the long run, you become a loser! Bear in mind that even taking today's "high" interest rates into consideration, you are simply being paid with dollars that are worth less and less. Unless there is *real* growth, your investments will yield a negative return. Most people just cannot afford the luxury of leaving money in bank accounts for extended periods of time.

Calculating After-Tax Yields

In order to assess the risk involved in any investment, you should compare the cost of investing on an after-tax basis to the capital growth needed to at least break even. Bear in mind that if a profit on the disposition of property is treated as a capital gain, only one-half is taxable. Thus, if you are in a 50% personal tax bracket, the maximum tax on a capital gain is 25%. The key point is clearly, however, the deductibility of such interest. Where such interest is non-deductible, you would require a much greater pre-tax return on investment in order to break even. This is illustrated below.

The results are somewhat shocking. If interest expense is non-deductible while capital growth is taxable, you require *twice* the return before taxes just to break even! In other words, non-deductible interest is expensive. A good example of such a

AN INDIVIDUAL IN A 50% TAX BRACKET BORROWS MONEY AT 18% TO INVEST IN A "GROWTH" INVESTMENT

	Interest Expense is Deductible	Interest Expense is Non-Deductible
Cost of borrowing (gross)	18%	18%
Less: Tax savings (50%)	9%	–
Cost of borrowing (net)	9%	18%
Annual capital growth required to break even (gross)	12%	24%
Less: 25% tax on growth	3%	6%
Annual capital growth required to break even (net)	9%	18%

40

situation is borrowing money to buy a summer house (or second home). Although this subject will be dealt with in more detail in Chapter Six, a few words of explanation at this point would be useful.

Most Canadians are aware that as a result of the November 12, 1981 Budget, it is no longer possible for a married couple to enjoy capital gains exemptions on two principal residences. Thus, borrowing money for a country house is an expensive proposition. As much as you might like to have one, you should realize that if you borrow at 18%, your second house would have to appreciate by 24% annually for you to just break even.

Interest Deductibility

When is interest deductible? Before the Budget of November 12, 1981, interest expense was always tax-deductible in cases where funds were borrowed for the purpose of earning income either from property or from a business.

In general, interest on money borrowed to acquire an interest in or finance the operations of a small business will no doubt continue to be deductible for tax purposes. However, there are some new restrictions which are being considered by the government pertaining to the deductibility of interest on money borrowed for investment purposes. The new rules have not yet been finalized and are subject to amendment. For 1982, there are no restrictions except with respect to money borrowed to acquire investments in deferred income plans such as registered retirement savings plans. This restriction is dealt with in Chapter Five. In 1983, we do not anticipate that there will be any serious restrictions on money borrowed for other investments. After that, it is anybody's guess. You must always make sure that you stay abreast of the tax rules concerning the deductibility of interest expense. You will also have to monitor movements in interest rates closely because these will affect the desirability of your investments. Remember, the lower the cost to carry, the more worthwhile the investment. Until there is a definite trend towards stability of rates and tax rules, we caution you to stay away from significant long-term debt commitments. In fact, until interest rates drop a few per cent lower, you may not want to borrow at all.

In some of the examples in this chapter we dealt with the idea of borrowing $50,000 at 18%. You will recall that the after-tax cost of carrying such a debt is as little as $375 a month. If interest rates were only 13%, a similar monthly commitment would cover $66,000 of borrowings. In other words, the lower the interest rate the greater the leverage.

Chapter Fourteen tells you how to make the best use of professional advisers. Here, we will just mention that you should be able to rely on your accountant to keep you up-to-date with all information related to income tax. Before borrowing always seek professional advice as to the tax consequences. This is the only way that you can determine the real cost of carrying your investments.

CHAPTER FOUR

Making the Most Out of Interest Income

To maintain your perspective and survive the investment climate of the 1980s, remember that you must always look at after-tax dollars. The only "real" dollar is the one that you can keep in your own hands, under your own control, after the government has taken its share of your earnings. As discussed in the previous chapter, you must therefore always differentiate between before and after-tax interest costs. In Canada, interest costs are only deductible where funds are borrowed to produce taxable income such as interest, rents, or business profits.

Ordinarily, you would not borrow in order to earn interest income. This is because if you are representative of the average Canadian, your cost of borrowing from lending institutions will exceed the rate of return that you could normally anticipate if you, in turn, relend these funds. Of course, you may be an exception. Some people can make a very profitable *business* out of borrowing money for venture capital loans. In other words, if you know of someone who is in dire need of third mortgage funds or interim financing for a construction project and that person is willing to pay 30% annual interest for these dollars, you might then be willing to use your line of credit to borrow the required funds at 18% in order to earn 30%. Such an arrangement, however, involves a substantial degree of risk and generally a large degree of expertise. You would have to be in a position where you can personally evaluate the borrower's strengths and weaknesses and, as well, evaluate the security of the borrower's collateral. Such arrangements are not suitable for most of us and will not be considered further in this book. Instead, we will concentrate on more conventional interest-producing investments, such as Canada Savings Bonds, obligations of public corporations and bank term deposits and savings accounts.

Throughout history, interest has been charged on borrowed funds in order to compensate lenders for the risk that they take and for the time-value of money. The risk is the possibility that the borrower will not repay the loan at the agreed-upon time. The lender's choices then are to aggressively pursue collection, seize whatever assets are available, or (as a last resort) to write off the entire amount outstanding as a bad debt. None of these approaches is very satisfactory, so lenders are normally particular about their clients and will charge a rate of interest commensurate with the risk in each particular undertaking.

In Canada, you and I can become lenders. We may not wish to take the risk of making the types of private loans described previously, but we can certainly take our money and lend it to any number of banks or trust companies. In fact, we can earn interest with virtually no risk at all. There have so far been (over the past many years) no bankruptcies or defaults among the chartered banks and very few trust companies have ever gone into default on their obligations. From time to time, mortgage companies which relend funds obtained from private sources do actually default, causing their depositors much loss and grief.

At the time this is being written, many Canadians have a substantial portion of their investment portfolios sitting in interest-bearing accounts with chartered banks, trust companies and other lending institutions. (In June 1982, former Finance Minister Allan MacEachen estimated personal savings at Canadian chartered banks to be in excess of $44-billion dollars.) As you will see, there are certainly some advantages to keeping a portion of your funds relatively liquid and earning interest. In fact, your own circumstances will dictate whether investments in bank accounts and other interest-bearing securities are a good idea for you. However, in the long run, a conservative "no risk" approach of keeping all or substantially all of your savings in interest-bearing investments *will probably cost you a fortune*. The "holding pattern" begun in 1981, which stemmed largely from fear of taking other investment steps, cannot continue forever. It is our prediction that no matter what happens to our economy, many investment dollars will eventually be forced to leave the security of the chartered banks.

On the one hand, the latest recession could lead to a full-fledged depression. Then, if prices for real estate, the stock market, gold or silver decline far enough, the astute investor will cash in his savings accounts and buy these properties. This will be done in expectation of capital growth from an eventual recovery. On the other hand, if *this* recession is only temporary — and we will find out whether this is in fact the case if interest rates continue to drop as they did in the fall of 1982 — investment funds could very quickly come pouring out of the bank accounts of the nation in anticipation of what might be the last great boom of this century. Whereas bank savings accounts or term deposits may have been your favourite investment alternative at a certain time, this is not to say that you shouldn't be flexible and ready to change direction at virtually a moment's notice.

You must monitor rates of interest as they continue to fluctuate and, as mentioned previously, your after-tax return on investment is what counts. Second, you must also monitor inflation. If the recession ends in 1983 and Canada reinflates, the dollar which you will then receive in 1984 or 1985 will not have the same value as the dollars that you lend out today. Therefore, *any interest rate that you charge must also compensate you for the loss of purchasing power*. If you can't get an after-tax rate of return equal to inflation, then stay away from interest-bearing securities.

Certainly, even the potential erosion of purchasing power can be minimized — depending on how wisely you structure your arrangements. As you will read in the next few pages, a great deal depends on your ability to take advantage of family members in low tax brackets to earn interest income on your behalf. However, if by the conclusion of this chapter you still find that earning interest income on your investment capital is the only alternative that you are comfortable with, you should at least restrict the length of time you will guarantee a borrower (even if it is a chartered bank) a specific interest rate. In other words, investing your funds in a long-term deposit can be extremely dangerous. For example, you could probably tie up funds to earn 15% on a five-year arrangement. Certainly, this may have some appeal to you if your tax bracket is low and especially if interest rates do decline to 12%. However, even if such a decline does take place, who is to say whether by 1985 the prevailing interest rate might not be 25% or 30%?

When Is an Interest-Bearing Investment
An Acceptable "Alternative"?

As mentioned in Chapters Two and Three, the first $1,000 of interest, dividends, or taxable capital gains earned by an individual in Canada on Canadian securities is exempt from tax. Since every family should have a cash emergency fund in any event, sufficient funds should be set aside in short-term interest-bearing accounts so as to take advantage of this "investment deduction". In fact, in a family of husband and wife, especially where both parties have income from other sources, the general rule would be to *double up* on the investment deduction.

To earn $1,000 of annual interest presently requires approximately $7,000 of capital at a 14% rate. So a husband and wife should each invest $7,000 in order to "double up". In previous years, if part of the investment deduction was not required by one spouse to reduce taxable income to nil, the benefit of the investment deduction could still be doubled by transferring the unused portion to the spouse in the higher bracket. Starting in 1982, however, the marital exemption is reduced by the amount of the transfer. It is therefore no longer possible for *one* spouse to get double the advantage. However, where both spouses are working and one cannot claim the other as a dependant in any event, there is still a significant advantage

(This example ignores the $1,000 investment income deduction.)

First assumption: An individual has $10,000 in term deposits

Interest at 16%	$1,600
Tax at 50% marginal rate	800
After-tax yield	$ 800

Second assumption: Inflation rate of 11%

After-tax dollars needed to maintain purchasing power	$1,100
Loss after one year	$ 300
Interest rate necessary to sustain purchasing power	22%

in such doubling up. Because of the investment deduction, the gross yield and net yield on the couple's total $14,000 investment would be identical. Since a rate of 14% is significantly higher than the prevailing inflation percentage, this is a good overall return.

Apart from an investment of funds sufficient to generate $1,000 of tax-free interest income, it does not make sense for the average investor to carry large amounts of interest-bearing securities on a long-term basis. The example above illustrates that today's double-digit yields are misleading when you take into account the effects of both taxation and inflation.

From the first example, you can see that the combination of income taxes and inflation will defeat you before you even have the chance to get started. Many people try to overcome this by compounding their interest, that is by reinvesting the after-tax interest which they receive each year. Theoretically, compounding your income should help you to break even. However, what many people don't realize is that *inflation also has a tendency to compound the erosion of your original capital*. The next two examples will show you the disastrous effect of inflation on the purchasing power of money which you retain in an interest-bearing investment.

EFFECT OF TAXES ON COMPOUND INTEREST

Year 1 interest ($10,000 × 16%)	$1,600
Tax at 50%	800
After-tax return reinvested	$ 800
Year 2 interest ($10,800 × 16%)	$1,728
Tax at 50%	864
After-tax return	$ 864
Growth in two years ($800 + $864)	$1,664
Equivalent to a compound rate of only	8%

The example above shows that you, in fact, compound your income at a rate of only 8%, not 16%, after taxes — and the example does not yet take into consideration the effects of inflation. The following example shows how inflation erodes the purchasing power of your capital on a compound basis at a far greater rate than you can ever hope to keep up with by reinvesting the interest you retain after tax. If the investor in the first example lost $300 after taxes and inflation in only the first year, he will literally lose more than double that amount in overall purchasing power after two years of compounding.

You can easily see that if we do get a "made in Canada" interest rate of, say, 12% or if North American interest rates

EFFECT OF INFLATION OVER TWO YEARS

Investment capital	$10,000
After-tax interest in Year 1	800
Inflation loss on $10,000 at 11%	(1,100)
Value of capital at the end of the first year	9,700
After-tax interest in Year 2	864
Inflation loss on original $10,000 plus $800 interest at 11%	(1,188)
Value of capital at the end of the second year	$ 9,376
Original capital	$10,000
Final value of capital plus interest	9,376
Real loss in two years	$ 624

decline to that level for other reasons, an investor's return will drop accordingly. If inflation then accelerates as a result of the availability of "cheap" financing, your loss will compound that much more quickly! The only rational approach, assuming you are interested in maintaining the purchasing power of your money, is to look into other vehicles more adapted to life in the inflationary fast-lane of the 1980s. Unless you can compound your after-tax interest at a rate that is greater than inflation in the long run, you will be a loser. Many investors have accepted such a loss over the last year or so without putting up any struggle. This has been the price that they have been willing to pay to avoid the even greater losses which could have resulted had they gone into real estate, the stock market or precious metals at the wrong time. In the long-run, however, a defeatist attitude of "Thank God I'm not losing more" should be avoided.

Exceptions

We do not wish to imply that all interest income after your first $1,000 a year is deficient. As you will see in Chapter Five, you will have ample opportunity to take advantage of conservative investment philosophies with very little risk and at reasonable rates of return under the Canadian income tax structure. Specifically, through the use of a registered retirement savings plan, deferred profit-sharing plan, or registered pension plan, you do have the opportunity to earn moderate amounts of interest income while deferring immediate taxes, thereby beating inflation. For the majority of Canadian, the RRSP is an integral part of the financial planning package. You will also see in Chapter Five that the RRSP is a valid investment even if you have to make your contributions with borrowed funds on which the interest is *not* tax-deductible.

Taking Advantage of the Family Unit

In many cases, interest-bearing investments can still comprise a significant portion of a family's portfolio even if the gross rate is not much in excess of the inflation factor — as long as the net yield is not eroded by taxation. Often families fail to utilize two major assets at their disposal. The first is the equity in the home, which is rarely drawn upon as a potential pool of investment funds. This will be expanded upon further in Chapter Six. The second major asset that many husbands enjoy is their wives. A wife often performs a multitude of valuable and indispensable services in the home without formally being paid. In cases where earned income flows into the hands of the husband only and it is he who then makes the family's investments, the penalty is generally taxation at maximum rates. Certainly, a family as a unit is much better able to provide for its collective needs when it can retain as great a percentage as possible out of each dollar brought in. Where a husband has a substantial earned income, the best planning is to ensure that the investment income is received in the hands of his wife, who is in the lower income tax bracket.

Take as an example a husband who has accumulated $100,000 of investment capital. If he simply makes a gift of these funds to his wife, who for purposes of illustration has no other income, the gift itself would not have any adverse tax implications (outside of the province of Quebec where there is a provincial gift tax). However, if the wife invests the funds to earn interest at 16%, this *income* is then taxed in the *husband's* hands in spite of the fact that the wife received it. This is because there is a tax rule that states that where an individual transfers property to a spouse, the income generated by the transferred property reverts back to the transferor. This "income attribution rule" applies as long as the transferor is alive, is resident in Canada and the transferee is his spouse. Even if the wife takes "her" capital of $100,000 and acquires shares in a public company, receiving a dividend of, for example, $10,000 in a subsequent year, that dividend will be taxed to the husband as well. In this case, the public company shares would be considered "substituted property" and the attribution rules apply to substituted property as well as to the original gift. Fortunately, there are some significant opportunities to get around this particular problem. The answer is a non-interest-bearing loan from the husband to his wife. There has never been any legal or tax requirement that interest be charged on a loan from one individual to another. The courts have held that a loan is not a transfer of property and income attribution would not apply. If a wife therefore borrows $100,000 and invests the proceeds, the income is then taxed in her hands and not in his. In fact, given an interest yield of 16% and an inflation factor of 11%, a good, conservative approach might simply revolve around such a loan coupled with an interest-bearing investment. This is illustrated in the example below.

NON-INTEREST-BEARING LOANS CAN SAVE TAX DOLLARS AND MAXIMIZE INVESTMENT YIELDS

Non-interest-bearing loan from husband in high tax bracket to wife with no other income		$100,000
Gross yield at 16%		$ 16,000
Less: Estimated taxes payable by wife	$2,500	
Tax cost to husband from loss of personal exemption	1,500	4,000
Net interest yield		$ 12,000
Loss of purchasing power on $100,000 due to 11% inflation		$ 11,000
Net positive "return" on invested capital		$ 1,000

A simple loan from a high-bracket husband to a wife who would otherwise be in a "zero" tax bracket can, as illustrated, produce an acceptable (if not spectacular) investment yield. *At least the purchasing power of the original investment is maintained.* Naturally, this would only work in cases where the wife is not otherwise taxable. If, for example, the husband's income is $60,000 a year (and he is in a 50% tax bracket), while the wife's employment income is $15,000 a year and she is already in a 30% bracket (before taking into account any interest income on the above borrowed funds), the results would be quite different. Although the loss as a result of taxes and inflation may be smaller than if the husband himself were to earn interest at 16% subject to a 50% tax rate, nevertheless there would still be a loss. In the long run, the combination of taxes and inflation would substantially erode the family's nest egg.

Structuring a Non-Interest-Bearing Demand Note

The use of a non-interest-bearing demand note from one spouse to the other is such a simple planning opportunity that most people overlook it. One possible reason for this is that it is not covered in any of the investment books that are published in the United States. This is because, for U.S. tax purposes, married taxpayers in that country generally file joint tax returns. It therefore becomes academic as to whether income is earned by a husband or by a wife. In Canada, however, the system is different. Married couples file separate personal tax returns and the object is to take advantage of the spouse in a low tax bracket.

The non-interest-bearing demand note need not involve a formal twenty-five-page legal document. A simple IOU is acceptable for income tax purposes and serves as evidence that a loan has been made between married persons. An example of this easily executed document is shown below.

The note should be witnessed, preferably by someone other than a family member. Certainly, a couple can have several notes outstanding at any one time. In order to be valid, cash funds should be transferred and not securities, real estate or other investments. A loan can remain open for an indefinite

A NON-INTEREST-BEARING DEMAND NOTE

I, Jane Doe, acknowledge the receipt of $10,000 (ten thousand dollars) as a non-interest-bearing loan from John Doe repayable in whole or in part within thirty days of demand.

_____   _____
DATE   (JANE DOE)

                                    _____
                                    (JOHN DOE)

                                    _____
                                    WITNESS

period of time. However, occasionally, it would be advisable to make very small payments against the principal. This should be done in order to avoid the "statute of limitations", which might otherwise make the loan invalid after a certain number of years has elapsed. Of course, if a wife repays part of the principal owing to her husband, she could presumably borrow back these funds on the following day under the same type of arrangement.

These types of loans are not restricted to husbands and wives but can be made to any adult. The concern, of course, must always be the control over the use of the invested funds and a reasonable assurance of repayment on demand. A parent might decide to lend money to a child over the age of eighteen, for example. The child must be a least eighteen years old for this arrangement to work since children under the age of eighteen cannot legally borrow money. If gifts are made to children under the age of eighteen, income generated by the transferred property automatically reverts back to the transferor for tax purposes.

The following example depicts a typical situation where a parent, by making a $35,000 loan to a child, can save up to $1,815 using 1982 exemptions.

EXAMPLE OF TAX SAVINGS RESULTING FROM A LOAN TO A CHILD

Assumptions:

- Parent has $35,000 of investment capital bearing interest at 15%, *over and above* the $7,000 needed to utilize his annual $1,000 "investment income deduction". He is in the 50% tax bracket.
- Parent has a child over the age of eighteen attending university. The child has no income and the parent uses his after-tax investment income to pay tuition fees ($600) and to provide support.

Note: Tuition fees are only deductible by a student, although the $50-a-month education deduction is transferable to a supporting individual whenever the student does not need it to reduce his own taxable income to nil.

ALTERNATIVE 1: No loan to child.

Interest income to parent		
(15% × $35,000)	$5,250	
Less: Income taxes thereon (50%)	2,625	
Net interest income		$2,625
Add: Tax savings from:		
Personal exemption for child (in 1982)	$1,220	
Transfer of education deduction		
(assume 8 months × $50)	400	
	$1,620	
$1,620 × 50% tax saving		810
Net cash flow		$3,435
Cash flow utilized:		
To pay tuition	$ 600	
To pay expenses	2,835	
	$3,435	

ALTERNATIVE 2: A $35,000 loan is made by the parent to his child. (The loan is non-interest-bearing, and is repayable on demand.) A term deposit is purchased by the child.

Child's tax position:

Interest income (15% × $35,000)	$5,250
Less: Tuition fees paid by student	600
Net income for tax purposes	4,650
Personal exemption (1982)	(3,560)
Investment deduction	(1,000)
Optional standard deduction for medical and donation expenses	(100)
Education deduction (8 months × $50)	* (400)
Taxable income	Nil
Taxes payable	Nil
Cash flow utilized:	
To pay tuition	$ 600
To pay expenses	4,650
Net cash flow	$5,250
Advantage of loan ($5,250 – $3,435)	$1,815

*The $400 education deduction could be transferred to the parent. This would result in additional tax savings of $200, thus increasing the advantage of the loan.

This saving, which results from capitalizing on the child's lack of income, is certainly significant in relation to a total investment income of $5,250. Multiply this benefit by the number of years that the child attends university, and there is a substantial advantage. The savings can be used to provide additional support for the child *or* for the benefit of the family as a whole. The demand loan feature should protect the parent in the event that the child decides to use the dollars for anything other than the purchase of a term deposit or similar investment. Presumably, your bank manager would witness the note, and in the event that the child tried to "cash in", it would be incumbent upon the manager to inform the parent of these developments. Of course, if the child is unreliable, you would not jeopardize your asset position even for the tax advantages.

If the ages of your children are such that one child is finishing university just as the next one is starting, you can see that the benefits of the above plan can be compounded. As one child graduates, the parent can demand that the money be returned, and the funds are then available to lend to the next child. Of course, if several children are in university at the same time, then a parent would need more money in the first place to compound the advantages.

Helping Your Children Pay Off Their Mortgages

Another variation of this same theme involves situations where parents have substantial investment capital while their children are forced to borrow money in order to subsidize the acquisition of their homes. Ironically, when the parents earn interest income they pay taxes on their yields. On the other hand, the children must pay the interest expense on their homes using after-tax dollars. Chapter Six will discuss ways of getting around this ridiculous situation, in order to maximize tax and investment advantages for *both* the parents and the children.

The Use and Misuse of Credit Cards

In spite of the benefits of having some of your assets invested in interest-bearing certificates (especially if the tax burden is low), a well-thought-out investment strategy must take into account your entire set of personal circumstances. Millions of people have accumulated large amounts of personal debts through the use of credit cards. There appears to be something psychologically pacifying about paying off the minimum amount on these obligations every month while keeping the remainder of one's investment funds in savings accounts or term deposits. The actual result of making such a choice is extremely expensive. As the example below illustrates, you can lose large amounts of real money because the interest which you earn on your term deposits is subject to taxation while the interest on credit card debts is paid with after-tax dollars. You should note, that this particular pitfall is unique to Canada. In the United States, credit card interest is tax-deductible, so it really doesn't matter to many Americans whether they earn interest income on the one hand and pay interest expense on the other. In the U.S., the "comfort" of having term deposits may override the fact the credit card interest is generally somewhat more expensive than term deposit income.

INTEREST AND THE BEFORE-TAX-DOLLAR ILLUSION

Assumptions

- Owe $5,000, with interest @ 24%
- Monthly blended payment is 5% of declining balance

Total payments in first year	$2,551
Principal portion	1,530
Non-deductible interest paid	$1,021
Earnings necessary to cover interest in 50% bracket $1,021 × 2 =	$2,042
Term deposit — $5000 @ 16%	
Interest at end of Year 1	$ 800
Tax @ 50%	400
Net income	$ 400
Lost earnings through non-deductible interest	$2,042
Recovery through after-tax interest income	400
Real loss at end of one year	$1,642

Once you realize that you can actually lose over $1,600 a year if your circumstances conform to our example, you would certainly make the logical choice—pay off your outstanding non-deductible interest obligations as soon as possible. In Chapter Six, we will examine an extension of this concept when it comes to paying down the mortgage on your home.

Investments in Bonds

Although most investments that bear only interest income will cost you money in the long run (given taxes and inflation) there is still a significant opportunity to actually make money if you are willing to explore the bond market. A bond is basically a piece of paper which gives evidence to the fact that a borrower has borrowed money and has undertaken to repay the debt along with a stated rate of interest. In general, bonds can be issued by governments, private companies and public corporations. For our purposes, we will concentrate on bond obligations of governments and public corporations. Certainly, if you wish to explore specific issues, you would have to seek expert advice from your broker. Fortunately, bonds are rated as to quality. There are two services—Moody's and Standard & Poor's—which evaluate the strengths and weaknesses of companies that have borrowed money in the bond market. The top rating would be AAA while the lowest rating is a CCC–. If you wish to be conservative, you can instruct your broker to consider only those that are at least BBB or better.

How the Bond Market Works

Bonds are issued from time to time as the borrower needs to raise capital. The certificates are usually issued in denominations that are divisible by 100. The rate of interest which each bond stipulates is based on the rate prevailing at the time the capital was raised. In mid-1982, if a corporation were to issue bonds in denominations of $1,000 each, it would have to be prepared to pay approximately 18%. The documentation would therefore guarantee the holder of the bond an 18% rate of return annually based on the face value of the bond certificate. Thus, over the life of the bond (which is also stipulated in the relevant documentation) the holder would receive $180 annually on each $1,000 bond. If the original purchaser holds the bond each year until maturity, he will receive an 18% rate of return on his invested capital.

However, once the initial sale takes place, the value of the bond will fluctuate on the open market to compensate for changes in the prevailing rates of interest. If interest rates go up, then an 18% return may become unattractive. The value of the bond will therefore decline. On the other hand, if interest rates drop, the value of the bond will increase and the bond will trade at a premium. Any time a bond is sold for more than the price which the buyer paid, the difference is treated as a capital gain. As such, only one-half of this profit will be taxed. Conversely, if the bond is sold at a price less than the buyer's cost, he will suffer a capital loss. Only half that loss is tax-deductible.

The "trick" to making money in the bond market is to take advantage of the opportunities bonds offer to earn *both* interest income and capital gains for the investor. In order to make this trick work, the investor must, from time to time, be able to predict a trend in the movement of interest rates.

Investments in Bonds Create Capital Gains

In this day of uncertainty and in spite of volatile interest rates, there may still be a place in your investment portfolio for bond issues. However, we must again emphasize that proper strategy does not dictate that you invest for the long-term prospects of receiving a stream of interest income. The situation in Canada is somewhat different from that of the United States. In the United States, there are many issues of tax-free municipal bonds attractive to investors in high income-tax brackets. However, this tax-free status does not extend to Canadian investors. In this country, there are at present no such local obligations which are free from tax. For many investors, an 18% bond represents an after-tax return of only 9%. Nevertheless, certain bonds can represent an excellent investment vehicle in Canada — as long as the object is to earn capital gains.

As mentioned previously, bonds are highly sensitive to

Assumptions: Public Company A issued a $1,000 bond @ 12% ($120) interest in 1978 which matures in twenty years. In 1982, the market rate of interest is 18%.

Therefore: The price of this bond will have dropped between 1978 and 1982 so that $120 interest now equals an 18% return on the current price paid by an investor on the open market.

Let X = Price to be paid for bond
$.18X$ = $120 (interest on bond)
X = $667

Thus, the discounted price for the bond is $667.

changes in the prime rate of interest because they are valued on the basis of the interest yields which they guarantee the holder. Thus, bonds which bear a low stated rate of interest are sold in the bond market for less than their face value. If the discount is large because the stated interest rate is low, the bond is referred to as a "deep discount" bond. The example above illustrates how the discount on a bond works.

If the $1,000 bond used in our example can now be purchased for $667 at a time when interest rates are at 18%, then the price will *rise* if the market interest rate falls to, say, 16%. The investor who paid $667 would then realize a capital gain if he sold his bond at that time. High quality, heavily discounted bonds can respond quite significantly to changes of only 1% – 2% in interest rates. However, again, you must view the investment as a speculative one most suitable for the individual seeking to combine capital gains and interest income — not the investor looking for a stream of income. The example on page 60 shows how you can gain or lose if the prevailing interest rate moves in either direction by 2%. Thus the question of whether or not you will make a profit on your bonds depends on movements in interest rates.

You should note that your investment objectives can be totally defeated if you move into the bond market too early and have to wait for interest rates to drop in order to create an ultimate capital gain. Even if you are successful in making the capital gain of $83 illustrated by the first case, you will only keep $62 after taxes. If it takes one full year to realize this profit, and the inflation factor in the meantime is 10%, your $667 will have depreciated by about $67 in purchasing power. In other words, what starts out as a tax-free capital gain can end up a "real" loss. Again, you must also keep in mind that even if you are earning an 18% return on your investment, the interest income of $120 a year is reduced to only $60 after taxes if you are in a 50% income tax bracket.

HOW INTEREST RATE MOVEMENTS AFFECT BOND PRICES

Assumptions: $1,000 bond originally issued to yield 12% is bought for the discounted price of $667. The discounted price yields an effective return of 18%, which is the prevailing rate of interest at the time of purchase.

ALTERNATIVE 1: Prevailing rate of interest then drops to 16%.

Let X = Price to be paid by *next* purchaser
.16X = $120 (annual interest on bond)
   X = $750

Vendor makes a capital gain of $750 – $667 = <u>$83</u>
Vendor in 50% tax bracket keeps 75% of $83 = <u>$62</u> after tax on capital gains.

ALTERNATIVE 2: Prevailing rate of interest then rises to 20%

Let X = Price to be paid by *next* purchaser
.20X = $120 (annual interest on bond)
   X = $600

Vendor incurs a capital loss of $667 – $600 = <u>$67</u>
Vendor in 50% tax bracket loses 75% × $67 = <u>$50</u> after tax recovery on capital loss.

Note: Where one-half of the capital loss exceeds $2,000 and the individual has no other capital gains, the excess loss is not deductible from other income but must be carried over to other years. (Capital losses are discussed in detail on pages 149–50.)

Certainly, if the prevailing rate of interest goes up instead of down, the investment becomes a tremendous loser! Given the destructive effects of taxation and inflation, any hope that the individual has of ultimately retaining the purchasing power on his original investment — even if he holds the bond to maturity and realizes the face value of $1,000 — is destroyed.

Again, coming into the market too soon or cutting your potential for capital gains too short by selling too quickly (having guessed correctly at a downward trend in interest rates) can mean that you will consistently lose ground. Besides your concern for liquidity in the 1980s, you must also be willing to pay very close attention to the timing of your investments. The old saying, "Time is money" holds true not only in business but as a guideline for your investment portfolio as well.

Outside of deep discount, high quality bonds there is one other category of debt instrument which presents an attractive investment alternative. To increase their marketability, some bonds offer more than just a competitive rate of interest. These are convertible bonds, which allow the investor to trade his security for common stock of the issuing corporation at a fixed price. A convertible bond presents the investor with an excellent opportunity to become a shareholder and to pursue capital gains through the eventual disposition of the company's stock. Where the issuing company has good growth potential, such bond issues are usually keenly sought after, and frequently many are completely sold out within a matter of days after their issue. A close working relationship with your broker is necessary to guarantee that you will be able to take action on such issues as soon as they come onto the market. You may not want to hold these bonds until such time as the conversion price is attractive, but only long enough to capitalize on the rising market price of the shares. This would happen if the company performs extremely well or if the stock market in general starts to go up. Alternatively, even if the market does not perform well, but interest rates drop substantially, the fact that these bonds may bear a rate of return better than the going interest rate can again provide you with a capital gain.

Summary

The primary danger in holding long-term interest-bearing investments is that after inflation and taxes you will be left with funds that are insufficient to offset the loss in purchasing power on your original investment. Certainly, you can take steps to maximize interest yields. You can take advantage of the tax-free $1,000 of investment income which you can earn annually and use deferred programs such as registered retirement savings plans (which are discussed in detail in the next chapter). Perhaps the most important step is to always consider the family unit. Throughout the 1980s, the immediate and extended family will benefit most through mutual cooperation. Non-interest-bearing demand loans should be used wherever and whenever practical. Within the prudent limits of cash flow, a certain portion of your investments should still be made with borrowed funds. You may want to consider high quality bond issues in order to create short-term capital gains. Within the confines of liquidity and short-term investment returns, you should find that you have a significant use for interest-bearing securities in your overall investment portfolio. Of course, any drastic changes in prevailing interest rates will require modifications to your strategy.

CHAPTER FIVE

Registered Retirement Savings Plans And Life Insurance Programs

In the previous chapter, you were advised not to make interest-bearing investments solely for the sake of earning such interest — especially where the income is subject to taxation at high rates. We stressed the need to plan for the family as a unit as well as to take advantage of opportunities to combine interest and capital gains. We also indicated that the strategy of earning interest income can be profitable as long as such income is tax-sheltered.

One of the best ways available to Canadians to earn tax-sheltered income is through a personal registered retirement savings plan (RRSP) program. This is probably the only interest-bearing investment that is safe to hold over an extended time. As you will see, the advantage of an RRSP is the opportunity to use untaxed dollars for your own investment portfolio while also earning a tax-deferred investment yield. You will see as well that an RRSP presents opportunities to earn other types of investment yields in addition to interest.

RRSPs exist because the Canadian government wants to encourage you to plan for your retirement. The Income Tax Act sets out certain rules which allow you to take some of your earned income and to exchange it for future benefits. This deferral is accompanied by specific tax concessions which will make it easier for you to finance your retirement program. The tax rules do, however, draw a distinction between encouraging realistic savings plans and the tax avoidance possibilities that would exist if the deferrals were overly generous.

Registered Retirement Savings Plans

Under the registered retirement savings plan program, an individual is allowed to set aside tax-deductible contributions if these are made in a given taxation year or within sixty days following the end of that year. The maximum annual amount is 20% of "earned income", subject to a dollar limitation of:

- $5,500 where the individual is not a member of an employer-sponsored registered pension plan or deferred profit-sharing plan, or
- $3,500 (minus the individual's contributions to a registered pension plan, if any).

Earned income is basically the sum of net receipts from employment, self-employment (business), pensions, rentals and alimony. Where an individual is not a member of an employer-sponsored pension or deferred profit-sharing program, the "magic" earned income required for full participation in an RRSP is $27,500. This is because 20% of $27,500 is $5,500, which is the maximum amount that qualifies for an RRSP investment in any given year (excluding retirement allowances and other special transfers).

The RRSP program is a fairly straightforward investment. Each year that contributions are made, they are tax-deductible. As long as the amounts are invested in qualified investments such as term deposits or guaranteed income certificates, Canadian public company stocks and bonds, Canada Savings Bonds, or mortgages, the income earned within an RRSP compounds on a tax-deferred basis. After several years of ongoing contributions, the available capital starts to snowball and the build-up of capital continues until retirement. At that time, you liquidate the assets in the plan and purchase an annuity that will provide you with a cash flow after your retirement. Although withdrawals from an RRSP are taxable, you will usually be in a lower tax bracket after retirement than previously.

The benefits of an RRSP are substantial. If, for example, you invest $5,500 a year annually at 15% compounded for thirty years, you would have almost $2.75-million at the end.

This amount could purchase an annuity that would provide a *monthly* income of $34,000 for the rest of your life. It is, of course, an open question of what $34,000 a month would buy given current levels of inflation — but that is beside the point, as you will see in the next section.

Should I Have an RRSP?

One of the most common questions executives ask is whether or not an RRSP is advisable, especially because of investment restrictions. Real estate is a non-qualified investment, as are precious metals such as gold and silver, and one cannot invest to any great extent in foreign securities. Despite the limitations placed on one's RRSP portfolio, an executive really doesn't have a choice — he *must* have an RRSP.

Let's examine the alternatives. For anyone in a 50% tax bracket, it becomes a choice of either having $5,500 earning income at a compound rate of, say, 15% to 18% each year or having half the capital ($2,750) tax-paid and earning income at a much lower rate (since unsheltered investment yields are taxable). Having twice the capital to invest at a substantially higher rate certainly makes an RRSP worthwhile. In dealing with the question of whether or not an RRSP is attractive, simply ask yourself, what better choice is there?

Interest on Money Borrowed for Deferred Income Plans

Until very recently, an additional advantage of an RRSP was that an individual who did not have the necessary funds to contribute could borrow for RRSP purposes and deduct interest incurred with respect to his investment. However, under the November 12, 1981 Budget provisions, interest on loans taken out after that date to finance registered retirement savings plans as well as other income-deferral plans is no longer deductible. On the surface, this appears to pose a substantial problem for the middle-income executive who borrows from a lending institution in order to make an RRSP contribution. Generally, that individual is one year behind, always paying for the previous year's RRSP, but at the same time, saving much needed monies towards his retirement. In fact, RRSP contributions in January and February 1982 (for 1981) were substantially less than anticipated by most insurance companies, trust companies and banks.

What few people realized in the winter of 1981–82 is that borrowing money to buy an RRSP can *still* be advantageous as a forced savings program. Consider the alternatives. If an individual in the 50% bracket borrows $5,500 to buy an RRSP, and places his funds in the plan to earn 16%, after one year he will have earned interest income of $880. Even if he were to take his earnings out of the plan and pay full taxes on this interest, his net yield would be $440.

On the other hand, borrowing $5,500 involves a commitment of $458.33 a month over a one-year period, not including interest. Given an outstanding loan of $5,500 at the beginning of a year and a balance which is reduced to zero by the end of the year, this is the equivalent of owing $2,750 throughout the year (see the illustration on page 67). Even if the interest rate charged by a lending institution is 20%, the cost of the loan is therefore essentially 20% of $2,750 or $550 in total. Even though this interest is non-deductible, it is still not overly expensive when compared to the investment yield on $5,500 in the RRSP *throughout* the year. In fact, the actual cost in this example is really only $110 ($550–$440).

Actually, the cost is substantially less. The previous example has assumed that the average loan outstanding throughout the year would be $2,750. If, on the other hand, a $5,500 RRSP contribution results in a tax refund of $2,750 (for an individual in the 50% tax bracket) and these funds are used when received (generally in July or August) towards an immediate reduction of the outstanding loan balance, the actual average loan throughout the year is substantially less. This means that the non-deductible interest expense is decreased accordingly. Therefore, in the final analysis, the cost of borrowing on a year-to-year basis for the RRSP is virtually nil. Keep in mind that after the first year, the planholder would then have $5,500 available to earn compound income in subsequent years. This procedure can be repeated year after year, in accordance with

BORROWING TO BUY AN RRSP MAY STILL BE A GOOD IDEA

Funds in RRSP		$5,500
Investment yield		16%
		$ 880

		Repayment over 12 months	
Funds borrowed	$5,500	⟶	$0
Average loan	$2,750		
Interest rate	20%		
Interest expense	$ 550		

If interest income is deregistered:

Interest received	$ 880
Less: Taxes (50%)	440
Net interest income	440
Less: Interest expense	550
Cost of borrowing	$ 110

Note: If a tax refund is received in July or August and is applied against the loan balance, the average outstanding amount becomes less than $2,750. There may, in fact, be *no* net cost of borrowing.

the concept of the "forced savings program" that was discussed in Chapter Three.

This discussion contains a valuable lesson. Any time the government makes a change in the rules, you must not only examine the theory but you must also take representative numbers and see what the impact of such a change really is. On the surface, a prohibition against interest deductibility on funds borrowed to buy an RRSP seems to be a severe restriction. And yet, in the final analysis, the cost, if any, is negligible.

Spousal Plans

If you agree, and we hope you do, that an RRSP is a valid means of both tax sheltering and building up investment capital, you may want to add a few refinements to your own plan. One that is worth keeping in mind is the "spousal" RRSP.

Since 1974, you have been allowed to split RRSP contributions between yourself and your spouse. This does *not* mean that you can double your limit and contribute up to $11,000. However, if your annual limit is, for example, $5,500, you can channel this entire amount into your own plan, into a spousal plan, or you can allocate in any proportions (for example, 50–50, 60–40, etc.). The only way that a married couple can add more than $5,500 each year to RRSP savings is where *both* husband and wife have earned income. Thus, if your spouse has an earned income of her own, she too can contribute to an RRSP, earmarking the funds either to herself, to you, or in any combination.

Let us examine a situation where a husband has an earned income while his wife remains at home looking after the children. What are the advantages and disadvantages of setting up a spousal plan? The first major advantage of splitting RRSP contributions is that over time, two separate pools of capital are built up. Eventually, each pool will give rise to an annuity. Since tax rates for individuals are graduated, the tax bite will be substantially less if the annuity is split so that the husband only gets part of the income while his wife gets the balance.

If the wife in our example returns to the labour force, she will then be able to contribute to an RRSP too. She may contribute either to her own plan or to a plan in the name of her husband. Assume that she chooses to contribute to a plan in her own name. Under these circumstances, her husband probably would then begin to contribute more funds to his own plan and less to hers. The point however is that the family should make every effort possible to make contributions which would result in the equalization of their post-retirement incomes.

The second advantage of a spousal plan relates to another tax rule. As an additional concession for senior citizens who have had the foresight to save for their retirements through deferred compensation plans, the first $1,000 of annual private pension income is tax-deductible. The $1,000 tax deduction generally applies only where the recipient of the pension is over the age of sixty-five. (Receipts from the Canada Pension Plan or the Old Age Security Pension do not qualify for this deduction.)

Thus, by splitting your RRSP with your wife you not only build up two annuities, you *also* double up on the annual $1,000 pension-income deduction.

The only disadvantage to a spousal RRSP might occur in the event that a couple gets divorced. Whatever funds a husband has contributed into his wife's plan would then belong to her. This would not necessarily create a serious problem, however. In recent years, most provinces have adopted family law provisions whereby assets acquired after marriage are divided equally in the event of a marriage breakdown. Thus, a property settlement would presumably take assets held by each party's RRSP into account.

There is really no reason not to use a spousal RRSP as long as one's marriage is reasonably solid. We don't see much point in being paranoid about what might happen many years in the future. On the other hand, if one's marriage is somewhat shaky, why look for trouble? It might then be best to forgo the tax benefits of this arrangement.

One word of caution. If you place funds into a spousal plan, you must be prepared to leave these dollars for at least a while. The tax rules provide that where a wife withdraws funds from an RRSP, her husband is taxed on any contributions made in his wife's name during the current or two preceding years. This "attribution" of income is designed to prevent a situation where a high-bracket individual contributes funds (on a deductible basis) to his spouse's plan and she, in turn, withdraws the money practically tax-free almost immediately thereafter. You cannot beat the system by causing your wife to withdraw "older" contributions first. Under the rules, the most recent contributions are considered to be the first ones withdrawn for tax purposes. Naturally, the attribution rule also applies where a wife contributes to her husband's plan.

No RRSP Annuity Before Age Sixty

You may not take an annuity out of an RRSP before you have reached the age of sixty. If you wish to withdraw funds before that time, you must make a lump-sum deregistration of your plan. Your are, however, allowed to reregister those dollars on which you do not wish to pay taxes, subject of course to any handling fees that may be charged by the trustees of the plan.

If there is some possibility that you will require funds before you are sixty, because of unforeseen circumstances or a low income year, you may be best off with one or two smaller RRSPs as well as a major plan which builds for your retirement. If you are in need of a few thousand dollars, you would simply deregister one of the small plans and make use of those funds after having paid your taxes. If you become unemployed and require funds to meet your living expenses, an RRSP is, in many cases, the first investment that you should consider liquidating.

Bequeathing Your RRSP to a Spouse

There are also some important rules which apply on the death of an individual. Essentially, if at the time of your death, you have rights under an RRSP, the value of these rights is included in your income in the year of death. To avoid this, you must bequeath your rights under your RRSP to your spouse. Otherwise you will be making a rather costly mistake — especially if you die late in a year and have RRSP income over and above other income earned in that year. Generally, your will should provide for a spousal bequest of an RRSP. If an RRSP is bequeathed to a spouse, the spouse then has a choice:

- She can pay tax on all or part of that which she receives and then have tax-paid money left over, or
- She can transfer funds into her own RRSP.

Before the November 12, 1981 Budget amendments, she was also permitted to transfer a portion of the inherited RRSP into an income-averaging annuity.

If you were to die and your wife had very little income in that year, it would probably be advisable for her to take part of the RRSP which she inherits directly into her income. In fact, she should be willing to pay taxes on as much as $100,000. The total taxes on $100,000 would amount to only approximately $40,000, and on an after-tax basis, she would have about sixty cents on the dollar available for reinvestment.

Any surplus RRSP funds could then be transferred into her own RRSP. While an annuity from an RRSP cannot be taken *before* age sixty, she could nevertheless wait until age seventy-one before making withdrawals. In addition, by placing an inherited RRSP into several separate plans, it appears still possible for the surviving spouse to make periodic withdrawals as funds are required. *This would provide the same benefits as an income-averaging annuity.* For example, if an inherited RRSP were rolled into ten separate RRSPs there appears to be no restriction against deregistering one a year for the following ten-year period. The surviving spouse would be able to use these funds to meet living requirements at a relatively low annual tax cost.

Bequests of RRSPs to Other Beneficiaries

If you die without leaving a surviving spouse, there is still an RRSP rollover if you leave RRSP funds to dependent children or grandchildren under the age of twenty-six. The rollover is $5,000 for each year that the dependent child or grandchild is under twenty-six at the time you die. This particular rule was passed by Parliament in response to a lobby from unmarried or divorced taxpayers who felt that they were being discriminated against. Unfortunately, for most people this amendment is probably not worth the paper it is written on.

Think about how it would apply in your circumstances if you were to die without leaving a spouse to receive your RRSP. In most cases, you would not have a substantial RRSP portfolio until approximately age fifty-five. This is because the compounding effect really only builds up in the last ten or fifteen years before retirement. When you are fifty-five, do you expect to have *dependent* children or grandchildren under the age of twenty-six?

Becoming a Non-Resident

Ironically, one of the best benefits that one can derive from an RRSP is reserved for an individual who becomes a non-resident of Canada. The worst exposure to tax on RRSP withdrawals by a non-resident is a flat rate of 25%. If one moves to a country with which Canada has a tax treaty, the rate is sometimes only 15%.

Temporary Residents of Canada

The RRSP can also be an excellent investment and tax-saving device for temporary residents of Canada. Take, for example, the situation of a geophysicist coming to this country to work on the Hibernia oil discovery. Assume that he takes a position with an oil company paying $70,000 a year and that he expects to stay in Canada for a three-year period. During those three years, the geophysicist should invest the maximum amount possible into an RRSP. He would get a deduction for tax purposes and would save over $2,500 of taxes each year. Then, when he returns to his own country, his worst exposure to taxation would be a flat 25%. Any time one can recover forty-five or fifty cents on the dollar when contributions are made and not pay more than twenty-five cents on the dollar a few years later, the saving is worthwhile.

What Kind of Plan Should I Have?

RRSPs are administered by trust companies, banks, and insurance companies. In addition, you are allowed to have a self-directed plan where you appoint trustees (or a trust company) and the trustees make whatever investments that you as planholder desire. Of course, all investments must fall within the acceptable tax guidelines discussed at the beginning of this chapter.

Traditionally, people wait until the end of February to purchase their RRSP for the preceding year. Many millions of dollars are spent annually by companies trying to promote their own particular plans. To attempt to compare all the different alternative investments is a full-time job for a qualified investment counsellor. Contrary to popular belief, most accountants and lawyers are not any better equipped to pick "the right" RRSP than you are. When it comes to selecting an RRSP, you cannot necessarily even rely on past performance. Remember that the performance of a particular plan is only a function of those people employed as fund managers. If a well-qualified investment analyst changes jobs, the plan that was number one last year might very well sink to number ten, while last year's poor performer can end up tops the following year.

The only concrete advice that we give to clients is that they invest conservatively. While purists will probably try to extract every last nickel of income, we tend to believe that a one or two per cent difference in yield is not going to make or break the average middle-income and upper-income investor in the long run. It is true that compounding at a return of 15% instead of 17% can result in a significant difference over twenty or thirty years. However, plan performances will often balance out over the long run and you may not even be aware of what you could have realized had you invested differently many years ago. So don't worry about that extra one or two per cent unless you have the time to pursue the top performers, even though the list keeps changing frequently.

Self-Directed Plans

Once you have been contributing to an RRSP for several years and have, perhaps, $15,000 to $20,000 accumulated, you may want to consider a self-directed plan. However, you should only do this if you are willing to pay the same attention to your RRSP that you would to other investments. This would enable you to take advantage of special circumstances as they arise. For example, in November 1981, the Government of Canada issued a savings bond which bore interest in excess of 19% for the first year. This turned out to be at least 3%–4% higher than alternative interest-bearing investments offered by insurance companies, banks or trust companies. Many people who had self-directed RRSP programs took the opportunity to convert their holdings into this special issue of savings bond.

On the other hand, anyone who took the opportunity in 1981–1982 to use a self-directed program for the purpose of playing the stock market probably found himself much worse off. Nevertheless, in a rising market, playing the equity market can result in substantial rewards. If interest rates continue to drop as they did in the fall of 1982 and the stock market continues to recover, we would certainly consider moving our interest-bearing investments within self-directed RRSPs out of bonds and into the equity market.

Insurance Companies vs. Banks and Trust Companies

Traditionally, insurance companies that administer RRSPs tend to charge the larger part of their fees for handling your money against the initial contributions. This is called a *front-end load*. By contrast, banks and trust companies tend to charge their fees in smaller amounts over the entire life of your plan. We once did a study comparing what we considered (at that time) to be an "average" insurance plan to an "average" trust company plan. Over a period of twenty-five or thirty-years, there was only a negligible difference in the assets available towards a post-retirement annuity.

Thus, when a client asks us to comment on the differences, we tend to say that in the long run, there is no real difference. However, if you are a short-term resident of Canada, or non-residency is imminent, we suggest that you stay away from *any* plan with a front-end load. This is because, on deregistration, you may find yourself getting less money than you actually put in. If you plan on leaving Canada in a few years, your prime consideration should be directed towards an RRSP that will yield the largest possible income initially, with the smallest administration charges. In addition, you should obtain an undertaking from the trustees that your money will be refunded on demand, and if there are any deregistration charges, these should be clearly spelled out in your agreement. Most institutions will either manage your RRSP investments for you or act as your trustee in a self-directed program.

Suggested RRSP Investments

Over the years, two schools of thought have evolved with respect to RRSP investments. The first group recommends investing money in interest-bearing securities or mortgages paying the best current yields. Other advisers suggest that you might be better off by investing in equity funds involving Canadian public company securities. The proponents of equities feel that capital growth will outstrip interest yields over the long run as long as you pick the right securities!

However, equity investments are thought by many to be unattractive because of the fact that all withdrawals from RRSPs are taxable as ordinary income. In other words, you do not get the advantage of the favourable tax treatment accorded to Canadian dividends through the dividend tax credit (see Chapter Eight). In addition, capital gains become transformed into regular income, while ordinarily, only one-half of capital gains is subject to tax.

At the time this is being written in mid-1982, the stock market is behaving somewhat erratically. Given high interest rates and a general slowdown of the economy aggravated greatly by the restrictions of the November 12, 1981 Budget, we do not recommend that RRSP contributions be made in the form of stock market investments. As long as interest rates stay high, we think that investors should take advantage of RRSPs which earn such interest. After all, investment yields in an RRSP compound on a tax-deferred basis and anything better than the inflation rate is a positive return. If the stock market shows signs of sustained improvement, an astute investor should be prepared to modify his strategy.

"Cashing in" an RRSP for a Life Annuity

Until just a few years ago, there was only one way to "cash in" an RRSP. The Income Tax Act required that an individual (over the age of sixty) use the funds accumulated in an RRSP to purchase a life annuity from an insurance company before reaching the age of seventy-one. The annuity benefits were then taxable as and when they were received. The only alternative was to make lump-sum withdrawals from the RRSP and become liable to pay income tax on all amounts received. In order to protect yourself in the event of an early death, you were also permitted to modify the ordinary life annuity by adding a "guaranteed term" rider. (A guaranteed term means that payments continue for at least that length of time even if the annuitant dies prematurely. However, any time an individual lives beyond the guaranteed term the payments will continue until the time of death.) The guaranteed term permitted under an RRSP life annuity was always up to fifteen years. In addition, you were also allowed to arrange a joint-and-last-survivor annuity program where payments would continue out of an RRSP until both husband and wife had died. Even the joint-and-last-survivor option could be structured to have a guaranteed term of up to fifteen years.

Over the years, the requirement that one deal only with a life insurance company at the tail end of a program did not appeal to many potential RRSP investors. Actually, the insurance companies have been somewhat unjustly maligned because of a very common misconception. If you are seventy-one years old and you go to an insurance company with $100,000 in your RRSP, you could probably find a company that would agree to pay you an annuity of approximately $15,000 a year if you did not opt for any guaranteed term. Of course, you would not ordinarily think that this is any bargain. If you are male, you are probably conscious of the fact that your average life expectancy is only seventy-two years. Thus, how would you feel about receiving only two years' worth of annuities, or $30,000 out of a $100,000 investment made initially?

If you agree with this reasoning, you have fallen into the common trap. While it is true that the average life expectancy of a male would be seventy-two years, this is only where the person for whom the computation is made is younger than age forty. Once one passes the age of forty, life expectancy goes up. You will find, if you examine a standard table of mortality rates (see page 88), that a seventy-year-old male has a life expectancy of *another eleven years*, and that a female of the same age is projected to live another *fourteen years*. Thus, an insurance company is not really mistreating you by offering $15,000 a year as an RRSP yield. In preparing calculations, the insurance company must budget for a payout of eleven to fourteen years—even without any guarantee. Since most people are not aware of this, insurance companies have acquired "bad reputations" somewhat unjustly over the years.

Naturally, if you retire when you are sixty-five and begin to take an RRSP annuity at that age, you can expect to receive substantially less than if you wait until age seventy-one. Also, a woman should expect to be offered a lower annual yield than a man, since she could be expected to live longer.

Other Options: Fixed-Term Annuities and Registered Retirement Income Funds

In 1978, the government opened up the RRSP annuity field to trust companies and two new options were introduced:

- A fixed-term annuity may now be purchased to provide benefits to age ninety and/or
- RRSP savings may be transferred into a new kind of investment vehicle — a registered retirement income fund (RRIF).

Financial and other institutions that were previously eligible to issue RRSPs are permitted to offer the new options. Such institutions include trust companies as well as insurance companies.

Typically, however, the government gave and took at the same time. The previous section explained that anyone issuing a life annuity to a seventy-year-old male must be prepared to pay out over an eleven-year period. Under the fixed-term annuity to age ninety, the same initial capital is paid out over a twenty-year period. Thus, the recipient of a fixed-term annuity (over twenty years) is penalized by receiving smaller annual payments than he would under a life annuity. The fixed-term option may therefore only be attractive to those individuals with other incomes and other assets who wish to pass on estates as large as possible to their heirs. Of course rates of return are subject to change from time to time and it is always necessary to shop around for the best possible deal before making a final decision.

Under the RRIF option, a specific fraction of one's total RRSP assets—capital plus accumulated earnings—is withdrawn each year to provide the holder with an annual income until he is ninety. The fraction is related to the age of the individual in the year and is simply equal to "1" divided by the number of years remaining to age ninety. As an example, for a seventy-year-old purchaser, an RRIF would run for twenty years. In the first year, with twenty years remaining, the holder would be required to take into income $1/20$ of the total value of the plan at the beginning of the year. After another year, $1/19$ of what is left would be withdrawn, a year later $1/18$ and so on, until the final year, when the individual reaches ninety, withdrawal would exhaust the fund. A participant is only permitted to own one RRIF. He may, however, if he so chooses, allot only a portion of his RRSP accumulations to the establishment of an RRIF and invest the remainder in any number of fixed-term or life annuities.

An individual may also base the term of an annuity or RRIF on the age of his spouse, if the spouse is younger, thus securing benefits for the spouse to age ninety. Should a person die before reaching ninety, the benefits under the new options, as well as under life annuities with a guaranteed term, could be bequeathed to a surviving spouse. Otherwise, as indicated previously, the value of any remaining benefits must be included in the deceased person's income in the year in which he dies.

Presumably, the fact that one would ordinarily draw more out of the RRIF each year is intended to allow the individual to keep pace with increases in the cost of living. Thus, in theory the RRIF is better than both of the other options. This is because there is a flexible rate of return, rather than a fixed rate, and increasing, rather than level, payments. However, in spite of some recent amendments in the legislation, the RRIF does break down somewhat in practice. This is because the payments made during the early years are much smaller than the yield which could otherwise be obtained under either of the two alternative options. In many cases, it is not until the individual is approximately eighty years old that the RRIF would provide a better annual return than a life annuity. However, if we ever experience a period of hyperinflation in Canada, together with an enormous increase in interest rates, the RRIF will no doubt gain in popularity.

Even today, the RRIF can be useful for people who have other incomes and other assets. In most cases, however, an individual would be more interested in maximizing his cash flow in the first few years after he retires. It is during this period that he might still be mobile and able to enjoy whatever comforts money can bring.

Life Insurance Programs

The topic of investment planning couldn't possibly be covered without some reference to the role of life insurance as part of the overall picture. As a bare minimum, you should insure your life so that there need be no forced sale of assets at the time of death solely for the purpose of paying income taxes. For that reason, some kind of permanent insurance is necessary and term insurance will not usually be sufficient. (A term policy will not help if it expires before your death.) Basically, the tax rules provide that upon death you are deemed to have sold all your properties at fair market value. The exception is where you leave property to a spouse. In such a case, the tax on capital gains will not ordinarily arise until the second spouse dies. From time to time, you should try to estimate the potential taxes owing as a result of death. Your accountant can assist you in putting together the figures. You would then apply combined federal and provincial marginal tax rates to the anticipated income. In order to be fairly conservative, you might assume taxes of about 50%. Taxes arising from deemed dispositions may be spread over ten years, but each instalment presently bears interest at 16% and the instalment interest is not deductible.

Of course, life insurance has additional uses beyond just paying taxes. Its uses are described in the next few pages. Before going any further, however, you should be aware that *nowhere* in this chapter is it suggested that life insurance is an investment. In fact, as you will see shortly, insurance is a *cost*. Its purpose is to provide protection as well as a source of cash when it is most needed.

One of the most important points concerning life insurance

is that the receipt of *benefits* arising on the death of the insured is completely *tax-free* (except in Quebec where there are still provincial succession duty implications). This is because life insurance *premiums* are generally *non-deductible*.

Insurance Programs Provide Income to Dependants

Many people rely totally on group life and pension programs instituted by their employers. This is a mistake, since the present level of such benefits will not generally provide adequately for either a middle-income or a highly-paid key executive. In some cases, these shortcomings are created by government regulations, while others are caused by restrictions imposed by insurers themselves. For example, assume that an executive has annual earnings of $50,000. His company program limits his coverage to 2½ times earnings under its group life package. Let us assume that this executive now dies and his widow inherits $125,000 of tax-free insurance proceeds. Assume that the funds are then invested at 16% to yield $20,000 a year. Compare these earnings (on a pre-tax basis) to the deceased's annual income of $50,000. If the widow wishes to retain her capital intact, she must make a drastic change in her lifestyle. The thought of a 60% reduction in the level of family income is certainly not particularly attractive.

What about an employer-sponsored pension program? Let us take the example of an executive age fifty-five who anticipates retiring at age sixty-five after thirty-five years of service. (Actually, such a long period of service would be extremely rare in practice.) Again, assume a present income level of $50,000 a year and—assuming a 10% annual increase in pay—a final income of $118,000.

Traditionally, most pension plans are based on the average of the highest salaries earned over a five-year period. In this case, the average of the best five years would also be that of the last five years, or $98,000. Assume that the pension benefit is 2% for each year of service multiplied by the average of the best five years. This would provide an annual cash flow of 2% multiplied by thirty-five years multiplied by $98,000, or

$68,000. However, as of 1982, government regulations permit a maximum pension of only $60,000 a year. As a percentage of *final* earnings, this works out to only 51% in our case. If the retired individual decides to take his pension as an annuity guaranteed for fifteen years, the annual pension would be only approximately $54,000, or 46% of the final year's earnings. If taken as a joint-and-last-survivor annuity guaranteed for ten years (assuming a spouse who is five years younger) the pension is only $43,200 or 37% of final income. Then, if we assume that the taxpayer dies shortly after having attained retirement age, we can again see that the spouse is faced with the prospect of receiving an income that is only a fraction of what was being received previously.

If you stop and think for a moment, a "standard" executive compensation program is not generally sufficient to meet your needs. Thus, the first role of the insurance you hold personally is to provide income to your surviving spouse and other dependants in the event that earned income from employment, business or a professional practice ceases.

A second use of life insurance is, as described previously, to pay income taxes arising from deemed dispositions on death and on other income generated at that time. Also, insurance proceeds can be used to pay debts owing at the time of death and debts created by virtue of death (such as funeral costs, executors' fees and professional fees).

Insurance Provides Liquidity

In addition, one of the most important reasons for carrying life insurance is to provide liquidity to an estate so that assets yielding little or no current income can be retained. Your family home is one example. This is especially important if you have borrowed money to acquire these assets in the first place. Many times this book has suggested that you consider borrowing money for investment purposes and financing your costs from surplus earnings from your job, business or profession. The actual amount that you decide to borrow depends largely on several factors, including the type of investment that you choose to acquire, the deductibility of interest and your own "comfort level". The concept of borrowing money makes sense for many people — *but only as long as they are alive.* If your earnings cease, so does the cash flow needed to maintain debt. You never want to be in a position where assets must be sold at fire-sale prices just because your estate can no longer afford to carry them. As we have seen, the investment market in every area tends to be somewhat cyclical, and if your heirs must sell at a time where your particular investments are depressed, there can be a substantial penalty. A general rule of thumb is that you should always carry sufficient insurance to *cover all debts owing at the time of death as well as debts created.* In other words, even if you don't adopt an aggressive investment philosophy, you should still insure your mortgage, car loans and any other personal debts. Then, additional insurance should be provided in order to maintain a flow of income so that your dependants do not have to suffer a reduction in their lifestyles. The amount of insurance required is not necessarily mind-boggling. For example, if you have a $50,000 mortgage against your house at 18% and there is insurance to cover that debt at the time of your death, technically your family could then afford to live on your take-home pay prior to death *minus* $733 a month (ignoring the inflation factor). The $733 represents the amount previously required to meet your monthly mortgage payments.

Other Uses for Insurance

One of the most underrated advantages of carrying life insurance is that it can facilitate distributions of an estate among family members. If, for example, you own a family farm or small business, you may wish to pass that on to one child rather than divide it equally among all your children. This is especially true where the one child is active in the farming or business operation. Leaving such an enterprise to be shared by all your children can create some serious inequities. Why should the one child who is active be forced to support inactive brothers and sisters? In addition, if the business can comfortably support one or two families, what happens when that business is then drained by the requirements of four or five families? In other words, it does not always make sense to give all your intended beneficiaries equal shares of each and every asset.

Does this mean that you must disinherit some of your children? Certainly not. The idea is to carry life insurance in sufficient amounts so that a family farm or business can pass to one child while the other children receive equivalent cash values from the insurance proceeds.

Life insurance can also be useful to meet obligations with respect to charitable bequests, or in special situations where you wish to provide for handicapped children or elderly parents. In addition, an insurance policy can help you achieve independence if you are contemplating a career change with attendant loss of employer-benefit programs. If you own a part-interest in a private business, life insurance is almost mandatory to assist the surviving partners in buying out the estates of those who die first.

Borrowing Against Life Insurance Policies

As time goes on, some insurance policies develop "cash surrender values". A cash surrender value is the amount which you would receive from the insurance company if you were to cancel the policy. In most cases, we would not recommend that you surrender your insurance—if for no other reason than because of the fact that the older you get, the more expensive it becomes to replace your coverage. In some cases, however, insurance companies will allow you to borrow against the cash surrender value at relatively inexpensive rates. If you borrow for investment purposes, the interest is tax-deductible. Unfortunately, the income tax rules surrounding life insurance policies are somewhat complex. Moreover, they are presently under review by the Department of Finance. Accordingly, we recommend that before you consider borrowing against any policy, you review the income tax implications with representatives of the insurance company that has issued the policy as well as with your own accountant.

Types of Life Insurance Products

Broadly speaking, there are two types of life insurance:

- term insurance
- permanent insurance

For taxpayers who maintain liquid estates and who require most of their protection in the early years, perhaps term insurance would be advisable. When it comes to a business situation, however, most advisers would opt in favour of a more permanent type of coverage. This is because most term insurance policies are calculated to expire when the holder reaches age seventy, whereas the average individual will probably not die until one or two years later. Term insurance therefore provides protection for your early needs while your children are young, but it is not adequate for long-range business planning and the preservation of property that is not liquid, such as real estate. When it comes to investment and estate planning, a good insurance agent is just as important a member of the team as your accountant or lawyer.

Generally, we recommend that in the decade between age twenty-five and thirty-five, while one is advancing in a career and at the same time beginning to raise a family, an individual should acquire term insurance to protect the family in the event of a premature death. Then, once the individual is more established, he should begin to transfer his coverage into more permanent-type policies. This is because the longer one waits, the more expensive permanent insurance becomes.

Characteristics of a Term Insurance Policy

As mentioned previously, term insurance tends to give the most protection for the least initial outlay. However, many term insurance policies do, in fact, expire by the time the individual reaches ages seventy. Thus, the one major deficiency is lack of *permanent* coverage. Nevertheless, if you are considering a term insurance policy, there are several special considerations. First, there should be a guarantee that you can convert and renew it without providing evidence of your adequate health.

Generally, term insurance policies tend to be renewable annually or every few years and to be convertible into whole-life insurance. You would want the right to obtain these benefits, especially if at some point your health should deteriorate and you would be unable to pass a medical examination. A guaranteed convertibility and renewability feature can easily be built into most term policies. You would also look for a provision which provides a waiver of premiums if you become disabled. This means that the policy would continue in force subsequent to a disability without your making any additional premium payments. Finally, you might also look for "double indemnity". This feature means that the policy would pay-off double if you die accidentally. This feature would be especially appealing to you if your lifestyle or job requires that you do a lot of travelling.

Permanent Insurance

There are many kinds of permanent insurance policies. Most common is the "whole-life" policy where payments continue until the time of death. As a variation, there is also the concept of "limited pay life" where your insurance premiums cease at a certain age (generally at the time of retirement). When we make recommendations for permanent insurance coverage to our clients, we generally suggest that the client not take any policy requiring insurance premiums to be paid subsequent to retirement. This is because, in many cases, one's cash flow tends to decrease once the "earned income years" are over. In addition to whole-life policies, permanent insurance also encompasses "endowment" policies and "single-premium" policies. Endowment policies have tended to become somewhat unpopular in recent years while (at least up until the November 12, 1981 Budget) single-premium policies have been gaining market acceptance.

An endowment policy provides a certain death benefit, or if one survives, the face amount is paid at age sixty-five (or seventy) together with any income which may accrue. Proceeds in excess of amounts deposited as premiums are fully taxable.

This vehicle has not been popular since other savings plans can provide better yields.

On the other hand, at least before taking income tax considerations into account, a single-premium policy may be the cheapest form of whole-life. It can be compared to the concept of paying cash for a house. A single-premium policy could be attractive if an individual has cash invested in a low-yield interest-bearing certificate and does not require current income. It would also be useful if an individual has an extremely high income in certain years and doesn't want to be burdened with paying insurance premiums later on in life. A good candidate for such a policy would be an athlete or an entertainer. A single-premium policy can also be useful as a gifting program, such as from grandparents to grandchildren. For example, a single payment of $5,000 could buy approximately $175,000 of fully paid-up life insurance for a ten-year-old grandchild.

However, one of the big problems that faces the life insurance industry in Canada today is that the federal budget of November 12, 1981 and the amendments of June 28, 1982 propose to tax the interest build-up on certain whole-life insurance policies issued after June 28, 1982. At the time this is being written, the government and life insurance industry representatives are still discussing how to proceed. It appears, however, that the single-premium concept may be rendered obsolete because of the tax deferral advantages such a policy offers.

Last-to-Die Policies

The "last-to-die" concept lends itself nicely to estate planning where the object is to pass assets intact to the next generation. Under Canadian law, a husband pays no tax on property he leaves to his wife and vice versa. It is therefore not necessary to pay taxes on death until both husband and wife die. (The only exception is in the Province of Quebec, which is the only jurisdiction which still levies succession duties at the provincial level.) A last-to-die policy can provide inexpensive insurance if one spouse is considerably younger than the other. It can also be useful if one spouse is not medically fit and the premiums to carry insurance on that person's life alone would otherwise be very high. As a variation on this theme, a last-to-die policy can be structured so that premium payments cease when the first spouse (or income earner) dies. The policy would still pay off at the time of the second death.

Evaluating Life Insurance Products

Of all areas involving business and investment concepts, life insurance is probably the least understood. As a perfect illustration, our own government is under the impression that a life insurance policy is an investment and that the interest "build-up" should be taxable. Actually, any life insurance product — even a single-premium policy — represents a *cost*. If one lives out one's life expectancy according to the mortality tables, the cost of premiums paid will exceed the benefits eventually received. As mentioned on page 79, you should be willing to assume this cost in exchange for protection in the event of an early demise, as well as the benefit of having cash available when it is needed.

To illustrate how an insurance policy operates, let us take an example of a forty-year-old male who wishes to have insurance coverage of $100,000. Let us assume that he opts for a whole-life policy at a cost of $1,100 a year. This means that each year for the rest of his life he will commit himself to insurance premium payments of $1,100 annually and on death (whenever that occurs) the policy will pay off $100,000.

There are many different models which we could have chosen. For our purposes, we have picked a very simple structure involving level (equal) annual premiums and a death benefit which does not fluctuate. The results of this analysis are, however, equally valid in analysing other insurance products as well.

In order to evaluate this particular proposal, we must first assume that after the age of forty a man will live for an additional thirty-three years. This is based on the standard

EVALUATING ANNUITY YIELDS — MORTALITY TABLE Male and Female Life Tables, Canada 1970–1972

Expectation of life in years

Age	Male	Female	Age	Male	Female	Age	Male	Female
11	60.19	66.93	36	36.90	42.76	61	16.27	20.58
12	59.22	65.95	37	35.97	41.81	62	15.61	19.79
13	58.24	64.97	38	35.05	40.87	63	14.96	19.01
14	57.28	63.99	39	34.13	39.92	64	14.33	18.25
15	56.33	63.02	40	33.22	38.99	65	13.72	17.47
16	55.39	62.05	41	32.32	38.05	66	13.12	16.72
17	54.46	61.08	42	31.42	37.13	67	12.54	15.98
18	53.53	60.11	43	30.53	36.20	68	11.98	15.26
19	52.62	59.15	44	29.65	35.28	69	11.43	14.55
20	51.71	58.18	45	28.77	34.37	70	10.90	13.85
21	50.80	57.21	46	27.90	33.45	71	10.38	13.17
22	49.89	56.25	47	27.04	32.55	72	9.88	12.51
23	48.98	55.28	48	26.19	31.65	73	9.39	11.86
24	48.07	54.31	49	25.35	30.75	74	8.92	11.24
25	47.16	53.34	50	29.86	24.52	75	8.47	10.63
26	46.23	52.37	51	28.98	23.71	76	8.02	10.03
27	45.30	51.40	52	28.11	22.91	77	7.60	9.46
28	44.37	50.44	53	27.24	22.11	78	7.19	8.91
29	43.44	49.47	54	21.34	26.38	79	6.79	8.38
30	42.50	48.51	55	20.57	25.53	80	6.41	7.88
31	41.56	47.54	56	19.82	24.68	81	6.05	7.39
32	40.63	46.58	57	19.08	23.85	82	5.70	6.93
33	39.69	45.62	58	18.35	23.02	83	5.36	6.48
34	38.76	44.67	59	17.64	22.20	84	5.04	6.06
35	37.83	43.71	60	16.95	21.39	85	4.74	5.67

mortality table that you will find on the previous page. This mortality table is the regular table used by most insurance actuaries. You should note, however, that special tables exist for groups such as non-smokers, who tend to have longer life expectancies than smokers.

Our hypothetical individual in this case has to be prepared to pay $1,100 each year for the next thirty-three years. In exchange, his estate will then receive $100,000. How does one compare payments of $1,100 a year with a lump-sum payment of $100,000 due at the end of thirty years? This is done using "present-value analysis". Very simply, the object is to ask two questions:

- What amount would have to be invested today at a reasonable rate of return after tax so that an investor could draw out $1,100 each year for thirty years and have nothing left at the end?
- What amount would that same person have to invest today at the same reasonable after-tax rate of return so that if he draws *nothing* for the next thirty years he would have $100,000 at the end?

The answers to both these questions can be obtained either from mathematical formulas or from tables. (If you are not a mathematician and/or do not have the tables available, your accountant should be able to assist you.) To continue the example of our hypothetical forty-year-old male, we'll assume that a reasonable rate of return on invested funds before taxes is 16%, or 8% after tax. The results of the comparison are shown in the following example:

A PRESENT-VALUE APPROACH TO LIFE INSURANCE PRODUCTS

Single amount today which can be invested at 8% (after-tax) to yield $1,100 (combined principal and interest) each year for 33 years	$13,678
Single amount today which can be invested at 8% (after-tax) and which will amount to $100,000 *at the end* of 33 years	7,890
Net cost of $100,000 life insurance policy	$ 5,788

At first glance, the results of the analysis on page 89 may be somewhat astounding. You would have to invest $13,678 today at 8% if you wanted a yield of $1,100 each year over a thirty-three year period. At the end of that time the entire $13,678 would be used up. On the other hand, you would only have to invest $7,890 today at 8% (leaving these funds to compound for thirty-three years) so that you could have $100,000 at the end. In other words, buying the life insurance policy for $1,100 a year involves a net present-value *cost* of $5,788. Clearly, life insurance is therefore *not* an investment.

On the other hand, before you cancel your insurance, you must understand that if the results did not work out as shown above, the insurance companies would all go bankrupt. In other words, if they paid out more than they took in, they couldn't stay in business too long.

Why then would anybody pay out more than what he hoped to obtain? The answer is, of course, protection. What happens if our hypothetical male age forty died *before* age seventy-three? He would then be paying $1,100 *less* for each year of decreased life-span. Also, his estate would receive the $100,000 proceeds that much sooner. On the other hand, if our male age forty *outlives* his normal life expectancy the cost of insurance becomes *even more expensive*. This is because he would be paying $1,100 a year for more than thirty-three years and would only receive the $100,000 death benefit at a later time. (However few of us are likely to complain about having enjoyed a longer life!)

The point, however, is that insurance provides a policy-holder with protection. What if *you* are the one who dies prematurely? What happens if your dependants require income at an earlier time than they would if you were to live out your normal life expectancy?

We hope that officials in the Department of Finance will read this particular chapter along with everybody else. Presumably, they too are interested in mapping out their own investment strategies for the 1980s. If they read these last few pages carefully, they will then understand one of the major points that we are trying to make. *Specifically, life insurance is a cost and not an investment and if any attempt is made to tax the interest build-up in* any *policy, the cost to the consumer simply becomes that much higher.* It is not the insurance industry that has been attacked by the recent federal budgets. Rather, it is the Canadian public at large.

How Much Insurance Is Enough?

Realizing that insurance is a cost, some of you may decide to "buy term and invest the difference". Buying term insurance at a relatively cheap cost and investing the difference can be the best move that you will ever make — *if you are sure that you are going to die prematurely.* However, what happens if you outlive your policy? This too may not be a serious problem, if by that time, you have substantial liquid assets and if the needs of your dependants are more than adequately met from other sources. On the other hand, if you have invested heavily in illiquid investments and your family enjoys an expensive life-style, term insurance is probably not the answer. At a bare minimum you should carry sufficient insurance to (1) pay off all debts owing if you were to die the day after the policy is taken out, and (2) provide enough capital so that the investment income that can reasonably be generated (without too much risk) will adequately cover your family's living requirements.

Of course, one of the biggest problems is inflation. If you died today and your spouse inherited $500,000 of insurance proceeds, she could take these funds and invest conservatively to earn 15% or $75,000 a year before taxes. While your wife could probably live on this income (even after paying tax) today, what about five years from now, ten years from now, or twenty years from now? On the other hand, if you were to carry double the insurance, your premium cost today would also be doubled. Is it worthwhile to deprive yourself and your family of disposable income today just for the sake of insuring a future? How far any one of us should go to obtain insurance coverage is a matter of personal choice. Certainly, the spectre of death (like taxes) is not fun to contemplate. However, in your overall investment strategy you may have no choice. *Your* life may not depend on it, but those of your family may.

CHAPTER SIX

Investing in a Principal Residence

Possibly the best investment that any of us can make is to buy our own home. However, as we have pointed out previously, one of the most important aspects of making any investment is timing. Historically, high inflation has created a tremendous increase in residential property values in many parts of the country. However, the real estate market is cyclical and if you can acquire property in a down-turn phase, you can probably get a much better deal than during a boom period. On the other hand, if you buy a home in a buoyant market but are forced to sell during a decline, you can get hurt badly. Certainly, anyone subject to frequent or sudden job transfers must be extremely cautious.

The general state of the real estate market in Canada is discussed in the next chapter. For reasons which will be explained later, we certainly cannot recommend real estate purchases as long as the economy continues to decline. The real estate market has fallen badly over the first six months of 1982 and, as of mid-year, has shown no signs whatsoever of imminent recovery. If you own real estate such as your own home today, now is also not the time to sell. You could expect to receive only a fraction of what you might otherwise get in a rising market. Probably the most important consideration which will be dealt with in this chapter and the next is the effect of interest rates on real estate investments.

In general the reason that we advocate home ownership is that all of us need a place to live. Of course, mortgage interest on your own home is not deductible — but, then again, neither are rental costs. When faced with a choice between non-deductible mortgage payments and non-deductible rent, you are still better off in the long run as an owner, so that *you* can gain from the appreciation, not your landlord.

Certainly, home ownership can be an extremely expensive proposition. If your mortgage payable is at 18%, and you are in a 50% tax bracket, you must earn a 36% pre-tax rate of return on your investment capital to make it worthwhile to carry this mortgage.

Proper strategy therefore dictates that you try to discharge a home mortgage as quickly as possible. Most mortgages will allow the borrower to prepay up to 10% on the anniversary date each year. If you make ordinary payments on a monthly basis coupled with only eight instalments of 10% of the original balance, your mortgage can then be eliminated within that eight-year period.

Mortgage Amortization

To amortize a loan is to extinguish it by means of payments over a period of time so that the debt is eventually reduced to zero. The most common amortization programs involve repayment schedules calling for identical monthly payments over the term of the borrowing with each payment consisting of a combination of both principal and interest. Initially, most of the payments are used to pay interest. However, as the principal amount of the debt decreases, more and more of the

25-YEAR $10,000 LOAN AT 18%,
WITH INTEREST COMPOUNDED SEMIANNUALLY
MONTHLY PAYMENT $146.64

Year	Payments Made $146.64 × 12	Interest	Principal
1	$1,760	$1,730	$ 30
5	$1,760	$1,710	$ 50
10	$1,760	$1,610	$ 150
15	$1,760	$1,420	$ 340
20	$1,760	$1,080	$ 680
25	$1,760	$ 160	$1,600

payments are used to reduce the capital amount. This is illustrated in the example on page 93, which shows a $10,000 loan at 18% with interest compounded semiannually over a twenty-five-year term. (Of course, this example is representative of a wide variety of situations. If your mortgage is in the $50,000 range, just multiply all numbers by five.)

Initially, each payment is almost all interest. Over the years, however, each instalment will contain less interest and more principal. This is because the borrower only pays interest on the outstanding principal balance of the loan at the time each payment is made.

In times of high interest rates, you might try to reduce your monthly payments by lengthening the term over which the loan is amortized. As you will see, however, this would be an extremely costly mistake. For example, what if the twenty-five-year term on the $10,000 loan in our example were extended to thirty, thirty-five or forty years? While the monthly payments would decline slightly, you would find yourself not only with a much longer payout but also with a *significant additional debt*. This is illustrated below.

AMORTIZATION OF $10,000 AT 18% OVER VARIOUS TIME PERIODS

$10,000 at 18%	25 Years	30 Years	35 Years	40 Years
Monthly payment	$ 146.64	$ 145.50	$ 145.02	$ 144.82
Annual cost	1,759.68	1,746.00	1,740.24	1,737.84
Total cost	43,992.00	52,380.00	60,908.40	69,513.60
Total interest paid	33,992.00	42,380.00	50,908.40	59,513.60

Monthly payment over 25 years	$ 146.64
Monthly payment over 40 years	144.82
Difference	$ 1.82
Total interest over 40 years	$59,513.60
Total interest over 25 years	33,992.00
Difference	$25,521.60

94

The results of our analysis are somewhat mind-boggling. By spreading the debt over forty years instead of twenty-five years, there is a monthly saving of only $1.82 in the required mortgage payments. However, you must not only commit yourself to payments over an additional fifteen years but *you are actually increasing your debt by $25,521.60.*

Mortgage Acceleration Savings

While extending your debt obligation can be extremely costly in the long run, paying down your mortgage from time to time by making extra payments is one of the best available methods to force yourself to save money. The schedule on page 96 shows the principal balance outstanding on that same $10,000 loan at the end of each year for twenty-five years where the interest rate is 18%. At the end of year one, the principal balance outstanding is $9,970, while at the end of year twelve it is $9,060. Therefore, if you were to repay $910 on the first anniversary of the mortgage, you would thus be eliminating *one-half* of the *total* annual payments which you would otherwise have to make.

In other words, if your monthly payments stay the same (which they would) and you make *no further* special payments against principal, your debt would be completely extinguished only thirteen years later. Given a special payment of $910 at the end of the first year, you would then only owe $8,860 at the end of year two, $8,610 after year three, and so forth. Of course, if additional principal payments were made at the end of the second year (and subsequently) the debt would be eliminated that much more quickly.

Certainly, many people view the thought of paying down as much as 10% of a mortgage each year on the anniversary date as somewhat of a fantasy. Most of us just don't have the extra cash to accomplish this — especially since we must use after-tax dollars. However, whatever you can pay down certainly will be helpful. If, for example, you have $700 sitting in your bank account and you notice that the annual anniversary date of your mortgage is approaching, why not pull these funds out

BALANCE OUTSTANDING ON A LOAN OF $10,000
AT 18% (ROUNDED TO NEAREST $10)
MONTHLY PAYMENT $146.64

End of Year	Amount	End of Year	Amount	End of Year	Amount
1	$9,970	10	$9,370	18	$7,100
2	9,940	11	9,230	19	6,530
3	9,910	12	9,060	20	5,850
4	9,860	13	8,860	21	5,050
5	9,810	14	8,610	22	4,090
6	9,750	15	8,330	23	2,960
7	9,680	16	7,990	24	1,600
8	9,600	17	7,580	25	0
9	9,490				

and apply them against the loan? Paying down a mortgage is not a glamorous investment. You could take the same $700 and buy one Krugerrand and one gold Maple Leaf (see Chapter Ten) and you would have an investment in gold. You could probably spend as much as a half an hour at a Saturday night cocktail party describing your "adventurous" purchase to your friends—how you went to the bank or coin shop, what the coins look like, and the ingenious place that you decided to hide them. Paying down the mortgage is not something that will make for cocktail party conversation. Nevertheless, it is sound investment planning.

Ideal situations to pay down a mortgage arise if you are the beneficiary of a small inheritance or perhaps win a lottery. Maybe the best opportunity a family has to accomplish this objective is where a wife who has been home for several years looking after young children rejoins the labour force.

Let us take a simple example. Assume that a married man is earning $50,000 a year and is quite capable of supporting his family. Now that the children are in school full-time, suppose his wife decides to rejoin the labour force and in her first year of employment will earn $14,000. On this amount, the wife will pay approximately $2,500 in income taxes and her husband will lose a personal exemption which will cost him about

$1,500. In other words, the after-tax retention on $14,000 will be approximately $10,000. At this point, the family comes to a very important crossroad. It could choose to use the extra $10,000 to expand the family's lifestyle. A new car can be purchased, or the family can treat itself to the vacation trip they have been talking about for years. However, if husband and wife can simply exercise a bit of restraint for *one year only* and apply the first $10,000 that the wife earns (after taxes) against their mortgage, they will have made a tremendous advance towards the security of owning a fully-paid home. Look again at the example on page 96. On a $100,000 mortgage, it takes twelve years until $10,000 of debt is extinguished in the absence of mortgage acceleration payments. We hope that the message is clear.

The Mortgage Term

Be careful never to confuse the *amortization* of a loan with its *term*. If you are told that a mortgage is to be amortized over twenty-five years, you must not assume that it has a twenty-five-year term. The term of a mortgage is the period of time which is given to a borrower before the lender can demand the principal balance owing on the loan. Until a few years ago, lenders did in fact make loans for long periods of time, such as twenty-five years, at fixed rates of interest. Today, however, mortgage terms rarely exceed three years. Thus, although the amortization schedule may reflect the payments necessary to discharge a debt over twenty-five years, the borrower, in most cases, must still repay the principal balance at the end of three years. Of course, the lender will usually renew the mortgage — at current prevailing rates. (Today, even one-year term and variable-rate mortgages are becoming more and more common.)

Again, examine the schedule on page 96. If payments of $146.64 are made monthly over twenty-five years, a loan of $10,000 at 18% would be extinguished. However, here is the problem posed by a three-year term. At the end of three years, the lender will want his money, and on a twenty-five-year loan, you will still owe him $9,910. To repay the loan you would probably have to commit yourself to another mortgage and borrow $9,900 (in round numbers). Assume that the new mortgage is for a further three-year period at the same rate and also with payments calculated to amortize over a twenty-five-year period. This is what your outstanding balance will be over the subsequent three years in round figures:

BALANCE OUTSTANDING ON A LOAN OF $9,900 AT 18% (25-YEAR AMORTIZATION).

End of Year	Balance
1	$9,870
2	9,841
3	9,811

At the end of this second three-year period, when you have to repay the loan, you may repeat the process. Each new three-year term will result in smaller monthly payments because the principal amount at the start of each succeeding term will be less. However, instead of amortizing the loan down to zero over twenty-five years, it may take over *one hundred years* to discharge the loan completely. *The only way a twenty-five-year mortgage can be paid off in full over twenty-five years is to arrange to have the principal balance owing each time a mortgage is renewed amortized for a period which is not longer than the remaining number of years in the original amortization.*

We do not, however, wish to scare you. While the compounding effect of interest can be somewhat disconcerting, keep in mind the appreciation factor. Presumably, your property's growth will also be compounding over an extended period of time. Also, short-term declines in property values should not generally panic you into selling at the wrong time.

Borrowing Money From Private Sources

With today's high cost of residential housing, more and more young people are finding it difficult to acquire their homes without some sort of family subsidy. Perhaps you may be fortunate to have a "rich relative" who would be willing to lend you money. First of all, your relative would probably be earning slightly less on his capital if it is in term deposits than you would have to pay if you were to approach a lending institution. Perhaps your benefactor might be persuaded to pass this difference on to you. In other words, if he is receiving 15% interest on a term deposit, he may be willing to accept a similar rate on a private loan secured by your residence. Moreover, he may also be willing to allow you to pay only interest until your income increases sufficiently for you to start discharging principal. In many cases, a private lender is quite content with an interest yield on his capital only. He does not necessarily *want* to receive blended payments of capital and interest. For him, there is the satisfaction of keeping his capital intact and not having to worry about reinvesting small payments of principal which he receives from you from time to time.

Sometimes, people will take advantage of the fact that interest income is taxable while the corresponding expense is not deductible (when funds are borrowed for personal purposes). For example, if an individual in a 50% bracket is earning interest at 15%, he is only netting 7½% after taxes. That same individual might be willing to lend money to a friend or relative at only 8% or 9% to assist the latter in buying a house, provided his interest is paid to him in *cash*. Often, the borrower won't object to such an arrangement because he will pay a substantially lower rate and he can't deduct his payments anyway. Thus, the borrower pays approximately only half the prevailing mortgage rate, while the lender·ends up keeping more than what he otherwise would have retained had he received "conventional" taxable interest.

Because any practice involving undeclared income is fraudulent, the reader is cautioned to stay away from such an arrangement. However, we have seen cases where mortgage loans are made at *no interest* but where the borrower makes an annual (non-compulsory) gift each year to the lender which is (coincidently) equal to 8%–9% of the original loan. This procedure is acceptable. You should note that gifts made are not deductible while gifts received are not taxable. (Persons resident in Quebec are, however, subject to the rules of the Provincial Gift Tax Act.)

Registered Home Ownership Savings Plans

If you do not already own your home and have no other interest in residential real estate, it would be good planning to take advantage of the Registered Home Ownership Savings Plan. Under this program, up to $1,000 a year can be contributed until $10,000 (plus interest) is accumulated. The maximum length of time that one can keep an RHOSP open is twenty years. If funds are withdrawn from this plan and are used to purchase a home that you will occupy, the withdrawal is tax-free. Contributions are only deductible on a calendar-year basis. You are allowed to contribute in the year that you acquire a home, although the contribution should be made before you take title to the property. You are permitted to move funds from one RHOSP to another, although once you have made a withdrawal you may never reinstate. In this respect, you are only allowed one RHOSP in a lifetime. Interest on money borrowed to acquire an RHOSP is not deductible.

As already indicated, you are not qualified to contribute to an RHOSP if you or your spouse have "an interest in residential real estate". This restriction covers more than situations where you already own a home. For example, if you have an interest in a multiple unit residential building as a tax shelter or even an interest in a Florida condominium, you are disqualified from participation in an RHOSP. You are however permitted to own vacant land or shares in a corporation where the corporation holds residential property.

In cases where parents wish to subsidize the eventual acquisition of homes by their children, the RHOSP can be an excellent gifting program, especially if a child is in his late teens or early twenties and is working (at a modest salary). For example, assume that a child is twenty-one years old and is earning $14,000 a year. Even at this relatively low income level, he is still in approximately a 30% tax bracket. In addition, the child is not likely to be thinking seriously about the possibility of buying a home for several years. However, if his parents make an annual gift of $1,000 and the gift is invested in an RHOSP, there will be a tax saving of approximately $300. These dollars could then be gifted back to the parents and the net cost of such a gifting program becomes only $700. An RHOSP can therefore be used very effectively to reduce the cost of providing children with a downpayment for a home.

Tax Planning Considerations With Respect To Principal Residences

On Habitual Renovation of Homes

From time to time, there are newspaper and magazine articles about people who have an interesting hobby. They buy older homes, move into them, fix them up, and resell them at a profit. If an individual undertakes such a venture only sporadically, he can still expect to qualify for the principal residence exemption for his gain on sale. However, if he develops the habit of buying, fixing and selling a different house each year, Revenue Canada officials will consider these transactions to be a business. As such, the *entire* gain could become taxable. A number of tax assessments have resulted from investigations initiated from information which appeared in newspaper articles. Thus, if you are a habitual renovator, you would be well advised to maintain a low profile.

Sale of a Principal Residence at a Loss

Historically, most of us have always assumed that a principal residence will appreciate in value. What happens, however, if the value of the property drops? Unfortunately, if a principal residence is sold at a loss, the loss is not deductible. The provisions of the Income Tax Act automatically deem any loss with respect to "personal use property" to be nil. Personal use property is defined as any property which is owned primarily for the personal use and enjoyment of a taxpayer and members of his family.

Changing the Use of a Principal Residence

To accommodate people who are subject to temporary transfers, the Income Tax Act permits you to move out of your home and still designate the property as your principal residence for up to four years. In order to make this election, you must remain resident in Canada and must not designate some other property as your principal residence. If the designated property is rented out over that time, capital cost allowances (tax depreciation) may not be claimed to reduce rental income, although all other expenses, including mortgage interest, are allowed.

If an election to continue to designate a property as a principal residence is not made, there will automatically be a deemed disposition of the principal residence at fair market value as of the date habitation ceases. The resulting gain will ordinarily be tax exempt, although any future growth in value will become taxable when the property is either sold or reinhabited. The election to continue to deem the property as a principal residence gives you a reprieve. If you reinhabit the property within the four years, the "chain" of ownership as a principal residence remains unbroken. If, on the other hand, the property is rented out beyond four years, there will only be a deemed disposition at the end of the fourth year. Then, only proceeds greater than the fair market value at the end of the fourth year would eventually become subject to ordinary capital gains treatment. The growth during the first four years would, however, be tax-free.

You can obtain an extension to the rule which would permit a principal residence designation to continue *indefinitely* beyond four years in cases where you (or your spouse) are transferred by an employer and later reoccupy the home. This is provided that the residence is reoccupied no later than one year following the year in which employment with that employer terminates.

All these rules are designed to provide tax relief where the property was first a principal residence and later became a rental property. Unfortunately, no similar provisions exist to alleviate the reverse situation.

If a rental property later *becomes* a principal residence, the owner has a problem. The rules of the Income Tax Act provide that at the time of change of use, there is a deemed disposition of the rental property at current fair market value. This will trigger recaptured depreciation and capital gains even though there is no change in ownership. The taxes will have to be paid without any corresponding in-flow of cash. The only consolation, of course, is that future growth in the value of the property will then be exempt from tax under the principal residence rules.

Since there is no way out of this dilemma, you should at least be aware of the problem. If real estate prices are moving up, you might wish to acquire a rental property rather than waiting until you are ready to buy a house for personal occupancy. A delay could result in the penalty of having to pay a much higher price for the property in the future. You might consider buying a duplex, living in half and renting out the other suite. When you eventually sell, part of your gain will then qualify for the principal residence tax exemption.

One step that should be considered to reduce tax exposure would be to refrain from claiming depreciation during the years that the property is rented out. You would have to weigh the alternatives for yourself—the potential tax benefits of having initially claimed depreciation against the detrimental effect of a subsequent recapture.

In times of falling real estate prices, you may decide that it is in your interest to claim depreciation during the period that your property is rented out. This would provide you with ongoing income tax write-offs. You might not be too concerned with the potential of being faced with recaptured depreciation later on. These matters should be discussed, according to your own circumstances, with your accountant. In most cases, depreciation cannot be used to create deductible losses for income tax purposes.

In some circumstances, you can save taxes by moving in when you first acquire a property, before you begin to rent it out. Then, technically, at the time you vacate the house and begin to earn rental income you can elect that the property continue to be your principal residence for up to four subsequent years. In this manner, if you reinhabit your home within that time, you can elect that the entire ownership period be considered as one of principal residence.

Of course, whether or not the house initially qualifies as being "ordinarily inhabited" is a question of fact. We don't think that it would be sufficient for you to buy a property and spend one or two evenings curled up in a sleeping bag in your living room in order to substantiate occupancy. To be safe from reassessment, a three-month occupancy (at a bare minimum) would probably be more realistic. For the house to qualify as a principal residence, it would also be a good idea if you arrange for a telephone listing in your name at that address and change-over billings for credit cards and other monthly accounts to that residence. Then, after several months, if you find that you no longer wish to live in that house because it is too large, too small or too expensive, there is nothing wrong with taking advantage of the rules by renting it out from that time on while electing to maintain a principal residence status for up to four subsequent years.

Partial Use as a Principal Residence

As would be expected, whenever an individual occupies part of his property and rents out the other part, the "housing unit" will consist of the portion occupied by him and the rental portion will be subject to capital gains treatment when a disposition takes place. If a housing unit is used for non-residential purposes, such as where a doctor carries on his practice using a part of his home, only that portion occupied by the owner as a housing unit will be eligible to be treated as a principal residence. Any gain on sale of the non-residential portion will be taxed.

Ownership of a Principal Residence by a Corporation

Perhaps one of the most important points with respect to the whole concept of principal residences is the fact that to qualify for capital gains exemption, a property must be owned by an individual and not a corporation. If a corporation owns residential property which is rented out to a shareholder as the shareholder's principal residence, the corporation will still be subject to capital gains taxes at the time the property is sold. Thus, it appears that there is a significant disadvantage to corporate ownership. In some cases, however, corporate ownership should be considered. While a decision can only be taken on the facts of each particular case, we have, over the years, developed certain personal guidelines that might be useful.

If you are considering buying a "conventional" home in either a low or middle price range in comparison to other housing in your municipality, our general inclination is to favour personal ownership even if you have a corporation which could make the acquisition on your behalf. This is because, if the corporation acquires the property, you will still have to pay a fair rent or face an assessment from Revenue Canada as having received a taxable benefit. The rent, of course, is non-deductible in the same way as the mortgage payments would not be deductible if the property were owned personally. Thus, either way, ownership is somewhat expensive, but at the time of sale, there is the benefit of receiving a capital gain tax-free if the property is in your personal name.

However, if you are interested in a more expensive house *and control a private corporation which qualifies as an active business for income tax purposes*, there might be a better alternative. The general tax rate on small business profits across Canada is only approximately 25%. (The low rate of tax applies to the first $200,000 of business profits annually and until $1-million, before tax, has been earned cumulatively.) A complete analysis of the Canadian small business tax rates is not relevant to this particular book. Nevertheless, you should note that the purpose of the low corporate tax rate is to encourage business expansion. The idea is to allow after-tax profits of seventy-five cents on the dollar to be used to finance receivables and inventories and for acquisitions of business machinery and equipment. Nevertheless, there is no actual requirement that the after-tax profits be reinvested in business-related assets. It is perfectly permissible to use these profits to generate investment capital instead. Thus, where a business earns large profits which are not required for expansion and where the owner would like to buy a high-priced home, he might consider corporate ownership. The corporation could pay for the house using 75% of its profits towards that objective instead of paying salaries or dividends and having the individual acquire the property with only fifty cents on the dollar after high personal taxes.

This concept can be illustrated with a simple example. Assume that a very successful insurance brokerage business is owned by an individual and that the business is incorporated. The business earns $300,000 each year after paying all operating expenses but before any remuneration to the owner-manager. Since the owner-manager lives very well, he takes a salary of $100,000 a year before taxes. At this point, he is already in a 50% personal tax bracket. The corporation, on the other hand, with pre-tax profits of $200,000, pays only 25% tax.

On each $200,000, after a corporate tax of 25%, the annual build-up of retained earnings is $150,000. After only four years, the corporation has retained profits of $600,000. Assume that the individual now wants to buy a home which would cost $300,000. Since an insurance brokerage business is not a heavily capital-intensive operation, it is possible that the corporation itself could spare the full $300,000 out of its retained profits of $600,000. The corporation then buys the home and rents it to the shareholder.

By way of contrast, if the shareholder wanted $300,000 to pay for his house personally, being in a 50% bracket, he would have to draw almost the full retained earnings of $600,000 from his company in order to net $300,000 after taxes. Thus, the "earning power" required to finance the acquisition of the home becomes substantially greater.

Given a $300,000 saving in cash flow from the very beginning, the shareholder may not be concerned that he will have to pay non-deductible rent to the company over the entire period of ownership and that the capital gain at the time of eventual sale would become taxable. After all, even if half the gain were taxed at the top corporate rate of 50%, the effective tax (on half the gain) would only be 25%. Moreover, in a depressed market where expensive properties may not appreciate that much, corporate ownership may make even better sense.

Granted, the foregoing example is somewhat specialized. Even if an individual "owns" a successful small business corporation, the opportunity to use after-tax corporate profits to acquire a residence is not necessarily available unless the company has no need for its profits for business expansion. In the previous example, if the business were an expanding manufacturing concern, it might not be desirable to reduce working capital by $300,000.

Loans by Corporations to Employees and Shareholders for Home Purchases

As an alternative to corporate ownership of a principal residence, which automatically results in the loss of a capital gains exemption, an employee or shareholder in a business might consider a corporate *loan* for the purpose of buying a house.

If a business makes a loan to an employee, there is nothing in the Income Tax Act requiring that the loan be repaid within any specific time frame — as long as the employee is not a shareholder of the corporation. Thus, a loan from an employer corporation to an employee can be made for an indefinite period and can remain outstanding as long as both parties agree. If the loan is ever forgiven, the forgiveness of debt would (at that time) create income from employment. This rule is to prevent tax-exempt and other non-profit organizations from making advances to their employees (instead of paying salaries) and forgiving these loans later on. A non-profit organization would not need a tax deduction, and in the absence of the above rule, an employee could escape taxation.

Where an employee is also a shareholder there are, however, some very strict repayment rules that ordinarily apply when a loan is made. The reason for these rules is that the government does not want shareholders borrowing money initially taxed at comparatively low corporate rates without the imposition of personal taxes. In the absence of any special rules, a corporation with profits of $10,000 would have as much as $7,500 of funds available for shareholders' loans after paying Revenue Canada as little as 25% of its profits.

The general rule on shareholder loans is that if a loan is outstanding on two successive year-end balance sheets of the company, it is retroactively included in the shareholder's income. Thus, the maximum length of time that a loan can remain unpaid is two years less one day. (The "two years less one day" would only apply if the loan were taken out on the first day of a company's fiscal year.)

One cannot subvert the system by simply repaying the loan just before the deadline and then borrowing back the funds. Other provisions within the Tax Act provide that "a series of loans and repayments" is equivalent to not having repaid the loan at all. In addition, one cannot use family members for purposes of taking these loans for extended periods of time. A loan to a member of a shareholder's family is basically the equivalent of a loan to the shareholder.

There are, however, several specific exceptions to the above rules, which provide the individual with an opportunity to borrow money for a longer period of time. The most significant of these is that a corporation is permitted to make a loan to a shareholder *who is also an employee* to acquire or construct a house for himself and his family to live in. The Income Tax Act does, however, require a reasonable repayment schedule to be decided upon at the time the loan is made and to be subsequently adhered to.

Thus, in the case of a privately owned company, one of the best tax deals available in Canada is the opportunity that exists with respect to housing loans. The first advantage of such a loan arises because corporate tax rates, as was mentioned previously, tend to be significantly less than personal rates. Where the employer is a privately owned company and pays only 25% tax, seventy-five cents out of each dollar of profits can then be used as an advance to the owner for purposes of buying a home. This is much cheaper than using only fifty cents out of each dollar of after-tax personal earnings.

Personal after-tax funds:

Salary to shareholder-employee	$100,000
Less: Personal taxes of 50%	50,000
After-tax funds available to purchase a home	$ 50,000

Corporate after-tax funds:

Earnings taxed in corporation	$100,000
Corporate taxes (25%)	25,000
After-tax funds available to shareholder as a loan for his home	$ 75,000

The second advantage is that the employee-shareholder obtains the use of corporate dollars *today* which he must only repay over a period of time, presumably with "cheaper" dollars because of inflation. A reasonable repayment program for the principal itself might be ten or fifteen years.

If you own a controlling interest in an incorporated business, you would be well advised to speak to your accountant with regard to such a loan *before* you purchase or build any residence. The residence need not be a city home. A country house (or second home) will also qualify as long as it will be owned primarily for personal use and could not be construed as rental property.

Note that the very generous provision in the Income Tax Act permitting such a loan applies only in situations where a house is being built or bought. It does not apply to the refinancing of an existing home. However, if you intend to make a major extension to an existing residence, it may be possible to get an advance ruling from Revenue Canada allowing a company loan for that purpose under the same favourable tax conditions.

Interest Implications of Loans

While the housing loan itself is an excellent benefit, a discussion of this topic is not complete unless interest implications are taken into account. There is no requirement that interest be charged in Canada on any loan from a corporation to an individual. However, where interest is not charged by the employer, it must be "imputed" as a taxable benefit at a prescribed rate of interest, which is adjusted quarterly, and added on to the individual's earnings for that year. At the time this is being written in 1982, the rate of calculated interest is 16%.

Before November 12, 1981, if a housing loan qualified as a "relocation loan" the tax rules permitted a corporation to make interest-free loans of up to $50,000 per family unit of husband and wife. There is, however, a budget proposal that repeals these special provisions for housing loans made after November 12, 1981.

However, even though interest must now be calculated on all new loans, whether they are relocation loans or otherwise, it is important to note that there is still an opportunity to derive a significant benefit. This is because the only cost to the individual is the tax on the amount added to his income — about half of what a private mortgage loan would cost.

In some cases, the employer's policy is to charge a low rate of interest on loans to employees. There does not, however, appear to be much logic in this practice where the loan, in turn, is to be used for personal purposes. Under such an arrangement, the employer must recognize interest income which is fully taxable while the employee gets no tax relief whatsoever for the interest paid. It would be better to reduce the employee's salary by the amount of the interest otherwise charged, to offset any loss to the employer. Coping with a taxable benefit is much cheaper than an actual outlay of cash. Wherever possible, senior employees should try to negotiate housing loans as part of their compensation packages. It is not necessary to control a corporation to obtain such a benefit.

Investing in a "Country" House

Although mortgage interest on a personal residence has never been deductible in Canada, the tax rules still provide you with quite an important incentive to own your home. The incentive is of course the fact that the capital gain on eventual sale is tax-free. In fact, until 1982, a married couple could enjoy *two* principal residences as long as the husband owned one property while the wife owned the other. As a result of the November 12, 1981 Budget, however, where a couple owns two properties, one of the properties will become taxable on any appreciation that is realized after 1981. In other words, it is now no longer possible to enjoy capital gains exemptions on two principal residences.

If you and your spouse owned two homes at the start of 1982, there are some tax planning opportunities which are worth noting. First, you should arrange an appraisal of the property which is *not* likely to be designated as a principal residence. The appraisal should be made as soon as possible, and obviously, if the appraiser is very generous (but realistic) in his figures, this will stand you in good stead. Second, the property not designated as a principal residence should probably be held by the family member (husband or wife) who is likely to be in a lower income tax bracket at the time that the property is sold. The purpose, of course, is to pay the least capital gains tax on sale. The person who holds the second property should not necessarily be the one who is in the lower bracket today. For example, if a husband is fifty-years old while his wife is thirty-five, and both are working, it is probable that the husband will retire well in advance of his wife. Under those circumstances, the couple should consider structuring the ownership of the second property in the husband's name. Then, if the property is sold subsequent to his retirement, the tax may be substantially less than if the wife were to sell it in a year while she was still working.

A third area of potential planning is to transfer the second property as soon as possible (before there is any substantial post-1981 appreciation) or to acquire it initially in the name of a family member who has no principal residence and is in a low tax bracket. If that family member occupies the property from time to time, he or she could designate it as a principal residence and make a tax-free gift of the sales proceeds back to you upon ultimate sale. Alternatively, if that person dies and directs the property back to you under his or her will, there will be no taxes arising at the time of death (because of the capital gains exemption for a principal residence), and you will then recognize a new tax cost for the house at its then-current fair market value. This is ideal planning in cases where an affluent couple who can afford two principal residences have parents who are apartment dwellers but who would spend time with their children in a country house during the course of the year. Of course, the children would have to trust the parents to bequeath the second property back to them and not to remaining brothers and sisters! You should note, however, that you may not make a transfer to an unmarried dependent child under the age of eighteen. In any event, these are matters to be explored together with your accountants and lawyers.

Is a Second Home a Good Investment?

The major difference between a "primary" principal residence and a "secondary" principal residence is the question of need. When it comes to a primary home, we all need a shelter to come into out of the rain and snow. As we said earlier, when faced with a choice between non-deductible mortgage interest and non-deductible rent, we would rather pay the interest cost in exchange for (tax-free) capital appreciation.

A country home or cottage is an entirely different situation. One usually doesn't "need" a second residence. If your lifestyle is such that you would actually make use of a cottage for a substantial portion of the year for personal purposes then, by all means, if you can afford it, go ahead and buy. Under those circumstances, if you are willing to use after-tax dollars to subsidize your ownership *and also pay capital gains taxes at the time of sale*, this is a personal choice that only you can make. The table on page 113 shows how much capital growth you actually require just to break even, assuming you are in a 50% tax bracket and borrow money at 18% to invest in a second home.

It is quite unlikely that a country house will appreciate on average by 24% a year. By repealing the rules permitting a husband and wife to enjoy two principal residence capital gains exemptions, the November 12, 1981 Budget has relegated the

CAPITAL GROWTH REQUIRED TO BREAK EVEN
ON A SECOND HOME

Cost of borrowing (non-deductible)	<u>18%</u>
Annual capital growth required to break even before capital gains taxes	24%
Less: 25% capital gains tax (25% × 24%)	<u>6%</u>
Annual capital growth required to break even after taxes	<u>18%</u>

second home to the status of a most *undesirable investment*. If you are interested in recreational property for only a few weeks each year, you might be better off channelling your investment dollars into a property which is purchased primarily for rental purposes and is only used personally on occasion. Under those circumstances, within limits as described in the next chapter, your interest expense will then be tax-deductible.

Timesharing — Another Alternative

If your lifestyle is such that there is ample activity in your hometown to keep you busy during most weekends and you only take vacations at specific times in the year, you may want to consider timesharing as an alternative to the ownership of a recreational property. Under a timesharing arrangement, you acquire an interest in recreational property for that part of the year that you want to vacation. You do not tie up funds (or borrowing power) in an expensive facility which will sit vacant during most of the year.

Types of Timesharing

Timesharing falls into two broad categories. *Fee simple ownership* is where you own your own week in the same way as you may own a house or any other real estate. You can keep it, sell it, rent it, gift it, or bequeath it to your children. The *right to use* category represents ownership for a specific period of time, usually anywhere from fifteen to fifty years. This is very much like owning a lease. The right to use the weeks may also be sold, gifted or bequeathed subject only to restrictions on the length of time under contract. At the end of the contract period, possession reverts back to the original owner.

From a Canadian perspective, timesharing makes sense because if you buy a week's use of property for personal purposes, you then tie up only a minimum amount of your investment capital or borrowing power in a project where your interest cost is non-deductible. In other words, instead of tying up $60,000 in a vacation property which would only be used two weeks a year, you could instead invest only $15,000 in timeshare units, leaving $45,000 of your resources or borrowing power available for other investments.

If inflation continues, both types of timesharing should appreciate in value. Thus you, as an investor, should be able to recover your investment and perhaps even make a capital profit. For example, under the "fee simple" arrangement, as land prices and construction costs increase, new units will become more expensive. This means that the value of a unit which is already built should be worth more in subsequent years. Even under the "right to use" concept, there is potential for appreciation. If, for example, you pay $8,000 for the right to use a condominium unit one week a year for the next forty years, you could expect to be able to sell that right for at least the same $8,000 twenty years from now. This is because, with inflation, a right-to-use for a further twenty years (from that time on) should be worth at least the same $8,000 that forty years' use is worth today.

Regardless of the type of timesharing week that is available (fee simple or right to use) all timeshare ownerships have a number of common financial obligations:

- Timeshare weeks are all priced differently. You pay more for a week in high season than you do for a week in low season.
- Every timeshare owner is obligated to pay an annual maintenance fee. The concept of paying maintenance fees is similar to the obligations which arise under normal condominium ownership. All of the expenses associated

with running the resort—insurance, grounds-keeping, utilities, building maintenance, cleaning costs, real estate taxes, and so on are divided among all of the unit holders, generally on an equal basis. Usually, an extra charge is levied as a reserve for furniture replacement. In some cases, such as where utility costs vary dramatically depending on the season, the users during the high cost periods will pay an extra charge.

- Generally, the purchaser of a timeshare week will pay cash for the week bought, although financing is often available. A downpayment would usually run about 25% of the purchase price and financing would be over a five-year term. At the present time, you might pay as little as $6,000 for a timeshare week during a low-season period. High-season rates may, however, be more than double this amount.

There are several ways of allocating the weeks of the year to the timesharer for his vacation. The most frequent ways are:

- *Fixed time*. The fixed-time concept means that you buy a specific time period which recurs every year. Of course, under a fixed-time arrangement, you would pay a premium to secure a time period in the peak holiday season. On the other hand, someone who prefers to vacation in the low season would generally pay less.
- *Floating time*. A floating-time project will allow the use of a given number of weeks each year. The actual dates would be determined under some type of reservation system. With floating time, all timesharers may purchase at a similar cost but would have to apply each year to reserve their vacation time. There is, of course, the danger that you may not be able to secure the period which you desire. In some cases, there might be an arrangement which would facilitate swapping time periods with other members.

In 1974, the first of several international exchange organizations was created to provide timeshare owners with an opportunity to exchange their intervals between resorts and between owners. Thus, if you own a week of timeshare in British Columbia, it may be possible in a given year to exchange that week for a week's holiday in Mexico, Hawaii or anywhere else. The opportunity to exchange is contingent on space being available at the other location. Thus, it is generally suggested that you list several acceptable alternative locations and even time slots as part of your application for an exchange. If you own a unit at peak vacation time, you are more likely to have your request for an exchange honoured than if you have a unit in low season.

A Major Pitfall

The big problem with any timesharing arrangement is the question of ongoing management. Remember that an owner of a timeshare week will share his unit with perhaps forty to fifty other owners. There is no guarantee that furniture or facilities won't be abused or that the timeshare promoters will actively manage over the entire term of the timeshare contract. In our opinion, the best timeshare arrangement would be where the units are connected to a resort with varied facilities and where the owners of the timeshare project are also the owners of the resort. In this way, there is a vested interest in maintaining the timeshare units properly. The users would presumably patronize the resort facilities, thus providing additional revenues to the owners.

Timeshares as an Investment

It is somewhat difficult to evaluate the investment potential of a timeshare. You could take the position, for example, that if a timeshare unit cost $8,000, you might be better off investing these funds at 15% interest and using the investment income to spend on a holiday. The only problem, of course, is that interest income is taxable, and if you are in a 50% bracket, what starts out as $1,200 annual interest income becomes only $600 after taxes. Also, with inflation, the value of your cash decreases by approximately 11% per annum (at current rates). Thus, the buying power of your capital suffers through erosion by inflation.

On the other hand, if you invest the same $8,000 in a forty-year vacation lease, the value of your investment should, for at least the first ten or twenty years, keep pace with inflation. Thus, the actual cost of the holiday becomes only the weekly maintenance charge. You avoid both taxable interest income and also the necessity of paying for a vacation with dollars that are not tax-deductible.

The major advantage of timesharing is, however, the one to which we referred previously. Specifically, it enables you to tie up a relatively small percentage of your borrowing power in an investment which is of a personal nature. This provides greater flexibility to acquire other investments.

Timeshare Ownership for Businesses

Timeshare ownership may also evolve into an important employee benefit program for corporations. A business might provide its employees with accommodations, as an employee incentive. The units could also be used for entertaining clients, for housing executives attending board meetings, and to generate rental income. If a timeshare unit were owned by a corporation and were used for business purposes, the corporation could capitalize the cost and depreciate it over the ownership period. In addition, interest charges incurred to finance the acquisition become tax-deductible as well as maintenance fees and other related costs. Where a timeshare unit is provided to an executive and/or employee for his personal vacation use, there would be, naturally, a taxable benefit to the individual. The taxable benefit under the Income Tax Act is supposed to be calculated as the value of the benefit to the employee — which may be substantially greater than just the annual maintenance cost paid by the company. On the other hand, if the facilities are used in conjunction with conferences and seminars, the adverse tax consequences may be reduced greatly or may even be eliminated.

A Look at the Future

It is possibly a little early to try to assess the long-term consequences of the timesharing phenomenon. Certainly, the concept does have appeal for Canadians—especially because of the fact that interest expense incurred for personal purposes is non-deductible and the cost of most vacation property is therefore quite expensive. It remains to be seen, however, whether timesharing units will actually appreciate by an amount at least equal to the inflation factor. If this is the case, the concept will probably become quite popular. Of course, as we mentioned earlier, timesharing is not advantageous to someone who has a holiday home and truly uses it all year round. We have been quoted statistics, however, which indicate that Canadians use their second homes *an average of only seventeen days per year*. Thus, for most Canadians (even wealthy ones), a vacation home becomes an expensive luxury.

CHAPTER SEVEN

Investing in Real Estate

Deductible Interest

For most of us, the primary residence is still the cornerstone of an effective investment portfolio. Certainly, if you achieve the status of having your house paid for, you can then at least enjoy the security of an important hedge against *both* inflation and recession. Even if real estate taxes or heating bills escalate sharply, the fact that you do not have to make mortgage payments will still make a very big difference in your lifestyle. Once the mortgage is paid, at the very least you then have the extra cash flow from your job, profession or business to improve your standard of living.

However, if you are interested in building up capital, you will probably never have a better opportunity to latch on to a large sum of dollars with which to pyramid your investment holdings than by using the equity in your home. Once your home is paid for, you may *then* borrow against your equity to obtain capital that you need for investments. If you borrow specifically for the purpose of making investments, your interest expense becomes deductible. Then, even if you are forced to borrow at rates of interest between 18% and 20%, if you are in a 50% bracket, this represents a net after-tax outlay of only 9% to 10%. If the investment that you purchase appreciates by an average of 13½% per annum you will be ahead of the game, even after considering taxes on capital gains. (Of course, if interest rates drop, you would require correspondingly less appreciation.)

Investment growth before tax on capital gains	13.50%
Less: Tax on capital gains	
($\frac{1}{2}$ × 13.50% × 50% tax bracket)	(3.37)
Net capital growth	10.13%
Gross interest expense	20.00%
Less: Tax savings in 50% bracket	(10.00)
Net cost to obtain capital growth	10.00%

The key point, however, is to establish equity in your house *before* you borrow for investment purposes, although you don't necessarily have to pay your mortgage off in full before you can create tax-deductible interest. Let us assume that the balance on your mortgage is now $40,000, but that your house is worth $120,000. You could easily refinance the house when the mortgage comes up for renewal for $80,000. Of this amount, half will be required to replace the financing previously owing. To this extent your interest expense will not be deductible. If, however, the remainder of the borrowed funds is used for investments, the interest on this amount will be deductible. You may be required to prove how you have applied your funds, but this should not be too difficult.

Note that there is no shortcut to be taken. If you inherit money and use those funds for investment purposes without having first paid off the mortgage on your home, you will *not* be permitted to argue that you *could have* paid off the mortgage in the first place and then borrowed for investment capital. In cases that have come before the tax courts, judges have insisted on a proper "tracking". If you take a shortcut, be prepared to suffer tax penalties.

The subject of interest deductibility has already been discussed in Chapter Three. Remember that the government is still considering the imposition of restrictions on the deductibility of interest in cases where investment revenues are insufficient to support the related debt. Certainly, as we recommended in Chapter Three, you must keep up-to-date with the tax rules. It is unlikely that there will be any serious restrictions with respect to Canadian residential or commercial real estate. On the other hand, we might expect some changes insofar as foreign investment is concerned. Only time will tell.

Leverage

As long as excess interest continues to be deductible, a real estate investment can produce a tremendous amount of leverage. For purposes of illustration, we will assume that an executive, business owner or professional earns $60,000 a year and is in a marginal tax bracket of 50%. He has a home which is worth $200,000 and he has paid off his mortgage. Suppose this executive then refinances his house and borrows $50,000 at 18%. The monthly payments based on a twenty-five-year amortization will be $733 a month. Then with the $50,000 in hand, the individual finds a $150,000 investment property and arranges a first mortgage for $100,000. The investment is such that it generates sufficient rents to pay operating expenses and cover the required first mortgage payments. The secondary financing of $50,000 is then initially covered by the individual's *excess earnings* from his job, business or profession—and not by the property itself.

As long as the excess interest is tax-deductible, the $733 a month "negative cash flow" reduces down to only $366. (For purposes of this example, we will ignore the small portion of each payment which represents principal.) Can an individual earning $60,000 afford to pay $4,400 in (after-tax) mortgage payments? Our assumption is that he can—if he wants to—since this represents less than 8% of his income. (This also assumes that the individual does not have other extraordinary debt obligations.)

Why, however, would anyone wish to borrow $50,000 for an investment where the income initially generated is so insufficient that such borrowing must be covered by other income sources? The answer, of course, is the anticipation of property appreciation. If the $150,000 investment appreciates by 10% over a one-year period, the investor would be trading an after-tax negative cash flow of $4,400 for a potential appreciation of $15,000!

Of course, the negative cash flow in this case is easily calculated while the property appreciation is speculative. There is no guarantee that rental property will appreciate each year by a factor equal to increases in the cost of living. Assuming, however, that there is no total collapse of the economy, and that inflation averages 10% each year over a medium-term period, it seems a fair bet that if the cost of living increases by 50% over five years, then real estate investments should keep pace. Then again, if we are faced with a severe recession and shortage in the money supply, the foregoing may not hold true. In fact, there are many investment advisers today who feel that real estate is not a good buy at this time. In fact, in late 1981 and early 1982 property prices in many parts of the country actually declined by as much as 30%.

The Risk Factor

Is it then worthwhile to risk an annual negative cash flow of $4,400 in anticipation of property appreciation averaging $15,000 a year? Well, certainly, a great deal depends on the "comfort level" of the individual and how he feels about the concept of borrowing. Is it really a strain to meet the monthly commitments? Of course, if rents go up and if interest rates stabilize (or decrease), over a period of time the additional rental revenues will cause most real estate investments to start carrying themselves.

As a general rule, we would not recommend any real estate project which would not be capable of sustaining itself within, at most, a five-year period. In the early stages, however, unless you put up a very substantial downpayment, it is difficult to find property that is self-sustaining.

Certainly, one of the most important variables to consider is the location of a potential investment, and when dealing specifically with residential real estate properties, you must consider rent controls. If there are artificially imposed rent controls on the one hand, while the cost of borrowing *increases*, you can be caught in a very tight squeeze.

Again, it must be stressed that the previous example assumes that the excess interest expense will continue to be tax deductible. However, the deductibility of excess interest is only certain for the 1982 tax year. After that, if the government persists in making some part of excess interest non-deductible, the cost of carrying a property may literally double! Obviously, if you have to gamble $8,800 against the potential of realizing appreciation of $15,000, this is certainly not nearly as attractive as the present structure where the government subsidizes your negative cash flow. Of course, if rental incomes increase dramatically over the next few years, the risk may again become quite acceptable.

Just to round out the picture, there is one further refinement to the concept of investing where there is a negative cash flow. You should note that in the first year, if you were to borrow $50,000 (at an interest rate of 18%) you would actually be required to pay out $733 a month to the lending institution and not only $366. The cost of borrowing is only reduced to half *after* your tax return is submitted and a refund of taxes otherwise payable is received. In order to make up for the difference, a sophisticated buyer will often borrow a little bit more than he requires for the actual investment.

In the previous example, the investor would have borrowed $54,400 and not only $50,000. The $4,400 difference would then have been placed into a special bank account and would have been used over the first twelve months to make up the difference between the required monthly payments of $733 a month and the $366 a month which he could otherwise comfortably afford from his earned income sources. Then, at the end of the year, when a tax refund was received, the special bank account would be replenished by $4,400 and these funds would again be available to subsidize the (hopefully decreasing) negative cash flow for the following year.

The technique of borrowing more than one's initial principal requirement is often used by real estate speculators as well. A speculator is someone who plans to hold a property for only a short period of time. Where that is the case, the buyer does not usually worry about rental revenues, and if the speculative property consists of raw land, there generally is no revenue, in any event. However, in order to subsidize the cost of carrying his property, a speculator will often borrow not only the principal which he needs to buy the property in the first place, but also an additional amount to cover short-term interest costs. Then, if the venture is successful, the property will be resold at a price sufficient to recover the interest incurred during the holding period and also to provide a profit back to the speculator. Of course, speculation and investment are two different things but some of the financing concepts are certainly common to both.

A Word of Caution

Since 1981, interest rates have skyrocketed in North America, making the cost of borrowing for real estate investment very expensive — even after considering the deductibility of interest expense. Traditionally, rent increases tend to lag behind changes in interest rates by one or two years. In other words, landlords may not always be able to raise tenants' rents at the same time that their mortgages come up for renewal.

In most cases, a rental property won't carry itself on the basis of rents paid unless the owner puts up between 30% and 40% of the purchase price. If you invest a lesser amount (in order to acquire a larger property investment in the first place) a negative cash flow will result. Until such time as interest rates moderate substantially and stabilize at lower levels (if this in fact will happen) extreme caution is advised.

Real Estate as a Tax Shelter

In the past, tax write-offs from a property (especially during a construction period) served to minimize the downpayment that you would otherwise need to buy into a project. Unfortunately, however, the government has seen fit to remove most of the incentives for new construction. First, the multiple unit residential building program with its special depreciation incentives has not been extended for construction starts after 1981. Second, tax depreciation (capital cost allowance) cannot be used to create or increase a rental loss except on already-built multiple unit residential buildings. However, since the Canadian capital cost allowance rate on a building purchase is only

5% (2½% in the year of acquisition) this is insignificant and will not serve to help an investor recover a worthwhile percentage of his downpayment. Finally, the role of real estate as a tax shelter has been reduced dramatically.

In prior years, the major tax shelters came from two sources—interest deductibility, which was dealt with previously in this chapter, and "soft cost write-offs" during a construction period, which will be covered next.

Soft Cost Write-Offs

Soft costs consist of several significant expenses associated with real estate construction which are capital in nature but may be written off for tax purposes in the year or years incurred. These include:

- Interest paid on borrowed money during the construction period.
- Expenses of borrowing money (such as mortgage-application and commitment fees and appraisal costs).
- Landscaping of grounds.
- Expenses of representation (for example, the costs of obtaining proper zoning approvals and building permits).
- Costs of site investigation to determine suitability for a project.
- Utilities service connections (such as the costs of obtaining power, telephone and water services).
- Real estate taxes and insurance during the construction period.
- General overhead expenses of a building contractor, such as:
  - a) office expenses
  - b) off-site supervision during the construction period, and
  - c) advertising for tenants

From an accounting standpoint, soft costs contribute to the total value of any project under construction. Also, one could not construct a replacement building without incurring these same costs. Thus, they are treated as long-term assets (capitalized) on financial statements, and are only written off through normal depreciation over the lifespan of a building. However, for tax purposes, soft costs are subject to an *immediate* write-off because of specific income tax legislation.

The term "soft costs" was originally used to distinguish these particular components of a construction project from the "hard costs" of construction—the bricks, mortar and direct labor. There is another tax term with respect to these costs which, in its own way, is just as descriptive. Soft costs are also known as "first-time write-offs", to indicate that these particular costs are incurred only *once*—during the construction period.

Soft Costs and Real Estate Developers

In the past, developers were able to pass on soft cost write-offs to investors in rental or commercial developments by involving the investors in the ownership of these projects during the construction period. The total of these soft costs often amounted to as much as 20% to 25% of the value of a project. The tax saving resulting from the deduction of these soft costs served to greatly reduce an investor's downpayment and to subsidize the net amount of cash required in order to purchase property. Now, these former tax write-offs must be added to the capital cost of land and building. To the extent that they are added to the building, they are subject to ordinary depreciation only. The only exception is with respect to "principal business corporations". A principal business corporation is a corporation whose main business is any combination of real property leasing, rental, development or sale. The term "principal" business is not defined in the Income Tax Act, but presumably the corporation's gross assets and gross income would be examined. If more than 50% of assets and income are related to real estate, the corporation would probably qualify. However, the key point to note is that *individual investors* may no longer participate in new construction projects on a tax-sheltered basis.

The Real Estate Investment Market After 1982

For the aspiring executive or entrepreneur, there appears to be much less opportunity in the real estate market in late 1982 than there was one short year ago. Without the tax preferences and tax incentives which existed previously, it is now a real challenge to accumulate wealth through real estate ownership. In the past, Canadians have relied heavily on the use of leverage to accumulate capital. This device (as already explained) involves borrowing against excess earning power in order to make investments. Under a tax system in which the government subsidizes one's interest expense through tax deductions, it is possible to acquire growth property at a cost within reason for a large number of Canadians. The future of this system is, however, in jeopardy.

By eliminating soft cost write-offs for investors on construction projects initiated after 1981, the government has made it too expensive to acquire *new* real estate investments because the downpayment becomes too high. No longer is a substantial portion of the initial equity recoverable during the construction period.

The only possible salvation would be a substantial long-term decrease in interest rates. Otherwise, present rental levels will make acquisitions even at current depressed prices unrealistic. The downpayment required so that a property may carry itself is just exorbitant. We have already seen that the number of transactions in real estate has decreased substantially as a result of the November 12, 1981 Budget provisions.

The government of Canada has been faced with two severe problems over the last few years. They are inflation and unemployment. The purpose for removing most of the tax incentives pertaining to real estate was to create a climate wherein only a few would willingly borrow or invest money. In bringing down the November 12, 1981 Budget, the government hoped that a decline in the demand for money would eventually result in decreased activity, with a corresponding decrease in the rate of inflation.

Technically, a decrease in the demand for money should

EFFECT OF LOWER INTEREST RATES ON REAL ESTATE INVESTMENT

Tax System with Soft Cost Write-Offs

Cost of property:

Land	$10,000
Soft costs	17,000
Building	43,000
	$70,000

Financing:

By way of mortgage at 18% (payments of $733 per month)	$50,000
Downpayment	20,000
	$70,000

Rental income — $733 × 12 months	$ 8,800
Less: Mortgage payments	8,800
Net cash flow	Nil

Investor's cash requirements:

Cash invested	$20,000
Less: Tax advantage of soft cost write-offs (60%* × $17,000)	10,000
Net cash required to "carry" a $70,000 property	$10,000

*Top tax bracket in 1981

Tax System Without Soft Cost Write-Offs

Cost of property:

Land	$10,000
Building	60,000
	$70,000

Financing:

By way of mortgage at 16½% (payments of $815 per month)	$60,000
Downpayment	10,000
	$70,000

Rental income—$815 × 12 months	$ 9,800
Less: Mortgage payments	9,800
Net cash flow	Nil

Investor's cash requirements:

Cash invested	$10,000

Net cash required to "carry" a $70,000 property	$10,000

have caused interest rates to fall and the cost of borrowing to become substantially cheaper. At the same time, given a dramatic decline in construction starts, rents should certainly have increased. The government probably projected that would occur even without any new incentives. This scenario is illustrated in the comparison on pages 128–29, which shows the effects of increased rents and declining interest rates.

While the numbers in these examples are purely hypothetical, they do show quite clearly that a 10% increase in rents coupled with a 1½% decrease in mortgage interest rates would make a property investment viable even without the tax shelter previously provided by soft-costs. In the second example, an investor could carry his investment with the same $10,000 downpayment as in previous years without having to resort to tax subsidies.

We should, however, consider the question of whether the government's program to reduce inflation without endangering the soundness of real estate investments was successful. In theory, removing the stimulus for borrowing should have led to a substantial decline in interest rates. On the other hand, as we have seen in the time since the Budget of November 12, 1981, the Canadian economy does not operate in a vacuum. If our interest rates had come down while U.S. rates stayed high, the value of our dollar would have fallen even further. In addition, the Canadian government has also experienced the same problems as the private sector. Because of declining revenues and increased costs, the government projects a massive deficit *which will require it to be the largest borrower of all.* If the government must go to the market to borrow money in tremendous quantities, private industry will then have to pay a premium rate to obtain its dollars. It is unfortunate when a private borrower must outbid his or her own government!

We have seen therefore that long-term mortgage interest rates have not fallen substantially in 1982. The pressures which this has created on business have resulted in many large projects being cancelled. In addition, there have been severe cutbacks in labour. This too has had an adverse effect on the real estate market since rents in many parts of the country have *dropped*. The combination of low rents and high interest makes real estate singularly unattractive unless property can be acquired at bargain basement prices.

At the present time, the removal of incentives for construction and development, along with high interest rates, is contributing to the increase in unemployment and making the recession even worse. It is quite possible that if unemployment reaches levels which are intolerable, the government will then move to introduce the necessary stimuli to get the economy rolling again. At that time, real estate may again become a more viable investment. Already, several provinces have moved towards subsidizing interest costs to assist the depressed housing and construction markets.

Specific Planning

Certainly, if you own an interest in real estate today we strongly recommend that you continue to hold onto it — if you can. Remember that even if there is a negative cash flow, such cash loss will continue to be tax-deductible. Ironically, if you try to sell you will probably not find a buyer.

On the other hand, if you do not own property today but are an individual who has a substantial amount of cash or borrowing power, you should probably not be buying. If the economy continues to decline, whatever you can acquire today, you may be able to buy for 20%–30% less in a few months' time. Look back at the examples on pages 128–29. If rents start to escalate while costs of borrowing decline, it may then be the time to jump into the market. Real estate developers will also re-enter the picture once they see the opportunity to make some money but, by the time their projects are finished, investors in already-built properties will have realized large profits.

As far as home ownership is concerned, if you are planning to buy a house you might be well advised to wait for a few months. If the economy continues to drop, you might get a much better deal a little later on. On the other hand, if you own your home already, our suggestion is to hang on. This is because renters will *eventually* be faced with higher rents, especially given the sharp decline in construction activity.

If you have the guts to speculate, you may do what some people are trying and that is selling their houses in the hopes of buying back equivalent properties (or upgrading) with less capital later on. This is certainly extremely risky, since on the sale of your present home you will probably incur a substantial commission expense which you have to make back. When you take this into account together with the renovation costs that almost invariably accompany the purchase of a "new" house, the ploy of selling and buying may turn out to be too expensive. In the meantime, try to pay off your mortgage over as short a period of time as possible, if for no other reason than to create a reasonable level of security in these troubled times.

The point you must consider is that a bad investment or an inopportune investment can often be worse than no investment at all. Certainly, real estate is an intriguing topic. The trick is to watch closely since the market never stands still. At the right time, a person who jumps in can do extremely well. You must never forget that real estate is an illiquid investment. It cannot be disposed of on the open market at a moment's notice in the same way as a publicly traded stock or bond. If you approach the 1980s in the same way as we do — as being a period of "ups and downs", you should begin to look to real estate as a relatively short-term investment. If interest rates drop low

MORTGAGE DEBT OF $100,000
Amortized Over Twenty-Five Years at Various Interest Rates

Interest Rate	Monthly Payment	Annual Cost
12%	$ 1,032	$12,384
14%	1,174	14,088
16%	1,319	15,828
18%	1,466	17,592
20%	1,615	19,380
22%	1,764	21,168

enough and the economy starts to rebound, you may want to consider buying. However, if high interest rates are then reintroduced, take whatever profit you can and get out before the next "bust".

In closing, we suggest that you examine the table on page 132. This table compares the monthly and annual cost to carry $100,000 of debt at various interest costs assuming an amortization over twenty-five years. As you might expect, there is over a 50% difference when we compare the 12% rate prevalent in 1979 to the 20% rate which many borrowers had to pay in 1982. Picture the rent levels needed to sustain these additional costs. That in itself will give you a clear picture of where the real estate market stands today.

CHAPTER EIGHT

Investing in the Stock Market

This chapter will outline specific strategies to assist you in making money in the stock market. If you stop and think for a moment, you will realize that there is no point in our recommending particular stocks to you. By the time you read this, the investment climate can be considerably different from the way it is at the time this is being written. It is also not our purpose to tell you what you should have done in bygone years. Books that reveal how someone else made millions of dollars are of little use for future reference. They may make you green with envy but they won't line your pockets with money. There are literally hundreds of stock markets across the world. For a few very sophisticated investors, the international scene may have tremendous appeal. If the stock market is down in Canada, it may be booming in Bombay. However, for most of us, investing outside North America goes far beyond our comfort level. Therefore, we propose to consider only strategies for dealing with the North American markets.

If you have gotten this far in this book, you don't need us to tell you that the stock market goes up and it goes down. The stock market is a prime example of the fact that people learn very little when they win. As the market goes up and people make money on even the most inferior and suspicious issues, they never stop to question the rationality of the process. As prices rise and money pours into the market it seems that these hay days will never end and that each day will see a new plateau of prosperity. However, in the last two thousand years, mankind has found no way to eliminate the business cycle. This means that almost everything in the universe works the same way—that which goes up will also come down.

Government intervention has made it possible for the periods of prosperity to be greatly extended and to postpone for a time the correction that must necessarily follow. For example, as interest rates were kept artificially low in the later part of the 1970s, this encouraged you to invest in the market. Eventually, however, government intervention has had a great cost. Recent corrections in the market reflect changes in corporate values as well as human psychology. For 99% of people who have dabbled in the market, it remains the single most exotic mystery in their business and monetary lives. Our main concerns are how to find a stock, when to buy it and when to sell it.

Receipt of Dividends

Before we deal with strategies for buying and selling stocks in order to make profits, it is worth exploring the stock market as a vehicle for earning income on an ongoing basis. Many stocks pay dividends to their shareholders and these dividends provide a flow of income which can be used on an after-tax basis either for personal living expenses or to furnish capital for additional investments.

In Canada, the receipt of dividends from Canadian securities is treated quite differently for tax purposes than the receipt of interest. Dividends received by an individual are included in taxable income, subject to a calculation which grosses up the amount received but also provides an offsetting dividend tax credit which reduces the actual tax payable. The dividend tax credit is provided for two reasons, one being that dividends are a distribution out of after-tax corporate earnings. If the system taxed the same dollar as income to both the corporation which earned it and the individual who ultimately received it, this would result in double taxation. Second, the dividend tax credit provides a major incentive for Canadians to invest in their own corporations.

The example on page 136 illustrates that taxpayers in all marginal brackets will retain more, after tax, from receipts of

COMPARATIVE AFTER-TAX RETENTION ON DIVIDENDS VS. INTEREST

Individual's marginal tax bracket	40%	45%	50%
ALTERNATIVE 1 — $100 Canadian dividends			
Cash dividend	$100	$100	$100
½ gross-up	50	50	50
Taxable income	$150	$150	$150
Tax in marginal bracket	$ 60	$ 67	$ 75
Dividend tax credit (combined federal and provincial)	50	50	50
Net tax	$ 10	$ 17	$ 25
Net retention: (Cash dividend minus tax)	$ 90	$ 83	$ 75
ALTERNATIVE 2 — $100 Canadian interest			
Interest	$100	$100	$100
Tax in marginal bracket	40	45	50
Net retention	$ 60	$ 55	$ 50
Ratio of after-tax retention Dividends : Interest	3:2	3:2	3:2

dividends than they would from equivalent receipts of interest. Essentially, you must earn one and a half times as much interest in comparison to dividends in order to wind up with the same after-tax dollars in your hands. Again, this example shows you something that is uniquely Canadian. By comparison, in the United States both interest and dividends are simply taxed in one's top marginal bracket.

You should note that this example ignores the first $1,000 of annual investment income, which is tax-free whether the $1,000 comprises interest, (grossed-up) dividends, capital gains or any combination of the three.

From this example, you should now understand that for anyone who is taxable, a 10% dividend is equivalent to a 15% (pre-tax) interest yield. In other words, a dividend yield is certainly much more attractive than first meets the eye.

It should be stressed that the foregoing example is only valid where an individual is taxable in the first place. Again, as illustrated in Chapter Four, interest-bearing securities can be excellent investments in cases where one does not have to pay taxes on the yields. This is provided that the stipulated yield is, of course, at least equal to the prevailing inflation factor.

The gross-up and credit system, which provides that 50% of all amounts actually received as dividends from Canadian companies is first added to income and is then deducted directly off taxes otherwise payable, has a very interesting by-product. Specifically, up to $36,000 of Canadian dividends can be received by an individual in 1982 *totally tax-free* as long as he or she has *no other income*. This is illustrated in the example on page 138, which uses average tax rates applicable across Canada.

The example shows a dividend of $36,000 that is grossed up by an extra $18,000. However, after applying personal exemptions and other deductions, the tax otherwise payable is completely offset by the $18,000 dividend tax credit. The net effect is to reduce taxes to nil.

Remember that the concept of tax-free dividends only applies where a taxpayer has no other income. If the individual in our example had an *extra* $1,000 from *any source whatsoever*, the taxable income would become $51,000 instead of $50,000. In this case, since he or she is already in a 44% combined federal and provincial tax bracket, the extra $1,000 of income would cost $440 of taxes. There would be no further dividend tax credits available to offset this additional burden.

Thus, if you receive dividends as well as other income, the other income "floats to the top" and gets taxed at your highest marginal bracket with no relief. If you have substantial other income, you should be aware that the tax advantages of Canadian dividends are reduced considerably. You should also note that there is no direct relationship between dividends and other income. Therefore, you could *not* receive, for example, $16,000 of salary and a further (tax-free) $20,000 of dividends. The interaction of various mixes of dividends and other

IF AN INDIVIDUAL HAS NO OTHER INCOME, $36,000 OF
CANADIAN DIVIDENDS ARE TAX-FREE

Dividend	$36,000
½ "gross-up"	18,000
Net income	54,000
Less: Estimated personal exemptions	4,000
Taxable income	$50,000
Estimated federal and provincial taxes	
On $31,000	$ 9,640
On $19,000 (tax bracket 44%)	8,360
On $50,000	18,000
Less: Dividend tax credit (combined federal and provincial)	(18,000)
Net tax payable	Nil

income must be determined on a trial and error basis with the aid of your own accountant in your particular province.

On page 50, we illustrated how a family of husband and wife could improve their investment yield in cases where the spouse in a high tax bracket makes a non-interest-bearing loan to the spouse who is not otherwise taxable. In that example, $100,000 was invested to yield interest of $16,000. The wife's estimated taxes were $2,500. If the investment had been a dividend-bearing security instead (with a comparable yield of 16%), there would, in fact, be no taxes payable on the investment income. In both cases, however, the husband would have to be prepared to lose a personal exemption for his wife. Of course, the key is comparable yield. In many cases, dividend yields on a pre-tax basis tend to be significantly lower than interest yields. As you will soon see, however, there are some notable exceptions.

Retractable Preferred Shares

If you are going to invest in stocks in order to earn dividend yields, the next question to ask is what type of security should you be choosing? The answer is generally one of several retractable preferred share issues which blue chip companies in Canada have issued in recent years in order to raise capital. A preferred share is one that bears dividends before the common shareholders receive any return on their investment. The fact that the share is retractable means that the holder has the right to demand that his share be redeemed for cash at the end of a stipulated time. In other words, unless the company runs into severe financial difficulties, the investor would get his money back at the end of this period. Thus, retractable preferreds are quite attractive since they combine all of the best features of both bonds and stocks. Generally, these shares have a limited life, which is usually five years. Sometimes, these shares also offer the option of converting them into the issuing corporation's common stock. Thus, if the corporation performs well, there is the potential for a capital gain. Alternatively, if prevailing interest rates drop, the dividend yield on these shares becomes more attractive. In such circumstances, a sale even before redemption can give rise to a capital gain. Many of these issues presently pay dividends in excess of 10%. In fact, yields of 15% to 20% are not uncommon. You would need a 20% to 30% before-tax interest return in order to equal this!

Borrowing for Stock Market Investments

If you borrow to invest in the shares of Canadian public companies, you are generally permitted to deduct your interest expense against other income after having initially offset as much interest as you can against your grossed-up dividends. Although the November 12, 1981 Budget contained proposals to limit the deductibility of interest expense in excess of investment income, the proposed restrictions have, at least temporarily, been postponed.

It is possible to get a tremendous advantage in Canada from the fact that the dividend tax credit can offset carrying charges which are significantly higher than the dividends received. The example on page 140 shows the receipt of a cash dividend of $10,000 where the investor has incurred carrying charges on

EFFECT OF DIVIDEND TAX CREDIT ON CARRYING CHARGES

Assumptions:
- Cash Dividend $10,000
- Carrying charges $15,000

Cash dividend	$10,000
Gross-up	5,000
	15,000
Less: Carrying charges	(15,000)
Effect on taxable income	Nil
Excess of carrying charges over cash dividend	$ 5,000
Less: Tax savings from dividend tax credit	(5,000)
Negative cash flow	Nil

these and other investments of $15,000. Because the dividend must be grossed-up by half, it can fully offset the amount of the carrying charges incurred in arriving at the individual's income. However, although none of the dividend is in fact taxable, the taxpayer is still entitled to claim the dividend tax credit against the taxes on his other income. In terms of cash flow, the individual will find that the excess of carrying charges that he has paid over the dividend which he has received, or $5,000, is fully offset either through a reduction in his other taxes payable or as a direct refund.

For many people, a well-balanced investment portfolio will include stocks bearing high dividend yields. This is because the cost of borrowing for all investments can be at least somewhat offset by the tax advantages of the dividend tax credit.

How to Find Stocks to Buy and Sell

Of course, the most difficult question concerning the stock market is which stock to buy, when to buy it, and when to sell it. In an effort to deal with this question, two diametrically opposite schools of thought have evolved. One of these is the school which advocates "fundamental analysis" and the other practices "technical analysis".

Fundamental analysis is a rational process which focuses on the value of the corporation whose stock is traded. The proper stock to buy is the one which is undervalued — where the value of the company's assets, income, or expectations of income is not fully reflected in the stock's market price. Those who practice fundamental analysis assume that the market will eventually recognize that this particular corporation's shares are undervalued and that therefore the stock price is eventually bound to rise. Alternatively, if the same approach indicates that a stock is overvalued, this may mean that the particular security is undesirable and should be sold.

Fundamental analysis is an approach which is most suitable for long-term holdings because there is really no way to determine *when* the market will recognize its "error" in having undervalued a stock in the first place. Thus, fundamental analysis is of limited use for investors who wish to trade or speculate. In order to locate an undervalued stock, you (or your broker) must be prepared to analyse corporate financial statements through a series of steps. These include the use of many arithmetic ratios to determine liquidity, financial strength, and profitability. You must also be willing to acquire knowledge of the industry itself, the products, the management philosophy of the company and many other factors which would have an impact upon the value of the stock price. Fundamental analysis can be very time-consuming and for the average person the arithmetical approach in itself is very tedious. Furthermore, once you have developed all the material, you must be able to interpret the results properly. The biggest drawback of fundamental analysis is that it does not indicate *when* to buy or sell other than to tell you that if you hold the stock long enough then, supposedly, the intrinsic value will be recognized by the market. Anytime you are forced to hold a stock which does not move for several years, it is both frustrating and expensive. The fundamental approach does not indicate when to sell for short-term profits nor can it be used widely as an indicator of when to "sell short" (see page 144). If you practice fundamental analysis, you may in fact find a truly valuable stock in terms of long-term appreciation. However, if you have to hold it for three years and virtually all of the growth in price takes place in the last six months, you must consider the opportunity loss in the first two and a half years of the holding period.

Today many people feel that fundamental analysis was better suited to times that were more stable and during which stock prices were subject to more rational rules of order than they are today. During highly inflationary times, it is quite possible for a stock price to rise appreciably strictly because of monetary erosion, inflation or sheer panic that the dollar is losing its buying power, rather than in recognition of the value of corporate assets and income.

One of the most significant factors mitigating *against* the use of fundamental analysis is the accounting information which forms the basis of much of the review. Accounting statements are generally based on historical cost concepts. In other words, asset values on a corporate balance sheet do not necessarily reflect the fair market value of these particular properties. Furthermore, different companies within the same industry may adopt different depreciation policies. They may also have different methods of recording certain potential liabilities such as pension commitments. There is sometimes a time lag between the end of a particular reporting period and the date on which financial statements are made generally available. In the interim, there can be severe changes in conditions affecting the market as a whole, the industry in which the corporation is active, or the company itself.

So, in the last few years an entirely different method of stock market analysis has developed, which perhaps is better suited to the fast-moving and more speculative economy we witness today. This is technical analysis.

Technical analysis makes an effort to determine what the trend of stock prices is at any given point in time and where they presently stand within that trend. It tries to predict the tops and bottoms of current trends that evolve from time to time. The philosophy behind this approach is that the market has its own distinct personality, which is a composite of the tens of thousands of living personalities which are involved in it on a day-to-day basis. Therefore, the actions of the market are more a product of psychology than logic. Technical analysts feel that investment success is dependent upon understanding and being able to interpret the indicators of what the market is presently doing. By its very nature, technical analysis tends to focus on the more or less short-term picture. It makes the assumption that it is inefficient for an investor to commit his money in expectation of a profit which may be several years down the road. Today's economic situation makes this a very persuasive argument.

Technical analysis informs the investor that he can make profits by either buying stocks (going long) or by selling stocks that he doesn't even own (going short). It neither moralizes nor is concerned with the intrinsic value of particular corporations but basically attempts to "go with the flow". Analysts who use this approach interpret what the market is presently doing and what it is likely to do in the near future by studying the highs and lows, the Dow Jones Industrial Average, the advance-decline line, and on-balance volume figures. If, for example, many stocks are reaching high points at which they have traded over the last few years, this generally is an indication that the market is moving upwards. Similarly, if more issues go up than those which decline over a particular period, this too is an indicator that the market is advancing. Fortunately, none of the indicators is particularly complicated and virtually all information is available on a day-to-day basis in the *Globe and Mail* or other large newspapers. Your stockbroker probably has the benefit of studies done by analysts in his firm who use this approach.

The purpose of this chapter is not to undertake a major exposition of technical analysis. In his book, *Granville's New Strategy of Daily Stock Market Timing for Maximum Profit*, Joe Granville required 340 pages to adequately deal with the subject. Basically, however, the purpose of technical analysis is simply to determine whether the market is truly gaining or losing strength—whether it is expanding or contracting. On that basis, "smart money" determines which times to enter and leave the market and which times to take a long or short position.

Selling Short

Most people don't recognize that more money can be made in the stock market as prices fall than during times when they are on the upswing. This is because prices tend to fall very sharply while they tend to rise rather slowly. However, the average investor generally does not take advantage of this fact and feels that selling short is only for the sophisticated investor. *The procedure for selling short is simply to sell a stock which you do not own. Then, the object is to buy back and "cover" your position when the stock price is lower. The difference represents profit.*

If selling short is so simple, why do few investors use this technique? The following examples illustrate why selling short will not appeal to the timid investor.

SELLING SHORT INVOLVES A GREATER RISK

SITUATION 1
• Purchase 100 shares at $30 per share
• Stock drops to $1 per share

Original purchase	$ 3,000
Sale	100
Loss before commission	$ 2,900

SITUATION 2
• short 100 shares at $30 per share
• stock rises to $200 per share

Original sale	$ 3,000
Purchase to close out position	20,000
Loss before commission	$17,000

When a stock is purchased and put away for future growth, an investor knows that, unpleasant as the prospect may be, the most he can lose is the total amount that he originally invested. However, when an investor sells short he has effectively borrowed someone else's shares and has sold them in the market. That is, he has sold something which he does not own in the belief that he can repurchase it at a lower cost. One cannot usually wait indefinitely to buy the stock back, and the investor must be prepared to meet certain cash requirements set by brokerage firms to maintain a balance between what he originally sold the stock for and the current day-to-day value. If the stock price begins to run contrary to his opinion, he will be forced to make a decision about committing further funds as margin or taking his losses by repurchasing the stock to close out his position. As Situation 2 illustrates, an error in judgement in this case can be very expensive. The investor potentially risks losing many times more than his original investment. If you are speculating in a security which is thinly traded (that is, not many shares are held by the general public) you run the risk of literally being bankrupted. This would happen if the stock price starts to climb and no one is willing to sell shares to you in order to cover your short position. Therefore, if you are going to sell short in the market (and we believe that you should—if the circumstances are right), you should only select securities that are widely traded.

Because of the risk in selling short, most brokerage houses do not widely advertise the opportunities to their clients. Your broker will, however, be pleased to answer all your questions if you bring up the subject first. Unfortunately, when the market is "bad", most investors would rather stay out completely than bet their money that the situation will get worse. Even those investors who hold shares that have dropped dramatically in value prefer to sit on their holdings rather than to sell out, take their losses, and start again. Most people are very reluctant to take losses. Hope springs eternal that the market will rebound and that the investor will get his money back. Selling short, as illustrated previously, involves far more decisiveness. If you don't take steps to eliminate your losses (as described on pages 147–48), you can be wiped out.

Brokerage houses prosper in good times and suffer greatly when the market is down. Of course, any lack of activity tends to result in reduced commissions. Consequently, many brokerage houses will try to "hype" the market. During 1981–82, you will probably recall having received many investment letters advising you that "in spite of the general market decline, our analysts recommend that you buy X Company Limited."

Technical analysts are disgusted by this kind of advertising—they argue that it is foolish to look for one or two stocks that will run counter to the general market when a lot more money can made if you go *with* the trend. Notwithstanding that the use of charts and indicators casts an aura of mysticism over the stock market, a great deal of what the technical analysts say makes good sense. As Joe Granville puts it, "the market doesn't care where you live." In Quebec and Ontario, investors tend to watch the stocks of manufacturing companies. In Alberta, the sun rises and sets on the oil stocks. In British Columbia, where the economy is tied into the performance of the lumber industry, MacMillan Bloedel and B.C. Resources are the stocks that are followed daily. And yet, investors in the East buy western stocks while investors in the West buy eastern stocks. In fact, Americans, Europeans, and investors in other countries also deal in Canadian stocks. If the economy is good, the market will rise. If the economy is bad, most stocks will go down.

When to Buy and Sell

Our suggested approach combines both fundamental analysis and technical analysis. First, try to determine the trend which the market is following. Don't fight it—go with it. Then, examine the particular issues that you should be dealing in. In a strong market, you should buy the strongest stocks while in a weak market you should shop for the weakest stocks. Again, for most investors trading should be restricted to those stocks that are widely held. Experience has taught us that speculative promotions are for insiders only. Of course, knowledge of particular industries and particular companies is also important. If oil prices are dropping on a worldwide basis, then oil stocks will drop dramatically in a bad market and won't go up in a good market. If a company such as Massey Ferguson is severely hampered by debt loads, it probably won't perform well even in a buoyant market. Again, go with the trend. Don't try to ferret out the one or two issues that are performing contrary to the general direction of the market.

From September 1981 to July 1982, there was a large decline in stock prices. Even profitable high technology stocks did not perform well. The reason, of course, is that if the market in general is contracting even stocks of profitable companies will not buck the trend to a significant extent. If you bought at the wrong tine, you must be willing to take your losses and go on to something else.

Remember that sitting on a depressed stock for a year or two carries a tremendous opportunity cost. Putting away stocks and forgetting about them is not the answer. In January 1979, Canadian Pacific, one of Canada's foremost blue chip stocks was trading at about $25.00 a share. During the boom which followed into 1980 and the first part of 1981, the stock reached a high of over $50.00. By July 1982, the entire gain had evaporated!

If you are not willing to play the markets in both directions, you should probably just stay away. On the other hand, if you have the proper temperament, you can make a lot of money selling short. All you need is an element of decisiveness and the discipline to limit your losses.

How to Minimize Risks of Selling Short

The first approach that you can take is simply to pay very close personal attention to the price movements of the stocks in which you have transacted and quickly close out loss positions. Of course, this is time-consuming and nerve-wracking unless your full-time occupation is investing. Therefore, a more practical approach is to use one of several artificial mechanisms to curtail severe losses. First, you can place "stop-loss orders" with your broker, which will automatically close out a short position if the market begins to run decisively in the wrong direction. In other words, if a stock begins to rise drastically in value, then a stop-loss order would allow your broker to buy back the shares before significant losses had been sustained.

Unfortunately, the use of stop-loss orders has a major drawback. The market frequently opens at a different price than it closed the night before, and in some circumstances this may mean that the limitation of the stop-loss order has already been exceeded before the broker even has the opportunity to place an order for the purchase of the stock. Also, there is an inevitable lag between the time when a broker places his request and the moment it is actually executed. There could be a movement of several points before your position is liquidated. If you use the device of stop-loss orders to provide protection, you must realize that this will ensure only the *approximate* loss which you would be willing to sustain.

A better approach might be to protect a short-sale position through the purchase of "call options". These will be discussed more fully in the next chapter. However, for the time being, you may note that a call option is simply an option or right to buy a stock at a particular price. Then, if the stock price rises, you exercise your option to acquire those particular shares. Being able to buy back the "short shares" at a predetermined price allows you to calculate your maximum potential loss. The purchase of a call option can provide you with insurance and eliminate all risks of major losses from selling short. This ideal method is, however, utilized by very few investors. First of all, it is contrary to human nature to believe in the possibility that one's opinion is seriously incorrect. Also, if the investor is right in his assumption that the price of the stock will fall, then the call option (and the commission paid) will become valueless. These extra expenses will reduce the overall profit which he realizes on the short sale. Thus, both ego and greed leave the majority of speculators open to significant losses in taking short positions.

From a practical standpoint, we recommend that for small investors, the use of stop-loss orders would be adequate protection. Even if a stock jumps by three or four points above the price at which you have asked your broker to cover your position, the loss will still be bearable. On the other hand, if you are investing large sums, you would be foolish not to protect yourself with call options. You should treat the cost of this in the same way as you would life insurance. After all, life insurance is a cost for protection. You don't usually hope that you die in order to collect.

Capital Gains and Losses

All too frequently, an investor puts himself into the double bind of being unwilling to liquidate and recognize loss positions while he is also reluctant to liquidate large capital gains positions because he knows he will have to face the tax consequences. This type of reasoning is highly self-destructive. It is far better for an investor to take his maximum capital gains, cut his losses and then make whatever tax arrangements are reasonable to protect himself from giving away a substantial portion of his net profits to the government. Few convenient vehicles are still available (following the November 1981 and June 1982 budgets) that would allow an investor to defer the tax on the receipt of substantial capital gains. However, one remaining possibility is the use of a "commodity straddle", which is described in the next chapter. This method is only practical if it is desirable to postpone the tax on a significant capital gain for one year since the investor would have to take into account the additional costs of putting such an arrangement into place. The small investor has no alternative but to pay the tax in the year in which profits are made.

One of the best ways to keep taxes down to a minimum is to again make use of the family unit along the lines described in Chapter Four. Specifically, you could lend funds to a spouse in a low tax bracket or to children (as long as they are eighteen years of age or over) and have these people make the investments for you. Then, if profits do result, the tax bite may not be that expensive. Of course, problems can result. If you make an investment and that investment is structured in the name of a non-working spouse or child in the late teens or early twenties, you lose your "downside" protection. In other words, if a capital loss arises, you do not get the opportunity to deduct it for tax purposes.

In dealing with capital losses, it is a good idea for any investor to have a basic understanding of the tax rules. In Canada, one-half of a capital gain is taxable while one-half of a capital loss is deductible. If you have capital losses, you may offset them against capital gains, and deductible losses in excess of capital gains may be offset against other income to the extent of up to $2,000 a year. Any excess capital losses beyond that limit may be carried back one year and carried forward indefinitely. They may be used against capital gains in the carry-over years and may also be used to offset up to $2,000 of other income in those years. If you have a large capital loss, there is certainly little comfort in the first place from being able to deduct only half, and in the second place, from being forced to spread that loss over several years. But that is just the way the system operates and there is not a whole lot any of us can do. Of course, this is just a general overview and there are certain exceptions and special rules which you may wish to discuss with your accountant.

Often, an investor would like to take a loss on a stock for tax purposes without relinquishing an investment he feels is a good long-term holding. Under these circumstances, there is the inclination to sell and buy back immediately. However, under the Canadian tax laws, if an individual sells a stock at a loss and then buys it back either personally, through his spouse or through a controlled corporation within thirty days of the sale, the loss will be disallowed. This arbitrary rule does not apply in cases where an individual sells an investment at a *gain* and then buys it back within a short time. Under these circumstances, the gain will immediately be taxable. Similar rules also apply where an individual moves stocks which he holds personally into an RRSP. At that time, he is deemed to have sold these securities at their fair market value. Any capital gains will be subject to tax, although capital losses arising on such a transfer will not be deductible.

One big plus under the Canadian tax system is that this country (unlike the United States) does not differentiate between "short-term" and "long-term" gains. In the United States, a short-term gain arises where properties such as securities are held less than a year. A short-term gain is fully taxable as if it were any other ordinary income. In the United States only 40% of a long-term capital gain is subject to taxation. For Canadian tax purposes, you are allowed to adopt capital gains treatment even on securities that are held for a short period.

This is provided that you are not a stockbroker by profession or otherwise connected to the stock market. If other individuals so wish, they can protect their capital gains treatment on Canadian securities for their entire lifetimes by making a "guaranteed capital gains election". If this is done, all profits will be treated as only half-taxable while losses will be deductible to the extent of 50%, as well.

Perhaps the best advice that we can give you in connection with the stock market is to concentrate on making profits first and worry about the tax consequences afterwards. The stock market is certainly a very interesting investment arena. The important thing to remember is that substantial profits can be made both in good times and in bad.

CHAPTER NINE

Commodities and Options

Commodities and options represent perhaps two of the most glamorous areas of potential investment. They are known for being the arenas of the sophisticated and the wealthy, who use them to make, or lose, fortunes. Apart from real estate, probably the greatest leverage is available here, and large asset values can be commanded through a small initial dollar investment.

Commodity trading originated as a method of providing farmers and manufacturers with guaranteed prices on products which they would buy or sell at future dates. By having a guaranteed price today, a manufacturer, in turn, is able to guarantee a price to his customers and know that his profit is assured. As long as he knows he will be able to take delivery of his raw material at a specified price for processing at a future date, he limits his risk. If the cost rises between the time he contracts to receive the material and the time of delivery or manufacture, then he is able to sell his contract at a profit. This profit would absorb the loss which is experienced in purchasing the material from his regular supplier at a cost that is higher than anticipated. On the other hand, if the value of the commodity drops significantly by the time the material is required, then the loss which is experienced on the contract is offset by the ability to purchase the material from the supplier at a price that is lower than anticipated. In other words, commodity trading provides a cushion against erratic price movements in unstable markets.

A commodity futures contract can be an agreement to *either* "make" or "take" delivery of a specific quantity of a certain commodity at a predetermined date. The dates of delivery may range up to more than a year into the future. In the last example, the manufacturer would be interested in the opportunity to buy a particular product at a predetermined price at a future time. An example of a contract to "make" delivery can be illustrated by taking a simple farming situation. Assume that a farmer grows wheat. At the time he plants his crop, or even before that when he buys his seed, he would like to be guaranteed a specific price for his production. He may then sell his future crop for delivery several months or a year later. Having a contract to deliver at a specific price would then enable him to borrow money in order to sustain his business operations.

Although the commodities futures markets originally arose to protect trade and commerce and to ensure stable markets, speculators soon entered the field by buying and selling contracts along with the end users. If a speculator then bought a contract for a specific commodity and the price rose, he could sell his entitlement at a profit. Of course, he would have to do so before the delivery date, since at that time, the particular commodity would only be desired by the end user. In other words, within the commodities market, profits and losses are made depending on price fluctuations from day to day. There is no end to the factors that can influence the changing prices of each commodity. These can include current price activities within world markets, monetary and political pressures, and even changes in international weather patterns. For example, if torrential rains in Argentina wipe out the current year's wheat crop, then world prices for this commodity could start to skyrocket upwards.

The further into the future that a commodity contract stretches, the larger the carrying costs associated with that commodity. These carrying costs include interest and storage because the commodity must theoretically be stored during the period until the contract expires. Apart from the factor of carrying charges, the prices for commodities can fluctuate violently from one moment to the next. This makes the market exciting but also dangerous for the amateur speculator. Because large amounts of money can quickly and easily be lost, the requirements to qualify for a commodity trading account are stiff. Generally, an investor must first be able to establish a personal net worth of at least $250,000 apart from his own home and life insurance. Then he must be prepared to deposit $10,000 in U.S. funds with his brokerage firm. At that point, he can specify and purchase the number of contracts for the commodity in which he is interested. He can either pay the full price for the contracts, which may be sizeable, or he can buy them on margin. The margin represents a very small proportion of the value of the contract and the downpayment can be met by drawing down against the deposit which he has made with the brokerage firm. Any excess funds can be left on deposit and will be maintained in U.S. treasury bills earning interest. The advantage of this procedure is that should the investor receive a margin call, or should he wish to use his funds immediately, he can transfer them directly out of his deposit account by a phone call to the brokerage firm. Commissions charged on commodity contracts vary depending on the commodity. For example a gold contract involves a commission of $90.00 while a contract in pork bellies costs $66.00 There is also likely to be a service charge of approximately $15.00 for small contract trades.

The example on page 155 outlines the benefits and dangers of margin. In a winning position, leverage can multiply your profits several times over. However, in an adverse situation, leverage can create large and rapid losses. Before the hypothetical 333% loss in our example was reached, however, the luckless investor would receive a margin call from his broker requesting that he post further funds in order to maintain his position. At that point the investor must decide whether to meet this demand or close out his position.

Futures contracts are expressed in units of commodities. For example, gold is sold in 100-ounce contracts while a cattle contract is for 40,000 pounds of cattle. Unlike stocks, every commodity has a daily limit to its potential price change. The limit is quantified in cents and is calculated from the previous

$3,000 U.S. margin will cover a 100-ounce gold contract
100 ounces of gold @ $400 U.S. per ounce = $40,000
Therefore, a $3,000 "deposit" will command $40,000 of assets

SITUATION 1

Purchase a 100-ounce contract on $3,000 margin
Price moves up from $400 per ounce to $450 per ounce

Purchase	$40,000
Close-out position	45,000
Gain	$ 5,000
Profit on $3,000	167%

SITUATION 2

Same facts but price moves down from $400 per ounce to $300 per ounce

Purchase	$40,000
Close-out position	30,000
Loss	$10,000
Loss on $3,000	333%

day's close. Because of the large quantities involved in any single contract, changes of only a penny or two can mean movements of hundreds of dollars per contract.

Is the Commodity Market for You?

Over the years, speculators have found that a market which experiences wide variations of price provides opportunities for earning vast profits. This is especially the case because of leverage—the ability to command a substantial amount of "product" with relatively few dollars down. However, you must always recognize that the use of leverage produces the potential not only for large profits but also tremendous losses. Over the years many investors have been severely hurt by placing their reliance on a market with which they were not familiar. As you will see in this chapter, there are several methods that can be used to protect yourself against an unlimited loss in the commodities futures market.

To begin with, if you do trade in commodities, you basically have two choices. You can either become an expert on a particular item or you can spread your risk by holding contracts in a variety of commodities. Any one trade should generally comprise only a small proportion of your investment capital. This would help to prevent disastrous losses if the market moves in a direction that you did not anticipate. At the outset, you should determine your approximate profit objective and, at the same time, set a limit on the loss that you are willing to accept. Certainly, the profit potential in any position that you take should be large in relation to the risk that you are assuming. We also suggest that you trade only in broad markets and use stop-loss orders to protect your position. These are dealt with later on in this chapter.

Selecting a commodity means spending the time to study the market. The best place to start is by locating a reliable, knowledgeable, and cooperative broker. That individual should specialize in commodities and should not be handling commodity accounts as a sideline to his other stock-trading activities. The person should be willing to spend the time to explain the market and its requirements to you as well as suggesting various commodities which you could watch if you decide you have an investment interest.

With that starting point, and a daily quotation provided by a newspaper such as the *Globe and Mail*, you are in a position to get a feel for the market. The illustration on page 157 is representative of what you will see in the newspapers.

As you can see, different commodities are traded on various exchanges and the price of a commodity can vary slightly between exchanges. Reading these quotations is not difficult once you become familiar with them. Let's take silver as an example; there are quotations here from two different exchanges each dealing with 5,000 troy ounce contracts. The prices are represented in cents per troy ounce, so a quote of 760.0 is equal to $7.60 per ounce.

Take the April silver contracts traded on the Chicago Board

Commodities

APRIL 14, 1982

Symbols for the exchange on which each commodity is traded appear in brackets after the commodity, followed by the minimum contract size and the monetary units used in the table. Open interest is the number of contracts outstanding each month and not liquidated by delivery of the commodity or by an offsetting contract.

Exchanges: CBT—Chicago Board of Trade, KCBT—Kansas City Board of Trade, CME—Chicago Mercantile Exchange, NYCSCE—New York Coffee and Sugar Exchange, NYC-TN—New York Cotton Exchange, NYM—New York Mercantile Exchange, NYCX—Commodity Exchange in New York, IMM—International Monetary Market of the Chicago Mercantile Exchange.

WOOD

LUMBER (CME)—130,000 bd. ft.; $ per 1,000 bd. ft.

—Season— High Low		High	Low	Close	Chg.	Open Int.
228.30	136.90 May	138.00	136.50	138.00	-.90	3,080
224.30	147.60 Jul	151.30	148.60	150.90	-.50	3,094
229.10	155.50 Sep	158.30	157.00	158.00	-.40	901
234.00	157.10 Nov	160.00	158.30	159.30	-1.00	531
233.30	165.00 Jan	168.70	164.30	167.10	-1.60	290
209.30	171.20 Mar	176.10	175.20	175.20	-1.00	52
198.40	183.60 May	184.00	183.00	183.60	-.90	21
201.60	189.00 Jul	192.20	196.30	196.50	-1.20	30

Est. sales 2,094. Prev. sales 1,429.
Prev day's open int 7,364, up 71.

METALS

PLATINUM (NYM)—50 troy oz.; $ per troy oz.

—Season— High Low		High	Low	Close	Chg.	Open Int.
624.00	296.50 Apr	364.00	360.00	364.00	+14.20	304
535.50	304.50 Jul	372.30	363.00	369.40	+14.10	4,892
533.00	312.50 Oct	379.50	373.00	378.60	+14.30	1,464
427.60	329.00 Jan	391.50	380.00	390.90	+14.60	306
410.00	342.00 Apr	400.00	396.50	402.20	+14.90	

Est. sales 2,539. Prev. sales 1,731.
Prev day's open int 7,213, up 109.

SILVER (CBT)—5,000 troy oz.; ¢ per troy oz.

—Season— High Low		High	Low	Close	Chg.	Open Int.
4542.0	690.0 Apr			760.0	+10.0	9
795.0	700.0 May			764.5	+9.0	5
4300.0	714.0 Jun	780.0	769.0	771.5	+9.0	1,222
4036.0	729.0 Aug			793.0	+9.0	522
3860.0	750.0 Oct			813.0	+9.0	472
3120.0	763.0 Dec	836.0	836.0	837.0	+9.0	631
2720.0	790.0 Feb			861.0	+9.0	801
2674.0	804.0 Apr			887.0	+9.0	1,380
2146.0	815.0 Jun	895.0	888.0	888.0	+9.0	690
1601.0	160.0 Aug			907.0	+9.0	248
1608.0	868.0 Oct			926.0	+9.0	248

Est. sales 590. Prev day's open int 6,677, off 8.

SILVER (NYCX)—5,000 troy oz.; ¢ per troy oz.

—Season— High Low		High	Low	Close	Chg.	Open Int.
3821.0	697.0 Apr	763.0	760.0	759.5	+16.0	73
2095.0	700.0 May	770.0	760.0	764.4	+16.0	12,813
764.0	714.0 Jun	777.0	777.0	773.3	+16.1	
2959.0	716.0 Jul	789.0	779.0	782.8	+16.4	9,556
2651.0	723.5 Sep	805.0	792.0	801.8	+16.9	2,540
1715.0	748.0 Dec	825.0	825.0	829.7	+17.1	3,351
1302.0	765.0 Jan	842.0	842.0	839.3	+17.3	751
1555.0	782.0 Mar	868.0	856.0	857.9	+17.5	594
1449.0	802.0 May	885.0	879.0	874.4	+17.7	404
1320.0	840.0 Jul			895.3	+17.1	22
1103.0	853.0 Sep			914.0	+18.1	54
1004.0	869.0 Dec			942.1	+18.4	44
942.0	890.0 Jan			951.5	+18.5	

Est. sales 9,300. Prev day's open int 30,205, off 140.

FOODS

COFFEE (NYCSCE)—37,500 lb.; ¢ per lb.

—Season— High Low		High	Low	Close	Chg.	Open Int.
149.00	80.50 May	133.00	132.10	132.57	-.41	3,077
149.00	81.50 Jul	124.20	121.50	122.40	-2.38	3,200
137.00	85.25 Sep	121.19	119.60	120.13	-1.54	2,099
131.00	81.35 Dec	119.85	117.35	117.31	-1.86	464
118.80	103.35 Mar	116.50	115.25	115.25	-1.36	130
116.90	115.00 May	115.00	114.50	113.75	-1.50	3

Est. sales 2,160. Prev. sales 2,106.
Prev day's open int 9,471, up 68.

ORANGE JUICE (NYCTN)—15,000 lb.; ¢ per lb.

—Season— High Low		High	Low	Close	Chg.	Open Int.
136.90	94.50 May	116.95	115.60	116.70	+1.10	1,475
139.00	101.00 Jul	119.50	118.00	119.45	+1.15	2,492
140.25	112.50 Sep	122.00	120.70	121.60	+1.10	1,238
161.50	115.00 Nov	123.10	122.50	123.20	+1.15	795
143.00	118.00 Jan	125.00	124.50	124.20	+.80	562
163.25	122.80 Mar			126.40	+.75	324
165.75	125.00 May			127.90	+.75	115
140.00	128.25 Jul			129.40	+.75	6
139.00	139.00 Sep			130.90	+.75	

Est. sales 580. Prev. sales 724.
Prev day's open int 7,417, up 166.

SUGAR, World (NYCSCE)—112,000 lb.; ¢ per lb.

—Season— High Low		High	Low	Close	Chg.	Open Int.
26.30	10.18 May	10.42	10.38	10.31	+.04	28,631
21.30	10.45 Jul	10.69	10.52	10.57	+.04	15,294
38.00	10.76 Sep	10.95	10.85	10.89	+.06	4,921
19.17	10.96 Oct	11.16	11.01	11.06	+.03	15,570
13.95	11.58 Mar			11.36		3
15.25	11.87 May	12.01	11.87	11.90	-.01	8,000
14.25	12.14 May	12.25	12.18	12.13	-.01	1,486
13.41	12.35 Jul	12.40	12.40	12.34		72

Est. sales 6,610. Prev. sales 8,112.
Prev day's open int 65,897, off 448.

COCOA (NYCSE)—10 metric tons; $ per ton

—Season— High Low		High	Low	Close	Chg.	Open Int.
2204	974 May	1675	1634	1670	+55	5,378
2496	1402 Jul	1679	1645	1673	+37	4,482
2436	1657 Sep	1725	1700	1720	+30	2,496
2403	1724 Dec	1777	1755	1774	+29	2,663
2295	1790 Mar	1826	1810	1826	+29	390
1899	1835 May			1860	+29	8
				1897	+29	1

Est. sales 3,665. Prev. sales 1,237.
Prev day's open int 15,419, up 98.

FIBRES

COTTON (NYCTN)—50,000 lb.; ¢ per lb.

—Season— High Low		High	Low	Close	Chg.	Open Int.
87.10	63.11 May	66.25	65.86	66.10	+.08	7,130
87.10	64.60 Jul	68.30	67.87	68.13	+.20	11,673
83.00	66.80 Oct	76.95	76.00	76.95	+.05	1,650
81.71	69.77 Dec	73.12	71.92	72.10	+.15	5,429
76.87	69.12 Mar	74.00	73.85	73.94	+.14	606
75.30	70.52 May			75.00	+.09	87
76.75	74.39 Jul			76.00	+.05	16

Est. sales 3,100. Prev. sales 4,308.
Prev day's open int 26,799, off 2.

of Trade (CBT), for example. During the time that contracts for this month have been available, they have traded as high as $45.62 an ounce and as low as $6.90. Contracts are available and have been traded only for those months that are listed. You can tell at a glance not only what the highs and lows have been for the season, but also what the daily price activity has been, because the change in value (cents per ounce) from the previous day's close is noted. The open interest is the number of contracts for that date which have not been closed out and remain open. However, this does not distinguish between contracts to buy or sell so you can't tell from this whether or not the majority are being held for delivery (long positions).

At the bottom of the silver quotations for each exchange, information is given to indicate the market activity, the number of sales and the previous day's open interests. In this example, "off 8" indicates that eight open contracts previously outstanding have been liquidated or closed out. Therefore, the purchase of, say, one hundred new contracts would be denoted as "up 100".

Once you understand how commodity prices are expressed and how they fluctuate, you should use a simple price movement chart as a tool in making any investment decision. At a moment's glance, such a diagram will give you an analysis of price movements as well as the general day-to-day pattern of these movements. This type of chart helps to indicate not only the direction of the trend of prices for that commodity but also an acceptable range within which price reactions can be tolerated without prematurely closing out a position. An example of a price movement chart is shown on page 159.

You would not normally look to establishing a position or closing out one that you already have unless prices have moved considerably out of the defined trading pattern that the commodity has established. It is not only the extent of the reaction that is important, but also its direction. Has there been a considerable break in the established routine which could indicate a change in direction for the prices of that commodity? A sudden major reaction could indicate a change in trend. If you liquidate your position too early and then discover that the

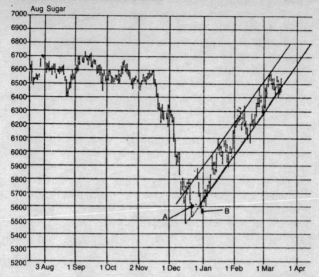

SUGAR PRICE MOVEMENT CHART

prices have merely experienced a minor reversal instead of a major change, you could then reinstate your position quickly to correct your error.

For instance, our hypothetical chart indicates that in mid-December the price of sugar began a change in direction, trending upward after quite a steep decline. If you purchased at that point (A), you would have predetermined the loss that you were willing to accept and, to a certain extent, the profit you anticipated. At point B, you would have considered whether this price met or exceeded your "loss resistance" selling limit. If not, then you would have continued to hold. With hindsight, in March this would have been a good decision. However, what if you liquidated your position at point B instead? You would have sustained a small loss but, as you observed the creation of a rising price trend, you could have reinstated your position in January and still have enjoyed quite a profitable ride. As the prices rose, you would have adjusted your expectations of

Commodities and Options   159

profit-and-loss limits in order to protect your gain. You could have fixed these by placing and replacing stop-loss orders, as will be discussed later in this chapter.

Whether you buy or sell, you should not establish a position when the current price trend is running contrary to your feelings with respect to a particular commodity. You should never add to a position in which you already have a loss. Once you have established a position, we suggest you should not add to it unless you are already experiencing a profit and no further contracts should be added unless all of your present holdings in that particular commodity are profitable. Sizeable gains can be made by pyramiding contracts during favourable trends which appear to have the potential for substantial further price movements. As the following example illustrates, additions to a position should never be larger than the original position taken. A conservative approach would be to add successively smaller amounts so that your overall position takes the form of a pyramid.

Date	Number of 100-oz. Gold Contracts	Price Per Ounce	Value	Margin
April 5	4 Oct. contracts	$394	$157,600	$12,000
April 12	3 Dec. contracts	402	120,600	9,000
April 14	2 Oct. contracts	403	80,600	6,000
April 19	1 Dec. contract	406	40,600	3,000
Total contracts	10		$399,400	
Total cash invested				$30,000

If the preceding approach is taken, and the majority of your positions are established at the most favourable prices, a moderate reaction should not have a disastrous effect on the total position. The following approach for accumulating contracts is unbalanced and should be avoided. Using previous values per contract, let's assume the following purchases have taken place.

	Number of	Price	
Date	100-oz. Gold Contracts	Per Ounce	Value
April 5	1 Oct. contract	$394	$ 39,400
April 12	2 Dec. contracts	402	80,400
April 14	3 Oct. contracts	403	120,900
April 19	4 Dec. contracts	406	162,400
Total contracts	10		$403,100

(The total margin would have remained the same.)

Here, the average price is most heavily influenced by the last purchase, and the investor would be very vulnerable to a price drop which could wipe out all the profits on his total investment. One of the interesting things about commodity prices is that once a trend is established, it frequently continues for some time. Therefore, if you develop the habit of taking small profits, you could be badly hurt in the long run. This is because your profits will be eroded by commissions and if you guess wrong only once in a while and you incur a substantial loss, that loss can eliminate all your gains. If commodities interest you, you have to be prepared to liquidate if prices start to go against your position. A successful speculator cuts his losses until he locates a solid upward trend and then capitalizes on it through pyramiding. He only closes out his positions when a major reversal in this trend has taken place.

THE STABILITY OF THE PYRAMID IS DETERMINED BY THE INITIAL PURCHASES

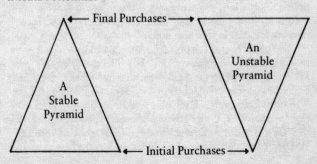

161

Safeguarding Against Commodity Losses

In the same way as you can protect yourself in the stock market, there are also methods to protect yourself against sizeable losses on commodity trades. One of these is to pay very close attention to the market and quickly close out positions as soon as a major trend reversal has been discovered. However, this can be very time-consuming unless you are a full-time speculator or are prepared to keep in touch with your broker virtually on an hourly basis. A second approach, therefore, is to limit your potential for losses through the placement of a stop-loss order. This is an order which you place with your broker at a specific limit in the opposite direction from your position. Then, if your commodity does not perform as expected or if the price trend reverses suddenly, as the commodity reaches that point, the stop-loss order is executed to liquidate your position.

The use of a stop-loss order will help you to minimize the possibility of taking a large loss and may help you to break the habit of letting your losses run. It can also protect an already profitable position by arranging to have it liquidated in the event of a trend reversal. The major drawback of a stop-loss order is that it may not always be executed at an ideal price or at the ideal time. As in the stock market, there is a lag between the time that a market order is entered and the point at which it is executed. Furthermore, markets do not always open at the same price at which they closed on the preceding trading day. Even though daily fluctuations are limited by law to prevent undue speculation, you must always remember that a change of even a few cents in the unit price can produce drastic consequences for your investment dollars.

The use of options as protection in commodity transactions is not generally practical. In the first place, options are not available on any commodities other than gold and silver. Gold options, as discussed in Chapter Ten, are available through the Winnipeg Commodity Exchange and the Montreal Stock Exchange. However, both of these markets are highly illiquid and therefore cannot be expected to provide an investor with reliable protection. Stop-loss orders are therefore the best means of protecting a commodity position, while the use of options is more practical in relation to stock market investments (as was discussed in the previous chapter).

If an investor is holding a profitable commodity position which he has purchased on margin, he has the advantage of being able to withdraw profits up to the margin limits without liquidating his position. Income tax will not be triggered by this but will only be payable at the time that the commodity contract is actually liquidated. The investor should note, however, that the profits that have been withdrawn should be kept available to meet any future margin calls on his commodity contracts.

Commodity Straddles and Their Tax Advantages

Many of the devices which Canadians have used in the past to defer taxes on their capital gains have either been eliminated or significantly defused as a result of the November 12, 1981 Budget. One of the few areas that has not, however, been touched is the "commodity straddle". Presumably, the Budget did not deal with these straddles because, to date, their use has not been common.

Using a commodity straddle to shelter a capital gain essentially involves purchasing a commodity "spread". The purpose is to move a gain from one year to the next for tax purposes. An investor does this by purchasing two contracts before the end of a calendar year at prices outside the range of present trading. One of the contracts is to buy a particular commodity and the second involves an offsetting sale. These contracts are for different months so it is important that the commodity chosen be one in which all months tend to move in the same price direction, like interest rate futures. Then, regardless of the direction in which the commodity price moves, the investor is able to create an immediate loss by closing out the losing position. He is nevertheless protected against a real loss by closing out the winning position right after the end of the tax year. The following example shows how this can work.

Current price of commodity: $100 per unit
Purchase: one contract to buy in July at $150
                    one contract to sell in September at $50

If the price of the commodity rises to $120 per unit, the September contract, in which you have contracted to sell at less than the current market price, represents a loss. In order to take this loss in 1982, you would close out the position by buying a contract for September at, say, $70.

	1 September contract sold	$50
Close-out:	1 September contract bought	70
1982 Loss:		$20

The gain is isolated in the July contract which you bought at $150. The price of the commodity for delivery on that date has also risen, so you close this out in 1983 by selling a contract for the same date as follows:

	1 July contract to buy	$150
Close out:	1 July contract to sell	170
1983 Gain:		$ 20

If the price of the commodity did not rise but dropped to, say, $80 per unit, then you would reverse the procedure to fix the loss and gain as follows:

	1 July contract to buy	$150
Close out:	1 July contract to sell	130
1982 Loss:		$ 20
	1 September contract to sell	$ 50
Close out:	1 September contract to buy	30
1983 Gain:		$ 20

In the first instance, at a price increase of $20, the investor would close out his sell position to incur a loss. In other words, the cost of a contract to buy the commodity at the same future date would have risen by $20. In the second case, if the commodity price dropped by $20 then he would close out his buy position since it would be trading at a loss from his purchase price.

As mentioned previously, the "winning" contract is left in place until the following taxation year. Therefore, an initial loss is created to offset capital gains which the investor has already earned while the gain is "recreated" in the subsequent year by selling the second contract. Thus, the gain for tax purposes is not eliminated, it is simply deferred. Of course, the deferral can be repeated year after year. If additional capital gains are made by the individual, straddles could become progressively larger. Naturally, there are costs involved in a commodity straddle. These include not only the price of the contract margins but the brokers' commissions on at least four separate contracts. Therefore, a straddle is practical only in situations where a sizeable capital gain is to be sheltered. You should also be aware that if the government finds that the use of straddles has become popular, they will probably move in some future budget to block the advantages. So far, this matter has not been an area of tension between Revenue Canada and taxpayers, although you should realize that the risk of assessment is something you must consider. However, you would not be essentially much worse off for having taken this risk since the taxes that you would have to absorb on a reassessment would be no greater than you would have had to pay in the first place. It is also interesting to note that commodity straddles can be used to effectively shelter not just capital gains but any type of taxable income. You might be well advised to discuss this point further with your own accountant.

Investing in Options

An option is unlike a commodity contract in that it is simply the *right* to buy or sell a specific quantity of a commodity or shares of stock at a specific date in the future. This market is possibly the most volatile of all and therefore is not a suitable arena for the amateur investor in most instances. However, as mentioned several times in both this chapter and the preceding one, options can offer a significant opportunity to ensure against losses in other investments such as stocks. In these instances, they can significantly reduce the risk that you would otherwise be subjected to. An option purchase price, also called the "striking price", is usually somewhat above the value at which the option can be exercised. This premium is exacted because the option offers a large potential for profit with a small and limited risk. If the price movement of a stock does not make it worthwhile to exercise the option by its expiry date, then the investor loses no more than the original cost of this option and its commission. Naturally, the premium to acquire an option is always largest when the option has a long period of time to run before its expiry. As that date comes nearer, the premium gradually declines to zero. As with commodity contracts, many speculators never exercise their options but liquidate them for either a profit or loss through the purchase of an offsetting option. The opportunities to make profits through trading in options can be illustrated with a couple of simple examples. You should first note that, as with the stock market, it is possible to use options to make profits when the market is either good or bad. If you feel, for example, that a stock will drop, you can sell a "put" option that will effectively provide for the sale of the stock at a high price, and if the value of that stock truly does decline the option will not be exercised and you will retain the money paid to you. On the other hand, if you feel that a stock will rise, you might buy a "call" option which would entitle you to buy the stock at a low price and provide a profit opportunity if the stock price subsequently increases.

Options can be bought at any time in the year, but are only available with specific expiry dates. The newspaper will give quotations for the price of a put or call expiring on those dates. However, the quotes will vary depending on the price anticipated for the stock at that future time, which may be above or below the current price. Often quotes won't be available at all for dates where no options were offered or none were traded.

Let's look at two examples of how options can work:

Stock trading in April at $43 per share
Purchase one call option on 100 shares in June @ $45 per share
Cost = $1.50 × 100 shares = $150
At the expiry date the stock closes at $50

Exercise option @ $45 × 100	$4,500
Sell stock for $50 × 100	5,000
	500
Less: Cost of option	150
Net gain	$ 350

If the stock did not rise to more than $45 by the June expiry date, you would lose a maximum of $150.

What happens if you sell a put?

Stock trading in April at $43 per share
Sell one put option on 100 shares in June @ $40 per share
Received = $4.50 × 100 shares = $450
At the expiry date the stock closes at $35

The person who bought this option from you would not exercise it since the stock could be bought in the open market for less money . . . you keep the $450 as profit.

What happens if the price of the stock moves in the wrong direction? If you have bought a call option, as mentioned previously, you simply would not exercise it and your loss would be limited to what you paid for it.

On the other hand, if you have sold a put option, the extent of the loss will depend on the circumstances. If you already own the stock which you have optioned (in other words, you have sold a "covered" option), then the loss can be no greater than the difference between your original cost and the exercise price ($40 per share), and this is cushioned to some extent by the $450 you have already received. If you had purchased the shares for less than $40 originally, you may not even sustain a loss.

However, if you have sold an option on shares which you do not already own, *you could be in a very costly position.* In this instance, you would have received $4,000 when the option was exercised but you would have to purchase the shares in the market for their going price, which could be far in excess of $40 per share. If you are speculating in "uncovered" or "naked" options, you therefore must watch the stock price closely and liquidate your position early enough to curtail significant losses. Thus, it is essential to trade uncovered options only on broadly held stocks so that, if necessary, your position can be easily and quickly liquidated.

Butterfly Spreads

An investor in the options market can reduce his risk through the use of spreads in the same way as he can when dealing with commodity contracts. One interesting example of this is the use of a butterfly spread. This involves four separate options and is only useful where there is very little fluctuation in a stock price. It is an interesting approach when a stock is simply stagnant — neither moving significantly upwards or downwards. The outstanding advantage to such a spread is that no matter what direction or to what extent the price of the stock should move, the loss is always limited to a specific amount which can be determined at the time the investment is made. In the following example we picked a stock that is currently selling at $60 a share. The investor purchases one "in-the-money option" at $50 that can be exercised several months in the future. An "in-the-money option" provides the right to acquire the stock at less than the current trading price. The same investor also purchases one "out-of-the-money option" at $70. Naturally, an "out-of-the-money option" is an option to buy the shares at a price greater than the current market price. Simultaneously, the investor sells two put options that are "at-the-money" at $60. The maximum profit is attained if, at the expiry date, the selling price of the stock is still $60. In this case the net gain is $9.

Many investors do not use this type of approach because they do not want to limit their profits by the cost of insurance. In the above example, a maximum profit of $16 is reduced to only $9 because $7 is the insurance cost, being the cost of the first two options purchased. In addition, if you are considering a butterfly spread, you must be wary of incurring extra commission charges. The butterfly spread is, however, one way in which an investor can trade in a highly volatile and frequently dangerous market while providing himself with maximum downside protection. Instead of looking at issues that fluctuate wildly, he simply concentrates on ferreting out those issues where there is generally very little price movement.

EXAMPLE OF A BUTTERFLY SPREAD

BCD Corp. selling at $60 per share
   A. Option to buy in May at $50 — selling for $14
   B. Option to buy in May at $70 — selling for $3
   C. Option to buy in May at $60 — selling for $8

Investor: buys 1 A and B option
          sells 2 C options

At expiry date: no change in BCD Corp. price — still $60

Profit position:

A option	—value $10	Loss	$ 4
B option	—value $ 0	Loss	3
C options	—value $ 0	Gain	16
Net gain			$ 9

If the price of the stock has risen or dropped significantly, then the losses are limited to a maximum of $1 because the investor has purchased options which partially offset each other in the first place.

Cash position:

Purchase of A and B	$17
Proceeds from sale of 2 C's	16
Cost of spread	$ 1
Limits maximum loss to	$ 1

Tax Consequences of Investing in Commodities and Options

In Canada, a gain realized on a futures transaction is generally accorded capital gains treatment. An exception to this is if you happen to roll up gains while trading in a commodity that is connected with your business or area of expertise. For instance, a lumber trader could well expect his gain on trading in lumber futures to be taxed as ordinary income. However, a taxpayer may also trade in commodities outside of his area of special knowledge. Thus, the same lumber trader should receive capital gains treatment on his profits from trading in oats, soya beans, silver or gold futures contracts.

Gains from trading in options may be given different tax treatments depending on the circumstances surrounding the trade. Gains from "covered options" will generally receive capital gains treatment. A covered option (as discussed on page 167) is one where the investor personally holds the shares or commodity to back up the option if delivery is necessary. He may be carrying an option on shares which he already owns or gold which he already has in storage. On the other hand, gains from dealing in "uncovered" or "naked" options will generally receive income treatment. In this case, an investor may have sold a put option on shares which he did not own. If the option is exercised, he will have to go to the market and buy the shares in order to cover the option which has been called.

As an alternative to capital gains treatment on futures contract trades, a taxpayer in Canada has the choice of electing income treatment. Of course, he would only do this in situations where he has had significant losses which he wishes to deduct in their entirety. Once he makes such an election it is effective permanently. In other words, the Department of National Revenue will insist on consistency of treatment.

Summary

As with the stock market, it would be useless for us to try to present you with particular opportunities to trade in various options or commodities. The business and investment scene changes too quickly for any specific investment advice to remain valid from the time that a book is written to the time you read it. However, our message should be clear. It really does not matter whether we are in the midst of a bull market or whether the bears are exercising their own brand of supremacy. Profits can be made in any circumstance. There is an old adage which says somewhat facetiously that profits are made by "buying low and selling high." In a bull market, you buy first and then sell; in a bear market you simply do the reverse — sell first and then buy back at a lower price. Commodities and option markets lend themselves to this with a greater degree of leverage than a standard investment through the stock market. Certainly, they require a degree of sophistication and attention which most investors do not initially have. Now it is up to you to decide whether you wish to include commodities or options in reshaping your own investment strategies for the 1980s.

CHAPTER TEN

Investing in Gold

Over the centuries, gold has been the single outstanding medium recognized in international financial exchange. This fact alone necessitates examining it as an investment. History has witnessed the rise and fall of many powerful civilizations; when all else of value lay in rubble, gold alone remained. To the present day, many people have credited their survival to having held substantial investments in gold. Gold is portable and can be bartered for food or, in fact, for one's life. Although we have not yet witnessed this phenomenon in North America, it has been true in Europe, Russia, Southeast Asia and Africa. Even in Canada, uncertain political and economic climates prompt most investment counsellors to suggest that every individual keep at least some investment capital in gold as a contingency.

Gold fever in North America began in 1974 when, after forty-one years, it again became legal for Americans to own this precious metal. At that time, gold was trading at $90 U.S. an ounce. By 1980, as a result of increasing inflation, low interest rates, and high demand by the countries of the Middle East, the gold price had skyrocketed to a high of about $850 U.S. Then, the market collapsed. Interest rates increased dramatically, making it very expensive for investors to tie up their capital in gold, and President Reagan made it clear that at least for the present, there would be no hyperinflation. The prevalence of high interest rates throughout the world, which has led to the present recession, has also prompted large sales of gold reserves by smaller countries who are now virtually bankrupt.

At the present time, it is very difficult to predict where the price of gold is headed. In fact, the price may not fluctuate to any great extent until interest rates decline substantially or until there is some kind of panic internationally. For example, a large-scale war would almost certainly send the price of gold spiralling upwards. Also, as mentioned in Chapter One, if smaller countries start to default on their obligations to American banks, and the United States is forced to reinflate, the potential hyperinflation could again create a tremendous demand for this metal.

Portability

It is rather odd that in North America today so many people look upon gold not as a hedge against inflation, but against disaster. In other words, if our civilization collapses, at least a holding in gold is portable—you can carry it with you. To some extent, however, if you think that gold is portable, you are sadly deluded. The average healthy individual can probably carry thirty pounds of weight without major discomfort, at least for short distances. At $450 U.S., thirty pounds (13.6 kilograms) of gold would be worth approximately $197,000 U.S. Essentially, this is all you can take with you personally. Of course, for some of us this sum represents a vast fortune. For others, this may be simply a small percentage of present net worth. Certainly, if you believe that the end is near and that ultimate salvation lies in holding gold, it would be best to consider arrangements for the movement of your holdings to "secure" locations before it is too late! Then, all you would have to worry about is getting to these locations if and when the need arises.

Who Holds Gold?

The Businessman

Aside from its function as a medium of exchange, gold has a considerable variety of uses. It is used primarily for industrial and fabrication purposes, with the single largest demand being jewellery manufacture. Businesses face the same problem with gold as with any other necessary raw material. How can a manufacturer guarantee that a price quoted today to a customer will cover the cost of manufacture six months to a year later? It is necessary to be able to assure the customer that he will be able to receive delivery of merchandise at the price in effect when his order was placed. In this instance, the manufacturer would hedge against increases in the price of gold by purchasing gold futures. He would do this not to make a profit, but simply to protect his position. It is not likely that the manufacturer would actually take delivery of the gold contract. Instead he would liquidate it at the time that his manufacturing commitments required him to actually purchase the gold in a cash market. At that time, he would again purchase a gold futures contract whose maturity was several months away in order to protect himself for the next season. If the manufacturer is forced to pay more for the actual gold purchased from his supplier than the price originally contemplated, he would liquidate his gold futures contract. The profit on the futures contract would offset the additional manufacturing costs. In other words, the manufacturer, while not really intending to make profits on gold transactions, also does not want to lose.

The "Survivor"

As mentioned previously, growing numbers of people have become alarmed by the decline of national and world currencies. These people are also accumulating gold, not as a hedge against inflation but against the complete collapse of the monetary system as we know it. If they are right, gold would become one of the few commodities which could be used to purchase the necessities of life. The "survivor" systematically accumulates this metal in its physical form and stashes it away without much concern over short-term fluctuations. He is willing to ignore the time-value of money and opportunity costs that he incurs by not investing in other ways in the interim.

The Speculator

The speculator is one of the most active participants in the market in terms of frequency of transactions. His inflation-protection strategy is to make money faster than the value of the dollar can decline. A speculator virtually never takes physical possession of his gold, but trades for many small profits through the purchase or sale of gold futures contracts. His transactions are highly leveraged and are short-term in nature. The small, less sophisticated investor may purchase gold certificates (see page 185) or gold stocks while still looking for short-term profits.

The Investor

The investor is a person who is willing to hold gold in either physical or paper form in anticipation of a major long-term price run-up. Ideally, the investor buys when the majority of people are selling and sells when the majority are anxious to buy. He is not always active in the market, but rather waits for major price distortions as a result of international events before making his move.

You may find it perfectly reasonable to combine several of these various motives because you may consider holding gold in different forms to meet different objectives. The strategy to achieve *your* aims should be flexible enough to meet changing circumstances. For instance, if you are holding gold as a hedge against disaster, you may sell a substantial amount of your holdings during a period of particularly high gold prices in order to repurchase it at much lower costs when the hysteria has died down. This could create a substantial increase in your "disaster fund". Of course, such practice calls for steady nerves.

Physical Forms of Gold Investments

Jewellery

In many countries where direct public ownership of gold is restricted or banned, personally-held gold jewellery is the most important store of portable family wealth. Jewellery, in these cases, has a distinctive use from that in North America where it is primarily worn as a personal decoration. Where jewellery is considered to be synonymous with wealth, it is necessary that the "karat" count (see below) be as high as possible so that if a sudden exodus is necessary, the family would not be left destitute and powerless to re-establish itself. This reasoning has certainly proven correct for many twentieth-century refugees, sometimes literally saving their lives.

Gold jewellery is distinguished in karats. A karat is an indication of purity, not weight. In terms of fineness, each karat represents a $1/24$ portion of pure gold. Therefore, 14 karat jewellery is 58% gold ($14/24$). The following table indicates karat counts and gold content of present day jewellery:

Karat	Purity	Origin
24	100%	Oriental
22	91%	Oriental
18	75%	European
14	58%	North American
10	41%	North American

From this table, you can see that jewellery, as we are familiar with it in North America, is largely an alloyed metal of *insignificant gold content*. It is produced for use in decorative design, not as an investment. When gold prices soared in 1980 to astronomical heights, many investors bought gold chains by the score. This left them with a large inventory of future Christmas gifts, but little in the way of a substantial investment in gold.

On resale, the artistic merits of gold jewellery are generally without value. Resale for gold content alone will not generally return even the purchase price. Undoubtedly, this is why the majority of private gold jewellery resales are made in pawn shops rather than jewellery stores. If you purchase gold jewellery while travelling outside Canada, it will be subject to import duties here and should be reported to customs as you cross the border.

Gold Bullion

Gold bullion is perhaps the best form in which to hold gold, at least for large investors. It is available in both bars and wafers. Bars are cast for larger weight sizes and wafers are usually usually stamped for smaller sizes. Values are determined by both weight (mass) and fineness. Precious metal weights have been traditionally determined in accordance with the troy system. The following table provides conversions to our better known avoirdupois and metric systems.

1 troy pound = 12 troy ounces
     = 13.17 ounces avoirdupois
     = .373 kilograms

1 troy ounce = 1.097 ounces avoirdupois
     = 31.103 grams

Most people are surprised when they first see a one-ounce wafer or coin. The size is generally larger than they had anticipated. This is because the troy ounce is approximately 10% heavier than the ounce with which we are normally familiar.

The face of every gold wafer or bar carries important information. The refiner stamps it with his name or logo and indicates his identification number. The one word "gold" may actually appear on the bar as well.

The purest gold bullion available has a fineness of .9999. However, because fineness to this degree is rare, banks usually accept fineness equal to or greater than .995. Naturally, the price will be adjusted slightly for any fineness of less than .9999. For all practical purposes, it does not matter how fine the bullion is that you purchase, as long as it is at least .995. In Canada, there is a sales tax on bullion only in New Brunswick, Nova Scotia, and Saskatchewan. You can buy gold outside these provinces and transport it back to your home without penalty.

When you purchase bullion, be absolutely certain that you buy it from an internationally recognized refiner. Otherwise, when you sell it, the dealer will often charge you a fee to assay the gold. The following is a list of some of the refiners who are well recognized in most gold markets. The first three are Canadian.

Englehard Industries of Canada Ltd.
Canadian Copper Refiners Ltd.
Royal Canadian Mint
Johnson Matthey Limited
Credit Suisse
Swiss Bank Corporation

Storage and insurance charges are also important considerations to holders of bullion. Even as fractions of the overall cost, these still represent real expenses which must be met while waiting for a long-term gain when the bullion is eventually sold. When considering commissions and related charges, an investment in bullion or wafers is one of the *least expensive* ways to directly acquire gold. Prices are widely quoted internationally, and bullion from accepted refiners is quickly convertible into cash. The major drawback to a speculation or investment in bullion is that it requires an investor to tie up his funds for an indeterminate length of time in an asset that pays no interest. Also, large gold bars may be portable but they are not divisible. Thus, if an investor sells, he must dispose of the entire investment at one time.

Gold Coins

Coins currently represent the most attractive means of accumulating gold for the average investor who wishes to enjoy physical possession. However, there is a great difference between bullion coins and coins with a numismatic (collector's) value. The value of numismatic coins depends, to a certain degree, on their gold content. However, this is usually a relatively insignificant factor. The "premium" on a numismatic coin, that is the spread between the gold content value and the selling price, is far higher than that of a bullion coin. The trading price of numismatic coins can fluctuate widely. These are basically a collectible, and their value is determined by a number of factors, including rarity, age, quantity in existence, and the condition of the coins themselves. As collectors' items, these coins are not always readily negotiable and certainly more knowledge is required in making a purchase. The rules which govern investments in collectibles (as explained in Chapter Twelve) apply here, as well. However, for the enthusiast with the time and money required, investing in numismatic coins can be a highly satisfying and rewarding investment strategy in its own right.

Bullion coins generally carry the lowest premiums. One of the major factors in their favour is that they have virtually no numismatic value—there is very little you have to learn about them. Bullion coins are produced in large quantities in several countries and their gold content is guaranteed. Certain countries, such as Austria, Mexico, Russia and Hungary have been issuing them for many years, but the ones with which you are most likely to be familiar are those produced in South Africa, and now, Canada.

The South African Krugerrand is possibly the world's most popular means of holding gold. These coins are widely accepted throughout most of the world and are as sound an investment as bullion itself. The Canadian government is now minting the "Gold Maple Leaf", which is identical in gold content to the Krugerrand. One of the major advantages of the Krugerrand, however, is that it can be bought in sizes that vary from one-tenth of an ounce to a full one-ounce coin. The following is a list of the premiums which would apply to the South African and Canadian coins:

Coins	Size	Premium
Krugerrand	1 oz.	6%
Gold Maple Leaf	1 oz.	6%
Krugerrand	½ oz.	8%
Krugerrand	¼ oz.	10%
Krugerrand	¹⁄₁₀ oz.	12%

Although the premiums increase greatly as the size of the coin diminishes, these smaller coins have several distinct advantages. First, you can easily accumulate them on a systematic basis without having to put out large amounts of cash. For this reason they represent an excellent opportunity to maintain a consistent savings program. Second, they represent handy coin "change" should it ever be necessary to barter for goods and services. Remember that if the time comes for you to exchange your coins for goods, it may not be possible to ask for change for a full one-ounce coin, let along a gold bar. Third, the variety of small sizes makes them highly portable assets. Therefore, the premium alone should not discourage their purchase, especially by the small investor. You should also note that bullion coins can be conveniently purchased at many locations across Canada, including coin shops. If you pay cash for your purchase, there are no records kept. You are not required to reveal your identity and if financial privacy is one of your aims this can be important. The receipt on this page represents the typical documentation for the purchase of gold.

Sales tax is payable on the purchase of bullion coins in British Columbia, Saskatchewan, Manitoba, Ontario, New Brunswick and Nova Scotia. Again, if you happen to be travelling and purchase these coins elsewhere, there is currently no law against transporting them across provincial borders. While gold bullion coins can enter Canada legally and without duty, there is really no advantage in buying abroad because gold has an international price.

```
          COINS
       THANK YOU

    0 3 / 0 3 / 8 2      DA TE

              3 7 7 . 0 0    1

              3 7 7 . 0 0   CA TL

    # 0 1 9 2
```

This particular "invoice" represents the purchase of a one-half ounce Krugerrand and two 1/10-ounce coins.

Although an investment in bullion coins is relatively inexpensive and quickly convertible to cash, a certain disadvantage still remains which attaches to all types of bullion. Specifically, this involves the nuisance of making a long-term monetary commitment. Certainly, bullion and coins represent good collateral. However, this requires lodging them with a bank or other lending institution and possibly defeating one of your major purposes in owning them — that of financial privacy and easy accessibility.

Coin Sets

Many coin sets are produced internationally as limited editions or commemorative packages. These generally would not be considered either a bullion or numismatic investment. Frequently, the gold content level is quite low and the number produced is quite high. These two factors combine to create a situation where the investor cannot liquidate his holdings for many years with any hope of recovering his original purchase price. Therefore, these types of coin sets cannot be recommended as investments in gold.

How to Buy Bullion

From the previous discussions, it is clear that establishing a holding in bullion means purchasing either bars, wafers or coins. If you are purchasing these solely for their gold content, they are available through various dealers across Canada, including banks such the Bank of Nova Scotia or the Toronto Dominion Bank, Guardian Trust, brokerage houses and coin dealers. For the most part, it is best to deal with a recognized source in order to assure the integrity of the product you are buying. If you get involved in a private purchase, particularly of gold bars or wafers, be sure to examine the refiner's stamp. Unless the gold was produced by an internationally recognized refiner, it should be assayed before the purchase is concluded.

Coin dealers and the main branches of financial institutions will usually be able to make purchases readily available to you.

However, small or suburban branch outlets of banks can frequently keep you waiting for weeks before you are able to take delivery of your gold. Furthermore, the time spent in purchasing is drawn out due to the necessity to ascertain an up-to-the-minute price on the gold which is being sold to you. Of course, cash-and-carry sales can be expected to be transacted on the basis of cash or certified cheque. Purchases of gold at certain business establishments can also create sales documentation which allows the purchase of the gold to be traced to you.

You should first ask yourself what type of bullion you want to buy and then decide what size. Gold bars, especially the larger ones, call for a large commitment of funds to a single purchase. Furthermore, some of the larger sizes may not be readily available and if you want physical possession of your gold, transportation and insurance can be an extra expense. As mentioned previously, a bar must be sold as a unit, which can be extremely inconvenient if your entire investment is tied up in only one large bar. Under these circumstances, you must then choose to be either fully invested or totally liquidated.

Wafers or coins are generally the best choice for most investors for a number of reasons. They are portable, negotiable, and can be easily accumulated over a period of time with a minimum periodic cash outlay. The higher premiums are thus outweighed by the convenience. There is generally less fuss involved in obtaining bullion in these forms, and much less time need be devoted to their resale.

The choice between wafers and bullion coins is an interesting one. Generally wafers may be available in a greater variety of sizes. However, all of the considerations with respect to refiners and the fineness of gold content apply here just as they do to large bar purchases. Coins are normally produced in a fineness of .9999. Thus, in terms of ease of purchase and resale, coins generally require less knowledge on the part of an investor and are therefore the more convenient form to deal with.

When the time comes to resell your gold, probably the most convenient means is to take it back to the dealer from whom you bought it. If you advertise your holdings for sale in the newspaper, you may be asking for trouble. Thieves read newspapers too!

How to Store Gold

The manner in which you store your gold will depend on whether you want to take physical possession of it and how quickly and with what certainty you would like to have access to it. If the gold is purchased through a bank or trust company, you need never take possession unless you feel that the bank will fail or ownership of gold will be made illegal by the government. Banks and trust companies will store your gold on your behalf, although possibly in another city. Of course, the institution will charge you a fee for storage and safekeeping. The fees will be calculated either on a flat-rate basis or as a fractional percentage of the value of the gold involved. Besides the inconvenience of an extra expense, the disadvantage of having your gold stored by an institution is that you cannot easily or quickly take possession of it. Therefore, many people keep their gold in their personal safety deposit boxes at their local bank branches. This would give you easy access and safety from all but outright government confiscation — which is still unlikely, at least at present.

If you are holding sizeable quantities of gold, a safety deposit box may simply be impractical. Keeping your bullion at home, however, carries its own set of problems. The first of these is safety, and the second is reasonableness. If you have significant holdings in gold, it may be worth having a safe built into your home. If properly concealed, this should give you some margin of security. People have gone so far as to store gold in their freezers which gives them ready access to "cold" cash. However, under no circumstances should bullion be left lying around in drawers. This practice only makes it accessible to quick and easy pilferage. Furthermore, if you are storing your gold at home, don't make it widely known to friends and acquaintances. Showing off your holdings at cocktail parties is obviously just asking for trouble.

In order to receive full value for your bullion, it is important that the total weight be maintained. Therefore, it is particularly important that wafers and coins be kept in excellent condition. Storage facilities must provide adequate room to accommodate the gold in individual wrappers. A worn bullion coin is simply not worth as much as one which is in mint condition. If portability is an important consideration to you, be sure that you have provided a reasonable means for making the transport physically possible. There is no point in getting a hernia while trying to carry your investments across the basement floor.

As a point of interest, a standard four-inch or ten-centimetre briefcase can hold perhaps up to *130 pounds* (59 kg) in gold coins. Of course, even if you could then lift that briefcase, the handle would only break off. If you have substantial holdings in gold, it is only reasonable to consider storing it in several locations — possibly in different countries. If outright failure of our national banks is not one of your concerns, then utilizing safety deposit boxes in several different locations makes sense. If ultimate privacy and safety is your goal, then you would be looking towards a much more sophisticated network of international safekeeping arrangements.

Paper Forms

Considerable amounts of money have been made by speculators and investors without coming into physical contact with the gold that they command. If you are a trader simply seeking a profit through gold price *changes*, then having physical possession of gold would only be a hindrance.

In fact, if you think that gold prices will decline, then you certainly wouldn't want to own it. However, you could still deal in gold in one or more of its paper forms to sell first and then buy back, hopefully at a lower price.

The various paper forms discussed in the next few pages represent entitlements to gold which is often stored in distant places without regard to the whereabouts of the specific investor. Also, there may be restrictions whereby the investor does not take title until a fixed date in the future. All of these paper forms do, however, serve their particular investment purposes — although they do not give you quick or ready access for physical possession.

Gold Certificates

Gold certificates can be purchased at several banks or investment houses during specific trading hours, generally between 10:00 a.m. and 1:15 p.m. daily. These certificates represent a personal entitlement to gold which is then held by the institution on your behalf. The gold may be stored locally, although, for their own convenience and security, the institutions generally hold it only in major cities across the country. Gold certificates are quantified in ounces with certain minimum purchase requirements. The Bank of Nova Scotia, for example, makes certificates available at a minimum of five ounces and up to a maximum of one hundred ounces. Certificates and all paper forms of gold, like the "physicals", are denominated in U.S. dollars, as are the commissions and premiums involved. A commission of one-quarter of a per cent and safekeeping charges are usually attached to certificates. A bullion certificate can be registered in your name and kept in your possession. It gives you the right to demand the delivery of the gold that you have purchased, or alternatively, you can cash it and obtain the market value of your investment at that time.

Certificates are, therefore, highly liquid and easily valued. They save you the headaches of storage since the certificates themselves can be kept in safety deposit boxes. A major disadvantage is that it can be awkward and time-consuming to try to take physical possession of your gold. Remember that your holdings are not segregated. You may also be incurring some risk if ever there is a bank failure, and it may be difficult to cash in a certificate drawn on a particular institution if you are outside the country. Interestingly enough, through some dealers in the United States, it is, however, possible to buy certificates and take delivery of the gold in centres outside North America.

Futures contracts are agreements entered into between investors and brokers for the *eventual* purchase or sale of gold. Futures contracts have several distinct advantages which appeal to both investors and speculators. First, as you read in the previous chapter, which provided a general overview of commodities investment strategies, a contract can be purchased on the basis of a relatively limited deposit. This deposit, or margin, which may increase if the price of gold starts to rise, allows the investor considerable leverage. In other words, he can command a large holding in the market on the basis of a limited deposit. If the investor is successful in predicting the trend of market prices, then the use of leverage can give him a profit of many times his original investment. Certainly, of all potential transactions in gold, there is the least carrying cost involved through the futures market.

Gold futures contracts can be purchased through major brokerage houses across Canada. As explained in Chapter Nine, you would have to establish a personal net worth of at least $250,000 and you would have to make a minimum deposit of $10,000 in U.S. funds. Gold futures contracts are denominated in ounces with the minimum purchase being 100 ounces. The commission charged in spring 1982 was about $90.00 per contract.

A contract can be placed to either buy or sell gold depending upon the investor's strategy. If you think that the short-term movement will be up, then you will want to buy a contract. Otherwise, you might consider a contract to sell. Each contract is purchased with a specific maturity date which can be from one month to one year in the future. During the month specified, the purchaser of the contract may take delivery of the gold if he has *bought* a contract, or he must make delivery of the gold if he has *sold* a contract. However, few contracts are ever held to maturity. Usually, an offsetting obligation that cancels out the original contract is purchased prior to the delivery month. The difference between the purchase price and the selling price represents the profit or loss. Naturally, investments in futures contracts have their inherent risks. The margin that you deposit on a contract does not limit your financial liability in this transaction. You are always expected to maintain a specific proportion of the original value of your contract on deposit. If the value of the contract begins to move in the wrong direction, you will be expected to put out larger and larger amounts of margin from your own pocket. Margin calls can be both unnerving and extremely expensive. Of course, you have the right to close out your position at any time by purchasing an offsetting obligation.

You should be aware that prices in gold futures can move very quickly and the market does not always open at the point at which it closed on the previous day. For example, in less than one week in July 1982, gold moved from approximately $310 U.S. an ounce to around $350 — a gain of almost 13%. Then in August there was a similar increase in the price. The combination of rapid price movements and high leverage can create enormous profits for some investors as well as producing staggering losses for others. Due to the effect of leverage, there is theoretically no limit to the amount you can lose at any one time. For instance, if you sell a 100-ounce contract in gold, this would indicate that you are anticipating that the price of gold will drop so that you will be able to buy an offsetting contract for less money in the future, and thereby make a profit. However, what if the price of gold starts to rise instead? Technically, it could do so without limits. Therefore, the purchase of an offsetting contract (necessary in order to avoid the requirements to make physical delivery of the gold by the maturity date of the sale contract) could be *infinitely expensive*. These chilling possibilities should be sufficient to emphasize that you would require not only substantial amounts of money to back your commitments to gold futures but also enough time to be able to pay close attention to the market. Futures traders generally do not hold contracts for long periods of time, but look for short-term profits and close out losing positions as quickly as possible.

Certainly, there are some ways in which you can provide protection for your investments. These include the placement of stop-loss orders, which is dealt with on page 162 in Chapter Nine and will not be repeated here.

To summarize the advantages, gold futures allow you substantial leverage without tying up large amounts of money. They are highly liquid and the important thing to realize is that the astute investor can profit equally whether the price of gold goes up or down — as long as he can predict the movement with reasonable accuracy. In other words, money can be made in good times and bad.

On the other hand, you must be aware that you are forced to deal in specific contract sizes and you should be certain that you have enough money bankrolled so that you can back up your margin account. Furthermore, recognize that trading must be carried out through your broker. If your nervous system and net worth are not attuned to this arena, then it is best to avoid it. However, for those who are willing to spend the time and the funds to acquire the necessary competence, gold futures can be a lucrative field and a challenging way to make money.

Gold Options

There is a distinct difference between a futures contract and an option. A futures contract is, in effect, a legal promise on your part to either purchase or sell gold at a specific price at a specified time in the future. An option, on the other hand, is not a promise to purchase or sell on your part but is the *right* to buy or sell at a fixed price. Trading in options can be profitable, and perhaps the most important consideration is that an option provides an investor with a *defined risk*. That is to say, the maximum risk is the cost of the option. If the price moves in the direction which you have anticipated, you exercise your option and take the gold. On the other hand, if you have guessed wrong in the price movement, you simply refrain from exercising your option and let it expire.

The only North American exchanges which handle gold option contracts are the Winnipeg and Montreal Commodity Exchanges. Major brokerage houses across Canada are loath to deal in these markets because they feel they are too "thin". In other words, there may not always be available buyers when you want to sell or available sellers when you want to buy. This can leave you in an uncomfortably illiquid position. The advantages of options are that, through leverage, you can command a sizeable investment while tying up only a minimal amount of your funds. Your risks are clearly defined since you can simply let your option expire but you still have the opportunity to make a substantial profit. On the downside, you must be prepared to deal in specific contract sizes (multiples of 100 ounces) and the prices will be slightly more expensive than for a futures contract. Options contracts are also less liquid and are not as negotiable as futures contracts. Quotations on options prices are available in the *Globe and Mail*.

Gold Stocks

When you purchase futures or options you are at least one step removed from direct contact with the physical metal. Through the purchase of gold stocks, you are at least twice removed. This is because you must rely on a broker to transact on your behalf in the shares of a company which is managed by other people who are involved in the production of gold. Here, you are investing more directly in the company, its finances, future and management, than in the metal itself.

The factors to keep in mind when considering investing in gold stocks are fundamentally similar to those discussed in Chapter Eight, which pertain to any investment in the stock market. The price per share will not only depend on what the outlook for the price of gold bullion is, but also on the grade of ore to which the mine has access. In addition, the costs of extraction must be considered. Beyond this, you must also examine the financial stability of the company and the quality of its management. Many large gold-mining companies are located in South Africa. This raises another important question, that of political stability. Furthermore, many gold-mining companies do not pay dividends.

Canada has many mines of excellent investment calibre,

including Campbell Red Lake and Dome Mines. One of the major advantages of this type of Canadian investment is that it can be deposited into your registered retirement savings plan and is basically the only way that you can hold gold in an RRSP. Dividends and profits from these types of investments within an RRSP will not be subject to tax until the plan is ultimately collapsed.

If gold shares are your interest, be sure to choose a knowledgeable broker who is an expert in mining share analysis and is also familiar with gold bullion price movements.

Tax Consequences of Transactions in Gold

Generally, profits on the disposition of gold, whether it is held in physical form or paper form, are subject to capital gains treatment in Canada. In the case of bullion, this is a result of administrative discretion. Since bullion has no capacity to pay interest or dividends and is held strictly as a speculation, whether short or long-term, any gains should theoretically be treated as 100% taxable income. However, it has historically been the policy of Revenue Canada to accept capital gains treatment on these transactions. However, you should realize that if you wish capital gains treatment on your gold transactions, interest on money borrowed to make your investments is not deductible. If you decide, on the other hand, to deduct interest expense you must be prepared to pay taxes on your full profits.

One of the advantages of gold futures contacts, under current Canadian tax legislation, is that an investor can choose either income treatment or capital gains treatment, and the choice does not have to be made until the time of disposition. Once made, however, the method must be applied consistently to all future transactions. Therefore, if you sustain a large loss, you may consider the use of an income treatment for this loss so that it can be totally tax deductible. However, this would also mean that any future gains would be subject to full taxation. Therefore, you should think long and hard before making a final decision. Perhaps, it would be advisable for you to meet with your accountant before filing a tax return for the year in which the sale took place.

Summary

It is evident that there are as many different ways of owning gold as there are different reasons for holding it. It is one of the few commodities that can be reasonably held in both physical and paper forms. Therefore, there is no reason why you, as an investor, cannot meet several of your objectives at the same time. You can accumulate wafers and coins as a portable, tangible store of wealth and also indulge your speculative desires by trading in gold futures. Gold and silver are the major investments which can be made by people at all income levels. While large purchases of gold bars, certificates, or futures call for substantial amounts of cash, the average investor can very conveniently accumulate gold wafers or coins in a variety of sizes to meet the demands of his or her pocketbook. This allows the smaller investor to acquire an increasing amount of a long-term investment which is also a portable store of wealth.

As with anything else, the key, of course, is timing. In general, see whether interest rates continue to decline. If this, in fact, does happen and inflation rates start to accelerate, there should be renewed interest in this metal. The sophisticated investor should also follow international political and economic developments. A large-scale war or the bankruptcy of smaller countries could, in the next few years, have a dramatic effect on the price of gold. In the long run, it is quite conceivable that gold will live up to its historical reputation as being the most practical and flexible of all investments.

CHAPTER ELEVEN

Investing in Silver

Although they are both precious metals, an investment in silver is not the same as an investment in gold. Nor is an investment in silver based on the same types of considerations as an investment in gold. The differences begin and end with two simple factors — supply and demand. While there is considerably more silver available than there is gold, silver unlike gold has a myriad of uses beyond jewellery. Silver production therefore tends to get "used up" while most of the gold which has been mined over the centuries is still around in one form or another. Thus, to call silver the "poor man's gold" is a great misstatement. There are so many market variables that it is quite possible for the price of one of these two metals to move up while the price of the other metal moves down.

The Demand for Silver

Like gold, silver has long been used as a medium of exchange, decoration and jewellery. It has always been in sufficiently limited supply to give it value as a store of wealth in itself. However, unlike gold, silver has several other unique characteristics which have drastically altered the demand for this metal over the last twenty years or so. As the technological revolution began to pick up momentum around 1960, silver emerged as perhaps the world's most versatile metal. Its uses may be summarized as follows:

- Silver is a better conductor of heat than any other metal. It is therefore suited for use in the production of heating elements and also has many other industrial and commercial applications.

- Silver has significant medical properties. Its antibacterial qualities make it particularly valuable in the fields of medicine and dentistry.
- Of all metals, silver is the best conductor of electricity. The electronics industry is therefore the second largest consumer of silver. The enormous growth in the production of semiconductors over the last twenty years has contributed significantly to this.
- Silver is more reflective than any other metal. This property was recognized centuries ago and so a thin film of this metal has been universally used on the backing of mirrors. Many more recent applications have sprung from the fields of space exploration and solar energy.
- Silver has excellent bonding properties, which have made it highly useful in soldering and for brazing alloys.
- Silver halides have a greater degree of light sensitivity than any other chemical. Because of this, silver is essential to and finds its greatest industrial use in all kinds of photographic applications.
- Silver is also utilized in various military applications such as the production of heavy-duty batteries. This creates considerable demand for it in the defence industry.

To understand the potential for silver as an investment, we should begin by understanding the two different kinds of demand. As prices increase for a commodity, one type of consumer will respond by simply buying less of that product. However, in other circumstances, large variations in the price of a commodity might have little effect on how much of it is purchased. The first type of demand, which is responsive to price changes, is called "elastic" and the second type, which is far less responsive, is called "inelastic".

Demand is generally inelastic when a commodity is *absolutely essential* or where there are no alternative materials which could reasonably be used in its place. It is also the case when very small amounts of a particular commodity are necessary for the production of a product and the cost represents only a small fraction of the overall price of the finished goods. It is therefore not only important to keep up with the changing areas of consumption for silver, but also to find out how these demands respond to significant price changes — especially in the light of overall economic conditions.

In North America, we have seen that as the value of silver began to rise, it started to disappear from use in coinage. We have also seen a considerable decline in its use in sterlingware and silver medallions. Therefore, the demand for silver in these areas appears to be highly elastic; however, you should recognize that these uses represent only a small proportion of general world consumption of silver.

Before 1980, many industrial applications for silver were considered to be highly inelastic. It seemed that no matter how high the price rose, the demand for silver in the areas of photography, medicine, and in the production of batteries continued to grow by leaps and bounds. However, the astronomical increase in price that occurred in early 1980 (bringing the price per ounce as high as $48 U.S.) finally had the effect of dampening demand even in these areas. The sole exception appears to be the demand for silver oxide batteries, which are used in defence despite the cost; governments are simply not willing to accept a less reliable substitute.

With the radical drop in the price of silver since early 1980, there have been substantial increases in demand in virtually all industrial areas. It is not likely that this trend will be reversed. Furthermore, U.S. President Reagan's emphasis on an expanded defence program in the U.S. will likely result in the consumption of huge amounts of silver.

There are also other factors which will affect international demand for silver over the next decade. One major consideration is the emergence of China as a major international industrial power with a population of over one billion. It is impossible to imagine that the Chinese will not begin to have a greater and greater impact on world markets in the 1980s. If, for example, China attains a greater level of prosperity and industrialization, this could result in the demand for vast quantities of silver.

Another interesting consideration is that an American mining company, Sunshine Silver Mine, announced in 1981 that they would begin to produce and market a one-ounce silver coin to be sold for its bullion content. Targeted towards investors, the new coin is designed to parallel the use of Krugerrands as a means of investing in gold. If the new silver coin should catch on in popularity, it could create a potentially large demand for this metal.

The Supply of Silver

While the demand for silver is anticipated to increase, silver is one of the scarcest of all known metals. Interestingly enough, silver is rarely produced from silver mines. The vast majority of the world's new silver production is derived as a by-product of other base metals such as copper, lead or zinc. For example, when copper is mined silver is removed from it through a wash process involving a catalytic chemical reaction.

As a result of the fact that silver is generally obtained as a by-product, the supply side of silver is considered to be inelastic; that is, market price variations cannot be expected to result in an increased or decreased production. Although access to more by-products would be desirable, the management of a mining operation can hardly justify massive steps to increase the extraction of the primary ores unless this would be profitable in itself. Since copper, lead and zinc are primarily used in the electrical and automotive industries, the production of these metals and, consequently, silver can be expected to be adversely affected by poor economic conditions if there is a prolonged recession.

To this point, it would appear that with demand outrunning supply, the price for silver should again quickly start to skyrocket. However, before you rush out and invest your life-savings, you must also note that world supply of most metals including silver comes largely from mines located in third-world countries. These nations have had a tendency to meet their own funding requirements by dumping large quantities of these metals on international markets. This depresses the price of the metals even in good economic times and tends to slow down the desire for increased overall production. The result of these offsetting factors has been that the production of silver has tended to remain relatively constant, increasing only minimally over the last twenty years.

There are various secondary sources for silver which have also been available to help meet the international demand. In the past, substantial amounts of silver have been recovered from coins which were withdrawn from circulation and melted down. However, in North America this process has fairly well exhausted itself.

A further secondary source of supply has consistently been the silver that was smuggled out of India and Pakistan. However, this supply has not been particularly responsive to periods of very high market prices. In other words, people in these countries have been reluctant to dispose of unusually large amounts of their gold or silver, which they hold in the form of personal jewellery. In these countries, such jewellery forms a portable and essential store of family wealth. Thus, the opportunity for short-term profits is simply not enough to encourage many people to dispose of larger quantities.

In interesting contrast to the Eastern philosophy, in 1980 millions of North Americans rushed en masse to dispose of personal silver possessions. The disposition of silver ornaments, jewellery and sterlingware created an enormous and extraordinary amount of silver salvage. Since large amounts were enticed into the market at that time, the salvage of silver from these areas is anticipated to be considerably below normal over the next few years.

Supply vs. Demand

The action of the silver market in 1980 provided many economists with one of their favourite examples of classical supply and demand. As the price soared, large amounts of silver came onto the market at the same time as consumers were finding this metal to be simply too expensive and were radically curtailing demands. For the first time in decades, there was a supply of silver considerably in excess of annual consumption. Now that the swells are beginning to die down from the great wave created that year, demand is moving back up and supply is slowly slipping back down. It is possible that the future will see increasingly large demands for silver in excess of the international supply.

In early 1980 the price of silver went up as high as $48.80 U.S. and then declined drastically. In April 1982 its price was about $7.20. This chaotic activity made millions for a few people and devastated many others. It is an interesting story, which is worth recounting.

In May 1978, the U.S. government began holding monthly gold auctions and certain bullion dealers bought large amounts of the gold offered. This was done as part of a clever speculative move. Prior to each auction, these dealers would short gold futures contracts. They would then cover their positions with the low-priced gold they were able to acquire at auction.

However, in August 1979 the bullion dealers were suddenly outbid by three foreign banks who took all the gold that was offered. This left the unsuspecting dealers with numerous short positions, financed through bank borrowings, which could not be covered. They were thus forced to buy in the open market and the world price of gold immediately shot up by $12 in one day.

You may wonder what this had to do with silver. However, prices of the two metals have traditionally had a strong tendency to move in the same direction. These dealers saw an opportunity to recoup their losses. They realized that the large jump in gold prices would inevitably affect the price for silver so they quickly bought silver futures. They were right, as the price started to rise.

Among the most famous of the silver bulls of this period were Nelson Bunker Hunt and his brother William Hubert Hunt. By January 1, 1980, they and their various corporations controlled more than 192 million ounces of silver. As the price for silver rose, the Hunts consistently withdrew their increasing equity and reinvested it in other ways, such as the purchase of a substantial amount of stock in a major brokerage firm through which they usually traded.

There were a few other major movers who held huge positions in silver. One was a senior executive in a commodity brokerage firm and two others were Lebanese multimillionaires. It is possible that large amounts of money used to make purchases came directly from the Saudi royal family.

The price of silver continued to rise until finally the commodities exchanges tried to discourage speculation by raising the margin requirements. These new rules were made retroactive and affected existing positions. This, in turn, quickly forced smaller speculators out of the market when they could not meet the higher margins. By October 1979, some bullion dealers had to put up millions of dollars each day to meet their margin calls.

The Chicago Board of Trade also tried to force the liquidation of some of these huge positions by setting a temporary limit of six hundred contracts per person, hoping that the result would be less frenzy and lower prices. Some holdings were sold but many were simply moved to another exchange.

World affairs were then in a particularly tense period. The U.S. hostages were being held in Iran and the Soviets were moving into Afghanistan. During these times people tended to hold a higher proportion of their wealth in precious metals, so in spite of new restrictions, the price continued to climb. However, the big added push in silver prices came as the result of a major blunder by the Peruvian government.

Peru mines large amounts of silver and hedges by shorting the market. This provides protection against the possibility of falling prices during the time the ore is mined, refined and sold. Unfortunately, in the later part of 1979, Peru shorted about ten million more ounces than it could possibly deliver, believing that the price of silver was bound to quickly decline. This proved to be a poor speculation and Peru quickly realized that it had to begin to cover its short positions. This pushed the price of silver up even higher and the Peruvian government eventually lost about eighty million dollars.

This frantic activity finally drew all kinds of short-term speculators into the market in the belief that silver was headed towards $100 an ounce. The exchanges began to impose further restrictions, and finally, on January 21, 1980, a major U.S. commodities exchange issued an emergency ruling whereby silver could only be bought to cover short positions (and not for accumulation). From that point, the prices of both gold and silver began to decline. Many late speculators were virtually ruined and several holders of large positions covered their margin calls at great cost and simply took delivery of their contracts. The Hunts alone were reputedly holding up to sixty million ounces of silver at the end of 1980 and may still have a large proportion of holdings even today.

Did the Hunts manipulate the market? The Commodity Futures Trading Commission, a U.S. federal agency, found no evidence of it. The Hunts themselves declare that they stopped adding to their positions in July 1979. Therefore, their holdings cost them an average of less than $10 an ounce.

Investing in Silver Bullion

Like gold, silver is available in bars of various sizes and shapes. These range from small one-ounce wafers to very large thousand-ounce bars. The smaller the bar, the higher the premium. As with gold, the premium represents the difference between the asking price of the bar and the actual value of the silver content. If you are purchasing bullion, you are generally better off buying the largest possible bar that you can afford in order to maximize the amount of silver that you get for your money. This is probably the best way to invest in silver for a wealthy investor who doesn't mind tying up his money for a considerable amount of time.

On the other hand, for the small investor, large bars of silver are simply out of the question. This is because such a purchase would require tying up perhaps $10,000 in a single investment which cannot be subdivided. That is to say, you must either retain the entire bar or sell it. There is no intermediate strategy.

All of the general inconveniences that attach to gold bullion apply to silver bullion as well. Unless purchased from an internationally recognized refiner, resale may be a lengthy and frustrating process involving the extra expense to reassay.

Silver Coins

The acquisition of silver coins, unlike their gold counterparts, is both simple and inexpensive. They are widely available at banks, coin shops and sometimes even antique shops. Prices are quoted as being so many times "over face". For example, if a silver dime is quoted at "5.2 over face" this means that it would cost you 52¢.

Face value coins are generally also known as "1966 silver", that being the last year in which currency coins with a high silver content were produced in Canada. These coins are usually quite worn, and in some cases their engraving may be indistinguishable. This makes them unsuitable as collectors' pieces. Silver coins dating back before 1967 are also available in thousand dollar lots known as "bag silver". This means that the contents of a bag will have a monetary value of $1,000. However, the purchase price may be several times higher and may even be in excess of the current quote "over face" on a coin by coin basis. Bag silver is not always available and in times of high prices may disappear from the market entirely.

As mentioned previously, the Sunshine Silver Mine in the United States now produces a one-ounce bullion coin. However, this is available only in the United States and is subject to duty if brought back to Canada. This is the only readily available coin which contains pure silver. Even 1966 silver coins and bag silver are adulterated by other alloys.

The choice between buying wafers or coins is entirely different in the case of silver than it is in the case of gold. If you buy gold wafers or coins, you are essentially buying pure gold. On the other hand, wafers are pure silver while coins are a silver alloy. Therefore, you are getting considerably more silver for your money through the purchase of wafers or small bars than you would through an accumulation of coins. Nevertheless, coins also have valuable investment potential and are attractive because they are so easily accumulated. In the past, coins have simply been culled from pocket change. They are often hoarded because they have at least a partial silver content, which makes them valuable as a hedge against economic disaster. They also come in very small, easily disposable units. Fortunately, silver bars, wafers and coins are usually available at such reasonable prices that it is possible to accumulate all of them for various purposes.

Numismatic Coins

Numismatic or collectors' coins include not only ancient silver, but also those of most recent and familiar vintage such as silver dimes, quarters, fifty-cent pieces and dollars. A collectors' coin must however be in reasonably good condition. Such coins are not included in bag silver, of course, but are sold separately in protective wrappers. They are graded according to the following categories.

Proof: These are special mintings of coins in limited editions for investment and display purposes. They are usually "double struck", that is they are struck twice and have a brilliant finish. These coins generally sell at very high premiums. As a result, they usually do not represent very good investments in terms of bullion ownership.

Brilliant Uncirculated (B.U. or U.&C.): Although these coins are not double-struck, they are not ordinarily used as currency. They include most of the bullion and numismatic coins produced today such as the Krugerrand gold coin or the twenty-dollar U.S. Double Eagle. If a coin is in brilliant uncirculated condition, it is best to keep it that way lest your investment value be eroded.

Extremely Fine (E.F.) Or Extra Fine (X.S.): While these coins may show some slight signs of wear, they are virtually uncirculated and still maintain their original fine finish.

Very Fine (V.F.): While the most prominent surfaces of these coins may be slightly worn, the details and design must still be quite clear.

Fine (F.): These are coins which show definite signs of wear from having been in circulation. Even some of the finer details may show wear, however all of these details must still be visible. This grading is the minimum standard for coin collectors.

Very Good (V.G.): The details of these coins are more worn but are still clear and distinct.

Good (G.): While quite worn, the design and inscriptions are still legible.

Fair (F.): The features and design may still be identified but the inscriptions are not easily legible.

Mediocre (M.): These coins are quite worn or are definitely damaged.

Poor (P.): Unless they are either rare or antique, coins in this category are usually not valued at more than their metal content.

Storage

Apart from bag silver, all coins, wafers and bars should be individually wrapped for storage as damage or wear will reduce their value. They can be stored in a safety deposit box or in a secure location in your home.

Silver may have a lower unit value than gold but it should be subject to the same standards of safety. This is especially so for silver jewellery, sterling flatware and servingware. These items should be appraised and insured. They are highly portable and are usually kept in easily accessible and visible places throughout the home. Sterling is a standard of purity that refers to any alloy of 925 parts silver and 72 parts copper. In terms of precious metal content, this makes sterling silver far more valuable, by comparison, than a quantity of 10 karat gold.

Paper Forms of Silver

Silver Certificates

Certificates entitling a purchaser to quantities of at least 100 ounces of silver can be purchased from most banks and coin shops. They are quoted in U.S. dollars, as is the one-quarter of a per cent commission and the one-quarter of a per cent safekeeping or delivery charge. Certificates entitle the buyer to either ounces of silver or in some cases, silver coins.

Like gold certificates, silver certificates have their pros and cons. They are certainly portable and are fully transferable but are not negotiable. In other words, you can transfer them to another owner but you cannot use them in payment of your bills. They do give you legal entitlement to a specific amount of silver. However, there is the question of "fungibility". Is your silver specifically segregated from everyone else's or is it mixed into one quantity against which you have the right to draw a specific number of ounces? If your silver is not segregated and is therefore "fungible", then you should be concerned about the financial stability of the organization which has issued the certificate to you. Should that institution go bankrupt before you take delivery of your silver, you may find that you are out of luck.

All silver certificates available in Canada are for delivery from depositories in Canada. However, if you happen to be travelling in the United States, it is possible to buy silver certificates which are drawn against depositories in countries outside North America, such as Switzerland. As with bullion, certificates brought back into Canada are not subject to customs duty. One of the largest disadvantages of a certificate is that it is necessary to put up all of the money required to cover the number of ounces that the certificate authorizes. This ties up funds which cannot then earn interest. Certificates are therefore more attractive to a speculator than they are to a long-term investor.

Silver Futures

Futures are, as explained in Chapter Nine, flexible contracts which allow you to buy, sell or even take delivery of a commodity. One of the most practical means of purchasing a large quantity of silver is simply to buy a futures contract and then take delivery. There is no sales tax on this transaction, and the only extra fee is the broker's commission. You can then avoid a number of problems, such as concern over safety, by obtaining a warehouse receipt and leaving the bullion in an exchange-approved depository. Although there is a small storage charge, the depository is likely a safer alternative than storing the bullion in your own home.

Furthermore, holding bullion in a depository makes resale a much more convenient matter. At that time, instead of selling the physical bullion, you simply "short the market". This means that you sell a futures contract for an equivalent amount of silver and then deliver the warehouse receipt to your broker. This eliminates all of the headaches over inspecting the name of the refiner, weight and fineness and avoids possible assay requirements.

As in purchasing any futures contract, you will have to work through a broker and be prepared to establish your credit worthiness. In mid-1982, a margin of $4,000 U.S. would allow you to carry a futures contract for 5000 ounces of silver. Contracts are also available for quantities of 1000 ounces.

The futures market is, however, the domain of the speculator, where even the most astute and experienced can be badly burned. As the Hunt brothers discovered, not only are there perils in the market itself, but the Board officials can change the rules to affect investors in the most extreme ways. Because of the convulsions that seized the silver futures market in the early 1980s, the average daily volume plummeted by more that 68% between September and December of that year. Public confidence in this market has still not been recovered two years later.

Options

The only market in Canada which handles silver options is the Winnipeg Commodity Exchange. As discussed in Chapter

Nine, most large brokerage firms will not deal in this market because it is too thin and is therefore illiquid. For the small investor, silver options would appear to be too expensive and lack sufficient liquidity to provide a safe investment.

Shares in Silver Mining Corporations

All of the considerations discussed in Chapter Ten in regard to gold stocks apply here as well. The likelihood of making a profit on your investment capital will depend just as much on the quality of the management of the company as on the market price for the ore itself. Unlike gold, silver is frequently found in "epithermal depositions". This means that the richest deposits of silver are located near the surface of the earth. Therefore, the deeper the mine extends, the thinner the deposit of silver will become.

These unique characteristics of silver deposits produce some specific concerns for the stock market investor. If you are considering investing in an operation that is strictly a silver mine, you should be particularly concerned about the "life" of the mine. How long can the mine be expected to operate at its present level of production? It is important to establish some knowledge of the expected reserves of silver in the ground. If these reserves are small, the mine's life will be short and the stock is therefore not suitable as a long-term investment.

Also, as mentioned earlier, silver is usually obtained as a by-product of other base metal mining. The four largest American producers of silver, Hecla, Asarco, Kennecott and Anaconda obtain virtually all of their silver as a by-product.

If you are interested in investing in a company that produces a base metal whose by-product is silver, you should be particularly concerned about the market for the main product of that mine. The markets for copper, lead and zinc can be quite volatile and, if its main market is depressed, no company is going to accumulate large stockpiles of unsaleable metal just to obtain silver as a by-product. Stocks of these companies should not be purchased on the basis of their production of silver. It is simply too risky.

Tax Consequences

In Canada, profits on the disposition of silver are usually subject to capital gains treatment. As in the case of gold, this is due to administrative practice, because silver itself does not have the capacity to produce any type of investment income as recognized by the Income Tax Act — that is, interest, dividends or rent. As a result, it is conceivable that at some future time, the rules may change so that an investment in silver would be considered to be held in speculation. However, unless you are a frequent and heavy trader in silver, you can, at present, rely on receiving capital gains treatment. It would nevertheless be worth reviewing the tax consequences pertaining to futures contracts, options, and gold investments as outlined in Chapters Nine and Ten.

Summary

Because silver has historically been more volatile in price than gold, it has been considered a market for speculators. However, silver is still the most moderately priced of all precious metals. This makes it both attractive and convenient for the small investor. It is readily available in either bar or coin form and is almost too easy to accumulate. Because of rapid changes in price, the opportunity for profit in silver is far more outstanding than in gold. A price movement in silver from $8 an ounce to $24 could triple an original investment in silver. However, for the same type of profit, gold would have to move from $400 to $1,200 per ounce.

On the other hand, although it may move proportionately higher, *silver also tends to drop proportionately lower and it drops faster*. Because of changing conditions in supply, demand and world economic conditions, as well as the uncertainty of interest rates, you must, in the final analysis, make your *own* prediction of where the price of silver is likely to go in the near future.

CHAPTER TWELVE

Those Marvelous Collectibles

The fascination with collectibles has grown at a phenomenal rate over the past ten years and has created a widely diversified industry worth hundreds of millions of dollars. The reason for this is twofold. First, the great increase in apparent affluence (that is disposable income) has made it possible for many to purchase objects of beauty. Second, many people have recognized the disastrous erosion of the purchasing power of money due to inflation. This has created the desire to exchange currency for valuable tangible assets.

Hyping the market has been the multitude of stories of dusty paintings purchased for mere pittances and sold for tens of thousands of dollars, or the trifling purchase of a second-hand tray that was subsequently discovered to be made of solid platinum. Some of these accounts have been so wonderful that they rival Grimm's Fairy Tales. Little mention is ever made of the great sums lost in the purchase of overvalued or fraudulent pieces of art. Collectibles may be extremely seductive, but such investments are too dangerous to be approached lightly.

To Have or to Have Not

It is only reasonable to expect that with all this avid interest in collectibles, many items of questionable value and content would begin to insinuate themselves into this category. You must first recognize that there is a distinct difference between true collectibles and memorabilia. In most cases, confusing the two will eventually prove to be both disillusioning and expensive for you.

It is difficult to define a "collectible". However, a definition should include a reference to rarity, antiquity, artistry and value. The concerns are essentially with the artist or craftsman, the age of the work and the subject matter. The artist's technical skill contributes to the quality of the creation as does his unique capacity to express thoughts and emotions through his work. The age of the item tends to be relevant as well as its character. The same subject may be dealt with many times by the same artist, but it should not approach the point of reproduction. These concepts are expanded upon later in this chapter as we discuss the valuation of collectibles. Rarity is one of the key components making up the value of old coins or stamps.

Memorabilia, on the other hand, includes items of charm but no real value other than that of nostalgia, such as matchbooks or thimbles. It would be wrong to say that collectibles are expensive and memorabilia is cheap. As paper money loses its value, there is invariably a rush into many types of assets. This often results in temporary increases in price coupled with much excitement, but in the long run, such an investment has little or no enduring worth. In many instances, the purchaser of nostalgia will find better use for his money and more satisfaction if he makes a substantial charitable donation. Sometimes, as in the case of collectors' plates, it is difficult to differentiate between collectibles and memorabilia.

The Speculator vs. the Collector

For years, collectors have harboured tremendous resentment against the dastardly speculators. These persons supposedly have little knowledge or appreciation of the works which they purchase. However, flushed with cash and eager for profits, they have driven the price of collectibles beyond the reach of many true collectors. The speculator is described as a Philistine whose sole motive is to pursue large gains by reselling works of art to even greater fools.

In reality, the fine line between speculation and true collection has now become highly obscured. In order to improve and expand his existing holdings, the collector now finds that he must be prepared to trade up his pieces in competitive and frequently expensive markets. The days are probably gone forever when huge collections could be established for reasonable prices over long periods of time. On the other hand, speculation and high prices have also flushed many superior artworks and antiques out of the old collections and into the auction houses again. Collectors cannot help but become speculators in these types of markets. In either case, these expensive investments are only for the shrewd, knowledgeable, gutsy and, generally, the very rich.

Nevertheless if you aspire to be a collector but have limited funds, you need not despair completely. It is perfectly legitimate to collect for the sake of collecting and not for investment purposes. If you want to collect a type of art because of your love for it but have little money, then look to specialized varieties, craftsmen or artists who may be temporarily out of favour. Try to collect specific items whose characteristics and history have personal appeal. Do not expect enormous profits from the resale of your purchases, although you may certainly enjoy them for their intrinsic beauty and appearance. If you eventually have the ability to move into more expensive markets, then you can use your basic collection as a stepping stone to more exquisite acquisitions. However, before you do anything, it is essential to come to a personal understanding of your motivation and expectations or you may miss a wonderful opportunity to appreciate beauty for what it really is.

The Pros and Cons of Collectibles

Although the emphasis of this chapter is on collectibles, many examples and references are to works of art. Certainly a mastercrafted sculpture is also a work of art although, technically, a piece of jewellery, a rare coin or an antique is not. However, you should realize that the discussions throughout this chapter apply equally well to *all* types of collectibles. The term "artist" will therefore include a master goldsmith, carpenter and sculptor; that is, anyone who makes their craft a fine art.

There are some very positive and intriguing benefits in owning a piece of art, a sculpture or an antique. You have the opportunity to live with it, hold it, touch it, enjoy it, and also to anticipate capital appreciation. You can perhaps draw some satisfaction from the fact that you have protected the value of your hard-earned dollars. You have the opportunity to meet interesting people and maybe even travel to exotic places. On the other hand, don't expect your friends to necessarily understand or appreciate your new enterprise and share in your enthusiasm. After all, not everyone can be enthralled by your collection of Zulu war masks!

There are serious personal considerations before you decide to become involved with art. Acquiring even a basic knowledge can be expensive and very time-consuming, although you may find it a fascinating experience. Apart from the danger of making potentially poor purchases, you may find that the market for fine art is quite limited because many collectors are not anxious to reveal themselves and thereby jeopardize the safety of their collections. Artworks, antiques, and stamp or coin collections frequently require extra care and extensive maintenance as well as insurance. Resale can also become something of a nightmare if markets are limited—the sale of a particular piece may depend on expensive transportation to distant cities. Government regulations may change to prevent the import or export of various works or artifacts. Ultimately, you may find that interest has simply shifted away from the pieces you have collected and that there is, in fact, no market for them all.

Doing the Basic Groundwork

Once you have decided that the world of collectibles is too intriguing to resist, you should be prepared to commit yourself to some basic necessities before actually entering the market. If you can restrain yourself, it is best not to buy anything at all— at least in the beginning. Instead, spend your initial funds on reference materials. Commit the time to educate yourself above the level of a rank amateur. This is absolutely essential in order to avoid the initial purchase of second-rate pieces or perhaps even an outright fraud. The discipline required in self-education will also tell you whether you are really interested in becoming involved in the collectibles market, which can be as demanding as it is dazzling.

You should talk to dealers and, if at all possible, other collectors. A good dealer is generally willing to give you a wealth of information if he sees that you are truly interested. Narrow your focus down to a specific area and read journals and magazines which give you the latest information on both the type of collectible and the market in which you can expect to be involved.

Investment Considerations

Once you are ready to move into the market and actually acquire your first piece, you will naturally hope that it is going to be a good investment. The best way to protect yourself, aside from extensive personal study, is to be sure that you only transact with reputable dealers. Beware of private purchases — especially if you feel you are being pressured into a quick decision. Don't expect to buy anything worthwhile at a bargain price, and at the same time don't regret passing up a purchase because you didn't feel sure of yourself. There will be other irresistible purchases available as you become more secure and knowledgeable.

Always buy certified quality, preferably backed up by documents detailing age, origin, creation and, possibly, ownership. Always buy the best collectibles that you can afford. Several small or less expensive pieces may make you feel that you are more involved in the market, however, you will generally find that they are likely worth less collectively than a single more astute purchase. Don't regret having a limited collection. Study the history, technique, subject matter, artist, school and period. This is not only personally satisfying but also results in a considerable amount of knowledge about the area in which you are involved. Your subsequent purchases should therefore be progressively more judicious.

You are frequently better off buying older pieces rather than those that are more modern. In most cases, rarity and history directly add to the value of the piece whereas more modern works might be replicated. Certainly, many present-day artists in Canada and elsewhere have produced very large quantities of works which are quite similar and of dubious holding value. It is also worth noting that fine art is not to be purchased out of newspaper columns which deal with items to buy and sell.

Should you purchase through a dealer or at an auction? Dealers often provide you with information that can be invaluable. If you buy from an established dealer, you are also assured of authenticity. Of course, you must pay for the dealer's time, expertise and overhead. Because of these, there is a mark-up on each purchase and you must expect to hold each piece for a considerable amount of time in order that the resale value (if you should choose to sell) will be at least equivalent to the retail price that you paid in the first place.

Many reputable dealers will guarantee to repurchase any piece from you for the price that you have paid or will give you full credit when trading the piece through them for one of greater value. This is certainly a practical way of accumulating a more valuable and sophisticated collection as time goes on.

Auctions are generally not for the novice. The auction which travels from city to city is not likely to be the place to expect to find investment-quality artwork or antiques. You should expect to buy pieces only from those auction houses in which you would consider selling pieces out of your own collection. In some cases, this could limit you to internationally recognized auction houses located in major cities. Naturally, travel to those locations can be expensive. If you are interested in coins or stamps, there are annual conventions of dealers and collectors which might be worth attending.

Information at most auction houses will be limited, but will generally provide you with the basic background on the piece in which you are interested and will often include a professional opinion as to origin and authenticity. However, remember that you are on your own and you may have to make some pretty quick decisions. Don't let the atmosphere and excitement carry you into a purchase that you may later regret. Get the auction catalogue early and narrow down your selection to those pieces in which you are really interested and then examine them personally, if at all possible. Auctions may command unusually high or low prices, so set your upper limits beforehand and decide whether or not you are willing to take advantage of what appear to be extraordinary bargains. Unfortunately, such good advice is often lost in the heat of competition. Before participating in an auction, it is wise to remember the old saying, "if you can't take the heat, stay out of the kitchen."

It is important to become familiar with import and export regulations that affect the type of pieces that you are collecting. Nothing can be more heartbreaking than to buy a beautiful piece of art in London only to find that you cannot import it into Canada. The same practical considerations apply when considering the sale of your pieces in another country. In this regard, it is particularly important to become familiar with the import-export regulations between Canada and the United States.

In Canada, a work of art may be imported duty-free if it is an original work with a value greater than twenty dollars. Antiques may be imported duty-free provided that they are more than fifty years old and are accompanied by documentation showing proof of age. There may be significant problems concerning the importation of certain types of materials, such as ivory or tortoise shell. These materials are related to endangered animal species and importation of such artworks may well require both export permits from the United States and import permits into Canada. If you intend to buy artworks outside Canada, it will save a multitude of headaches to be fully informed about specific government regulations beforehand.

Exporting to the United States creates its own nightmare of complications. Again, any work made of any material related to what is now an endangered species may require elaborate efforts beforehand to provide the proper permit, if indeed it is even obtainable. In this case it is best to contact the U.S. Fish and Wildlife Department well in advance before concluding any plans for sale or auction in the United States.

All these complications may be enough to convince you *not* to buy art of an international nature but rather to concentrate on national or local artists. The advantage is that you are dealing with known Canadian artists in a recognized market. Certainly, many works by Canadian artists have enjoyed considerable appreciation both locally and internationally. Collecting Canadian works also saves the nuisance of travel precautions and expenses to far distant markets. On the other hand, be aware that you are dealing with a relatively restricted market in Canada and you may find that some of your pieces, if sold overseas, will bring only a fraction of their local value. If one of the reasons you are attracted to investing in collectibles is their physical portability across international borders, you may well find that local or perhaps even national art will be of limited value to you.

In fact, the value of a work of art can vary dramatically from region to region. In preparing this book, we sent a questionnaire to ten art dealers located in different cities throughout Canada. We explained that we would be writing a book on investment strategies and that we would be dealing with the subject of collectibles. We asked each of them to recommend six living Canadian artists whose works presently sell in the $3,000–$5,000 range where the dealer believed that there was excellent opportunity for capital appreciation over the next ten years.

The results of our small survey were somewhat surprising. In only two or three cases did the same artist appear on more than one list. It seems that many art dealers will specifically promote those artists whose works they sell. Also, dealers in eastern Canada tend to promote eastern artists while dealers in western Canada support western art. We therefore conclude that it is quite difficult to predict the identity of *the* Canadian artist or artists for the 1980s.

One alternative is to purchase for personal enjoyment and consider that any significant appreciation is purely a bonus. On the other hand, you may decide to look at collectibles primarily as an investment and therefore must consider not only the practical concerns we have been discussing, but also the value and quality of a piece.

Valuing Collectibles

No discussion of investment in collectibles is complete without a consideration of how art is valued. Is an item "worth" $2,000 or $10,000? The answer depends on the quality of the artist or craftsman and the work itself.

The quality of an artist is judged by his unique creativity and, arising from this, the amount of influence he has had over his peers. Also, consideration must be given to the culture in which he was involved and the historical era during which he worked. This involves noting the movement to which he belonged and the subjects with which he dealt. Certainly, all of an artist's works are not of equivalent value. The difference in the quality of the works can vary greatly throughout an individual's career. For instance, during a certain period, a particular artist may have painted portraits while later on, he may have switched his attention to seascapes. The subject matter of the work will also be particularly important. Is it the type of subject for which the artist is well known, or if it is unusual for this artist, is it particularly good? Aside from these points, does the piece have striking visual impact? That is, does it have colour, movement, line, and so on that are outstanding? Consideration must also be given to the physical condition of the work itself. Clearly, a piece in very poor condition, even though created by a well-known artist, will command a lower value.

All of these criteria, even though many may be highly subjective, contribute to a determination of the quality and the value of any collectible. Beyond this, the investor must consider the marketplace with which he is dealing. Through an examination of publications, catalogues and auction records, an investor can derive some idea of the value the purchasing public places on the works of a specific artist or craftsman. Since all of the judgements necessary to determine the value of a collectible are largely based on experience and education, most investors find that they must rely heavily on a knowledgeable and trustworthy dealer. Many investors consult several dealers before concluding any purchase.

Collectibles as a Medium of Exchange

An increasing number of people are beginning to recognize one of the major advantages of investing in collectibles. This is the ability to use art, sculpture, jewellery, antiques, and stamp or coin collections as a medium of exchange. Certainly, this quality has been understood by people outside North America for hundreds of years. Collectibles are portable, exchangeable, and in many instances very difficult to trace beyond an original purchase. Such pieces are frequently used for the purpose of barter or sweeteners in business transactions of every size. Naturally, there are income tax regulations governing this type of exchange but they are extremely difficult to administer effectively.

Income Tax Aspects of Investing in Collectibles

The tax consequences of making profits on the disposition of collectibles will differ depending on the nature of the investment. Art, jewellery and stamp or coin collections are generally presumed under the Canadian Income Tax Act to be purchased primarily for personal use and pleasure and they are referred to as "listed personal property."

Listed personal property includes an interest in or a right to any print, sketch, drawing, painting, sculpture or other similar work of art. This category of property also includes jewellery, rare folios, manuscripts or books, as well as stamp or coin collections. For the purposes of administrative expedience, the tax cost of any such property immediately before its disposition is deemed to be at least $1,000 and the proceeds of disposition for the property are likewise deemed to be a minimum of $1,000. Therefore, individual transactions involving works of art where the purchase and sale value are both less than $1,000 will not give rise to any taxable income under the Canadian tax provisions. Values in excess of $1,000 will, however, create either taxable capital gains or allowable capital losses on disposition.

You should note that gains and losses on listed personal property are treated separately from those which arise from other capital properties, such as marketable securities. Losses on the disposition of listed personal property are deductible — but only as an offset against gains from other similar property. If losses exceed gains in the same year, the excess may be carried back to the preceding year, but again can only be applied against listed personal property gains in that year. Any remaining excess losses may be carried forward and may be deducted in the same manner any time in the subsequent five years. At the end of that time, any unabsorbed loss from listed personal property is no longer available as an offset against appropriate gains. Also you are not able to deduct $2,000 of excess allowable capital losses on listed personal property against other income in a year.

There may be instances in which a set of pieces has been acquired, such as a set of coins or sculptures. On disposition, the previously mentioned $1,000 limitation will apply to the *entire set* if the individual pieces have been disposed or in two or more transactions to one person or to a group of related persons. In other words, it is not possible to double up or triple up on the $1,000 exemption by simply selling a set one piece at a time. In the event of the sale of individual pieces to a group of unrelated persons, the $1,000 rule would, of course, apply to each item.

If you have a taxable gain on sale, the income tax rules permit you to reduce your gain on the disposition of privately owned artworks by the expenses incurred for storage, safe-keeping, insurance, appraisals and any interest costs that were incurred on money borrowed to buy them in the first place.

In certain circumstances, a taxpayer may actually be in the business of trading in art. This is not a simple matter to establish and would depend, in part, on the nature of the operation, the time devoted to it, the frequency of transactions and of course, the likelihood of the venture becoming a profitable operation. If trading in collectibles is actually a business, generally all expenses would be fully deductible as they are incurred. The works of art would represent an inventory, and a gain recognized on their disposition would be fully taxable while all losses would be deductible in full.

Until about a year ago, businesses could purchase works of art or antiques and depreciate them to reduce their taxable incomes. Of course, these assets generally tended to appreciate rather than depreciate. As a result of the 1981 Budget, it is now no longer possible to claim depreciation on works of art or antiques purchased after November 12, 1981. However, this restriction does not apply to the first purchaser of an artwork produced by a living Canadian artist. Judicious choices in this area could give a business not only a valuable long-term investment but also an immediate income tax savings.

If one dies, the tax rules decree that a deemed disposition of all artworks at fair market value has taken place and that any net gains be reported on the final tax return unless there is a bequest of the property to a spouse. If property is left to a spouse, gains are deferred until such time as the spouse dies. You cannot avoid these rules by gifting artwork or other collectibles to family members in your lifetime. A gift is also deemed to be a sale at fair market value, which would create an immediate capital gain at that time.

However, in spite of these rules, it generally appears that compliance in this area is weak, at best. So far, Revenue Canada does not seem to have taken many steps to enforce the rules, except perhaps in cases where the taxpayer is known to have a substantial collection. While we certainly do not advocate tax fraud, we do recognize that the degree of honesty between an individual and his government is a personal matter. Whether or not your estate will in fact be burdened by taxes resulting from deemed dispositions of your collectibles may, in fact, depend on the degree of publicity which accompanies your holdings.

Summary

An investment in collectibles can be not only exciting and satisfying but may also produce a considerable financial reward for the astute purchaser. However, you should recognize that monetary gains in this area are not easy to come by. For the successful investor, collectibles offer a unique opportunity to combine a variety of outstanding characteristics including enjoyment as well as financial gain. For some Canadians, the ability to combine portability, high unit values, and the retention of purchasing power in one asset makes collectibles a worthwhile and practical store of wealth.

Unfortunately, most profits in collectibles are only made in times of high inflation or where there is a large interest on an international level. However, when there is a recession most markets are "down". It is rare that collectibles will appreciate rapidly in times such as these. In fact, the investor with cash may be better off waiting until he feels that the low has been reached, when there may be some excellent bargains to be had. Some collectors however may take the opportunity to improve their collections by "trading up." They might exchange one or two lower quality pieces and some cash for one better piece. In the stock market, commodities or options, we have shown you that proper investment strategy will allow you to make money as the market moves in both directions. Certainly, this is not an easy feat when it comes to collectibles. It is unlikely that you can count on selling a piece of art during a boom period in order to buy it back again during the next recession. Thus, for most people, collectibles should only comprise a small portion of an investment portfolio.

It is not possible to recommend any one type of collectible with any guarantee of outstanding investment performance in the future. Certainly investments in rare stamps have done very well over the last few years but past performance alone should not encourage you to become an avid collector if you are not already interested in the subject. Follow your interests but temper them with a common-sense investment approach if you hope to reap monetary gains as well as pleasure.

CHAPTER THIRTEEN

Financial Privacy

As government intrudes further on the rights of individual citizens, people turn increasingly to ways of preserving their limited privacy. This desire is often nothing more than a case of the individual wanting to keep the ball in his own court so that he may exercise some control over his own financial security. The more that people must question their confidence in their government, the greater this interest becomes. Assuming that privacy is, and ought to be, a right of the individual in a democracy, then we should examine what information the government can obtain and how the individual can maintain control over his own assets.

Government Access to Information

In Canada, the Department of National Revenue has the right to request information with regard to tax returns without having to supply a supporting reason. Its job is to police the legitimacy of returns, statements of income and claims for expenses. This may be as simple as a request for supporting documents or as detailed as a full-blown audit. Certainly, people with lower incomes are much less likely to be questioned. Also, those whose affairs are uncomplicated, for example, whose incomes are mostly derived from salary, are not likely to attract queries.

A special investigation can be initiated for any one of several good reasons. Routine government audits of corporate records may uncover irregularities which encourage a more extensive investigation, or specific disclosures may be made by third parties which indicate major omissions. No investigation of this nature is undertaken lightly or without Revenue Canada having substantial reason to believe that significant amounts of tax dollars can be recovered. It is certainly impractical and expensive to pursue minor amounts. However, not all audits need to be profitable ventures for the authorities to be willing to spend time and money. Investigations may, in some cases, be a matter of righteousness and law enforcement.

During the course of an investigation, the Department of National Revenue has the right to examine and confiscate all records. They can have access to all bank records, which by the way can stretch back over several years and are retained by the banks on microfiche. Normally, the Canadian Income Tax Act gives the Minister of National Revenue four years in which to reassess a taxpayer's return. However, where fraud or evasion are suspected, there are no time limitations. The authorities can go back as far as they believe is warranted and reassess every return up to the current year.

In the event that no records are available, Revenue officials can estimate what your income should have been. They do this through an assessment of "net worth" based on the value of your personal holdings, your home, your investments, and the flow of money through your bank accounts. If your net assets reflect a lifestyle that could not have been sustained through the level of income which you have been reporting on your tax returns, then they will estimate what your income must have been. It is then up to you to provide evidence to the contrary. Since this type of net worth assessment is painstaking, it is not undertaken unless the authorities feel that there is good reason to believe that they have a case. However, as in all instances in dealing with the tax department, the onus is on the taxpayer to prove his innocence.

In many situations where a taxpayer has significantly understated his income, he may be able to make a voluntary disclosure *before* the government completes its assessment of his situation. At that point, Revenue officials are generally willing to negotiate and will accept an income figure which is somewhere within the realm of reality. This often represents something of a trade-off. The government may suspect that not *all* taxable income has been revealed, however, they recognize the advantages in saving time and expense by accepting a compromise. These types of voluntary disclosures, of course, are only pertinent for those individuals whose incomes were not easily traced or documented in the first place. Too often, this type of income arises from less than legitimate sources.

Evasion vs. Avoidance

In most provinces in Canada, individuals with taxable incomes over $55,000 must pay taxes to the government of at least 50% out of each additional dollar earned. We must also contend with sales taxes, real estate taxes, gasoline taxes and "luxury" tax on such items as cigarettes or liquor. Frustration with overtaxation encourages people to respond in anger. Even legitimate planning for tax minimization means extra expense and dissatisfaction if the government insists on changing the rules arbitrarily without clearly thinking out the results of its efforts (as was the case on November 12, 1981).

Some people respond to these problems by trying to withdraw from the system in order to preserve their privacy. They attempt to simply ignore the existing rules. However, the vast majority of people derive most of their incomes from salaried employment. This in itself makes it nearly impossible for them to ignore the system. If, however, you derive any significant portion of your income from sources other than salary, you may be able to practice effective tax *avoidance*.

There is considerable difference between tax evasion and tax avoidance. Tax avoidance, when skillfully practised, is that which helps to make you rich. On the other hand, tax evasion can put you behind bars. There is an excellent and well-known quotation by Judge Learned Hand which states, "Over and over again courts have said that there is nothing sinister in so arranging one's affairs as to keep taxes as low as possible. Everybody does so, rich or poor; and all do right, for nobody owes any public duty to pay more than the law demands; taxes are enforced exactions, not voluntary contributions. To demand more in the name of morals is mere cant." This represents the essence of tax planning and perhaps tax avoidance is best described as *(legitimate) tax minimization*.

On the other hand, tax evasion represents the results of efforts and schemes which are outside the realm of acceptable tax planning. It involves fraudulent documentation or taking advantage of the fact that there is no documentation surrounding particular transactions. Examples include the failure of a waiter or cabdriver to report his tips, or the lack of disclosure of trading profits in gold and silver coins bought and/or sold through coin shops.

We must recognize that all systems require rules of order so that both taxpayers and the government may reasonably come to agreement and at all times generally know what to expect of each other. The practice of tax evasion is outside these rules, and in many instances, is so poorly planned as to have no hope of success. Never underestimate the facilities and the experience of the government. While Revenue officials have not yet succeeded in mastering mind-reading, they certainly have access to expensive computer capabilities, and it is often not a difficult matter to locate income which has not been reported.

Our tax system is functional because the majority of people are honest. Not every return is checked in detail just as birth certificates are not questioned for all children claimed as dependants. Those who are not honest are generally not clever and take the most obvious approach, by omitting income or exaggerating expenses.

The penalties for tax evasion include, of course, the collection of all taxes outstanding as well as interest and penalties associated with these amounts. These interest and penalty charges are not tax-deductible. Imprisonment is also a possibility where large amounts of money are involved. Claiming ignorance of the regulations is not going to help you. The only instance in which you are going to have a defensible position is where the matter in question is subject to interpretation.

Knowing The "Grey Areas" Can Save You Money

There are many situations where the tax consequences of particular transactions are unclear. These grey areas include the nature and taxability of various types of income, such as whether a profit from a sale of a parcel of land should receive capital gains or (ordinary) income treatment. Disputes arise where a taxpayer has disclosed his income at the time he originally filed his return and the Department of National Revenue has responded by stating that it does not agree with the taxpayer's method of computation or the amount which is taxable. In most cases where the taxpayer has a defensible position it is to his benefit to file aggressively and claim the type of tax treatment which is most beneficial to his circumstances. At no time does this represent tax evasion. Rather, it is the essence of the process of communication and disclosure between a citizen and the government. In many cases, the use of a knowledgeable tax accountant or lawyer can result in the savings of many hard-earned dollars (see Chapter Fourteen).

Tracking Income and Expenses

Tracking is a process with which any auditor is familiar. It means being able to trace income or expenses back to supporting documentation. Your $20,000 of stocks could have come from any of several sources, including an inheritance, savings of after-tax dollars, borrowed funds or through a loan from a spouse. All of these are legitimate and you are only required to be able to associate the investment with a reasonable source of funds if so requested. Tracking, therefore, means documents or the creation of paper.

Revenue Canada uses the processes of tracking and matching to trace the flow of income from one taxpayer to another. This can easily be done with computer programs which register, for instance, the T-4 employment income as reported by an employer and trace it to each individual employee to see that it is reported on his or her personal tax return. Such matching is also typically done to associate a deduction for alimony payments to the recipient's return, which must report the receipt of that same income. Any discrepancies, of course, immediately result in an examination and it remains for the taxpayer to explain why the income was not reported.

Tracking procedures are also employed for investigations which do not require the use of a computer. The more documents, papers or records which exist, the more easily a flow of income, expense or cash can be traced. This is why failing to report income for which you've received a T-4 makes so little sense and why successful tax evasion is really a complicated and time-consuming process. Good tax planning is a much more intelligent alternative.

You should note that tracking is not only a tool to be employed by the Department of National Revenue. It is also useful in protecting yourself against a successful reassessment. For example, documents which support loans between spouses (see pages 50 to 52) or business expenses should be carefully maintained for a period of several years. Of course, the more complicated and intricate your financial affairs become, the more careful you should be that supporting evidence is carefully documented. Personal records should generally be kept for at least four years and business records for no less than seven.

So much paper is generated in our society today that it is difficult to avoid circumstances which would allow significant sums of income to be traced to you. For example, assume that you inherit $10,000. There may not be substantial documentation as far as this transaction is concerned since there are no longer any estate taxes or provincial succession duties (outside of the Province of Quebec). Assume, then, that you take your $10,000 and acquire a parcel of vacant land. Unless you are a developer, interest and taxes on vacant land are not deductible in Canada and therefore, your ownership of this property is not something that would ordinarily appear on your income tax returns. Finally, assume that this land is held for five years and then is sold for $100,000. Of course, there are deeds which would probably indicate both your cost and selling price but unless your affairs are audited in detail it is unlikely that Revenue officials will ever see these documents. Assume that you therefore decide that there is a good chance of not getting caught if you fail to report your $90,000 profit. To this point, we admit that your chances are pretty good but then where do you go from here? Your funds could not then be put into a bank account, or the banking records themselves would indicate that there has already been a flow of unreported income. For example, if your $100,000 of "capital" generates $15,000 of interest income (reported in the following year by the bank on a T-5 slip) you will then get a letter from Revenue Canada asking you to explain the source of your investment capital. You can see that the web becomes more tangled as you go along.

Basically, you cannot conveniently obtain unreported income, keep it or spend it, without creating some kind of record. Even if you use these funds to buy yourself a house or a fancy car where there are generally few income tax records, you are still open to a net worth assessment. In fact, we are aware that during one audit of a Mercedes Benz dealership in a major Canadian city a few years ago, Revenue Canada officials took a listing of all customers who bought their cars for cash. The presumption, of course, is that an expensive purchase would not normally be made by an individual carrying large cash sums on his person. If someone has nothing to hide, they would ordinarily pay by cheque.

In contrast, barter is the one type of exchange that is extremely difficult to trace or administer. Where goods are exchanged for services it is extremely difficult to isolate or value them. This is a factor in the increasing popularity of collections of artworks, gold and silver. However, by its very nature, barter is extremely difficult to carry out on a large scale and it is therefore often of limited practicality.

Moving Assets Out of Canada

The avalanche of interest in moving assets outside of Canada results from the desire for personal privacy as well as a perceived need to maintain the security of these assets. Some people feel that the Canadian economy is perilously close to a collapse as government deficits keep mounting and business failures increase by leaps and bounds. While this way of thinking is relatively new to the majority of Canadians, spreading assets is the accepted wisdom among affluent people in many other countries. In many instances, storing assets outside the country of residence has been the key to self-preservation during periods of war and financial catastrophe. Fortunately, at this time, it is still reasonably easy for us in North America to make these types of arrangements. Whether it is really necessary to do so, is *your* decision.

Portability of assets is discussed elsewhere in this book. The main problem is that at the time that you may desperately need to move your assets, you are least likely to be able to do so. The most logical approach, therefore, is to arrange to put your assets where you want them in the first place, rather than at a later, more inopportune time.

The motivation to move assets out of Canada should not specifically be to avoid income taxes, since Canadian residents are subject to tax on their world incomes no matter where earned. Your real interest should be in maintaining the security of some of your assets by putting them in a country whose financial and political attitudes are different from the way ours are presently or the way you see them developing in the future. It is also possible that this other country's attitude towards taxation may be considerably different from that of Canada.

It is important that you clarify in your own mind exactly why you might want to move assets to another country. Variations in these reasons can greatly influence the type of arrangements that should be considered. If your concern is a potential currency collapse at home, then it is likely that the use of a Swiss bank account would be more practical than, say, an investment in U.S. real estate. If you are concerned about the political and economic climate in Canada and believe that the United States represents greater investment potential, then an investment in U.S. real estate may be more practical than an "offshore" bank account. Thus, all of your motives and desires must be fully considered before any specific decision can be taken.

Moving Assets to the United States

Canadians usually choose to move assets to the United States by either opening U.S. bank accounts or by investing directly in U.S. real estate. In both cases, they then have a specific sum of money isolated within the boundaries of the United States. A deposit in a bank account in the United States differs from an account which is maintained in American dollars at a Canadian bank. The only reason to consider a bank account in the United States is that it is in another country. It can provide funds for use while you are travelling and can also furnish a store of security if the Canadian government ever imposes currency export restrictions. Income earned on your funds is nevertheless taxable in Canada and records of your account would likely be made available to officials of the Canadian government if requested. If moving funds to the United States has some appeal, you will find that a U.S. bank account is not only easy to open but is also relatively accessible. Most people today are familiar with keeping their own bank accounts so there is nothing exotic in their workings.

An investment in U.S. real estate should be evaluated in the same way as you would any other real estate investment. The fact that it is located in the United States may give you some degree of psychological security in that it is situated outside Canada; however, it is subject to the tax regulations of both Canada and the United States and can create tremendous problems in compliance. Also bear in mind that real estate is generally an extremely illiquid investment.

Many Canadians have bought real estate in the United States with the intention of eventually moving there and making it their residence for at least part of the year. Naturally, any income that is earned from the property will be taxable in Canada and if the individual leaves this country on a permanent basis, the value of an investment in foreign real estate, as well as that of any additional holdings in other countries, will have to be considered for tax purposes upon departure.

On the whole, we believe that U.S. real estate represents more of an interesting investment than it does a means of securing your assets outside of Canada. This is so because Canada and the United States are so closely interrelated that moving assets into the United States does not entirely protect you from what you anticipate may happen in Canada. The Canadian and U.S. economies are so closely associated that protecting yourself against North American decline generally means looking beyond North America itself.

Moving Assets to Switzerland

The major alternative to opening a bank account in the United States is to open one in Switzerland. Spreading your risk by maintaining part of your wealth in Switzerland has much to recommend it because of that country's past history of financial security and government restraint.

Swiss banks can make three types of accounts available to you in the same way that you would use them at home. The first is a current account where the balance may be maintained in one of several different currencies including (but not limited to) Canadian dollars, U.S. dollars, or Swiss francs. These accounts generally do not bear interest, but the entire balance can be withdrawn at any time without penalty.

If you are concerned about earning interest, then a Swiss franc deposit account is more suitable. This is similar to the typical savings account but, because the franc is so stable, the interest rate paid is very low. The objective of having Swiss francs in a deposit account, however, is not usually the receipt of interest income. Instead, such an account represents the opportunity to benefit from fluctuations in the valuation of international currencies. The stability of the Swiss franc has made it a particularly attractive investment which may appreciate considerably as the values of other currencies decline.

As with Canadian banks, custodial accounts are also available. These are opened for the purpose of storing and safekeeping investments such as stocks, gold, silver, etc. You pay a very small storage and insurance charge and the bank brokers your investments for you. You can also purchase investments in other countries through your Swiss bank account. However, because the commission charges are usually so much higher than if you bought these investments directly, you have to consider what your purpose was in opening the account in the first place.

In several major cities across Canada there are consultants who will make arrangements and open accounts with Swiss banks on your behalf. Also, the Swiss Bank Corporation (Canada) has offices in Calgary, Toronto, Montreal and Vancouver. They will open an account for you directly in their affiliate bank in Switzerland.

Using a Swiss bank account will probably be no more trouble and will likely cause you less grief than you have in dealing with your regular Canadian bank. The Swiss have a fetish for efficiency. Your correspondence will be in English, your bank statements will be easy to read, and your instructions carried out promptly. By sending a telegram, you can easily instruct the bank to buy or sell any type of security in which you are interested. You will receive confirmation of all transactions and you can increase your account by simply sending bank drafts or money orders. Withdrawals are also handled efficiently and a transfer of funds can be effected to or from anywhere in the world that you choose.

It is no secret that the Swiss are careful to maintain the privacy of their customers. An account maintained in your name would not be subject to the scrutiny of any foreign government unless a court order could be obtained to extract information about your account. Such a court order would not be issued unless evidence could be presented to prove that a crime has been committed. Even then, bank secrecy would be maintained unless that crime is recognized by Swiss law. The Swiss have never imposed laws against owning gold, transacting in securities, trading in commodities or any other financial activities which have, at various times, been restricted by other governments. In addition, it is worth noting that simple tax evasion is not considered to be a criminal offense in Switzerland. However, matters of fraud and extortion fall outside the realm of mere tax evasion.

Several times in the past decade, the Swiss government has

imposed a so-called negative interest tax on new bank deposits. This was done to stem the tide of money which was flowing into Switzerland from other countries. This penalty was, however, removed on November 29, 1979 and there are presently no limits on the size of accounts which may be opened. Also, when sanctions have been applied in the past, they have been directed primarily towards new accounts or to large additional deposits. Therefore, it is unlikely that existing balances would be affected if such a tax is again imposed in the future.

Tax Havens

A tax haven is a country which does not impose income tax either on a personal or corporate level. Such locations include, for instance, Costa Rica, the Grand Cayman Islands or the Channel Islands. Until 1976, it was generally possible for a Canadian to place his investment capital into a corporation set up under the laws of a tax haven country. The investment income generated by such a corporation was not subject to Canadian taxation until it was brought back into Canada. However, in 1976, the law changed and rules were introduced so that the investment income of a *closely held* foreign corporation is, from that time on, attributed back to the shareholders at the time the income is earned.

In retrospect, however, perhaps the government did not go far enough in tightening up the rules. The attribution of income does not apply to investment income earned by a foreign corporation as long as no single group of five or less unrelated Canadian shareholders controls the company. Thus, offshore investment funds which pool together capital contributed by *many* taxpayers are starting to gain in popularity. These can offer a substantial tax deferral as well as an overall tax reduction.

The basic idea of such a fund is to put together a number of unrelated investors (more than five) who combine to become shareholders in a company that will be managed from a tax haven. It is important that the managers not be resident in

Canada. Once the investment capital is placed into such a corporation, the fund may invest in a variety of securities, including Canadian as well as foreign holdings. Generally, such a set-up is suitable for an investor who will not require either his capital or his investment income within the following few years. Thus, income earned may be reinvested to earn additional income. Then, as long as compounded earnings are not returned to Canada, this income will also escape taxation.

If the fund is public and the shares are widely held, the profits may be left to accumulate in the tax haven corporation thereby resulting in a constantly increasing share value. If a particular investor eventually decides to redeem or sell his shares, his profit (representing his accumulated earnings) will usually be taxed as a capital gain. Thus, even in the final analysis, only *one-half* of the accumulated earnings accruing on behalf of each investor will be taxable.

In most cases, such a fund will require a minimum investment of between $25,000 and $100,000, although it is quite conceivable that several investors could pool their funds to acquire a single unit.

The advantages of such an investment can be illustrated with a simple example. Assume that a taxpayer in a 50% bracket makes a $100,000 investment which provides a pre-tax yield of 14% compounded semi-annually. After taxes, this would ordinarily work out to a net return of only 7%. After ten years, he would have a total of $199,000 of investment capital.

On the other hand, if the investment yield is not eroded by taxes, the initial capital of $100,000 invested at 14% would amount to just under $425,000. In other words, the return after ten years is more than double. After fifteen years, the net return is almost triple. Even if the investment is then cashed in and returned to Canada, where an effective tax of 25% is applied against the capital gain (that is, a 50% tax on half the gain) the after-tax difference in the repatriated investment is still very substantial.

Several public "offshore" funds have been marketed in the last few months offering the advantages just described. Of course, before you think about participating in any particular fund, you should ensure that the people administering the investments are ethical and reputable.

It should be noted, however, that individuals and their families cannot legitimately attempt to earn investment income through closely held offshore corporations without Canadian taxes being imposed. This is because of the Canadian income tax rules already mentioned, which would require "passive" income to be reported in the hands of the Canadian investors as it is earned.

Whether one can escape Canadian taxation on *business income* by using corporations set up in tax haven countries depends on the nature of the specific activity. If there is no real business reason for an offshore corporation, again the rules of the Canadian Income Tax Act will force such income to be reported for Canadian tax purposes when it is earned. Offshore corporations do carry a degree of glamour and prestige. From a practical standpoint, however, they are not really of much relevance to most Canadians.

CHAPTER FOURTEEN

Choosing a Professional

Locating and working with a professional, be it an accountant, doctor or lawyer, can be both time-consuming and expensive. In too many instances, it is also a frustrating and unsatisfactory experience for the client. This chapter is not designed to give you the traditional advice of dealing only with people of high integrity and long-standing reputations. Instead, we hope to provide you with some practical information on how to use a professional, what to expect, what *not* to expect and how to stay in control of your own affairs.

When to Seek Advice

Not everyone needs the ongoing services of an accountant, lawyer or tax specialist. However, there are certain instances in each person's life where expert advice is required. Too often, serious problems are created because the individual does not want to incur the expense of seeking professional help even if he knows that it is really needed. Very often, it then becomes virtually impossible to undo the damage that has already been done. Thus, if you know that you are approaching a situation which could have major tax or legal implications, then by all means, seek advice *before* you have committed yourself irrevocably to a course of action. If you are adequately prepared and can explain your situation thoroughly and completely, then your fees will be kept to a minimum.

If you are about to receive any large sum of income or if you are planning to join or leave a business, then we suggest that you contact an accountant *before* the event actually takes place. In fact, many people regularly have an accountant review their financial affairs once every few years just to be certain that they are taking advantage of every possible opportunity to protect their financial well-being. Certainly, a tax and investment check-up becomes virtually mandatory when there is a substantial change in the law such as that which came about as a result of the November 12, 1981 Budget.

What to Expect

In dealing with any professional, you should expect the work to be performed promptly and competently, and to be explained to you, as well, in unmistakable everyday terms. Certainly, the cost of professional services can be expensive, but if you are provided with the necessary information and protection the cost is certainly worth it. Since part of your fees is a payment for service, you should expect a high degree of attention whenever you deal with any professional. The professional should show interest in your individual perspectives and an understanding of your individual desires. You must recognize that in many cases, there is simply no single solution that is correct in the circumstances and that a choice must be made that will best suit you as an individual.

You should also expect the professional to provide you with technically reliable information and to tell you in which instances further research will be required. When it comes to research, professional help becomes expensive and it is in your best interest to define your situation as carefully as you can so that unnecessary work is not performed.

When you are looking for advice, a high degree of technical capability is *not* necessarily the most important characteristic of the professional you choose. Instead, the key is a sharing of personal rapport. No matter how qualified a person may be, if you simply feel you are not able to communicate with him or explain your true feelings, or if that person is simply not interested in your affairs, then you are most likely dealing with the wrong adviser. A lack of interest on the part of the professional could leave you with technically sound advice which is simply not tailored to your personality and interest. For example, a professional investment counsellor might feel that your best potential investment at a particular time is to buy a certain stock in a South African gold-mining company. However, if you are uncomfortable in investing in the Canadian stock market at the best of times, you certainly wouldn't feel happy committing any portion of your funds overseas. In other words, the only proper advice in many cases is that which you as a client can reasonably expect to live with and follow.

In any given situation, there is a considerable span of tax and financial advice that can be given, ranging from the most conservative to the most aggressive. Often, the average accountant in public practice does not have the time to develop an expertise in tax and he may provide you with information that you feel is too conservative. If you look for specialized advice, be sure that you clarify your expectations and the type of planning that you would feel most comfortable with. If your own accountant cannot help you, ask him to recommend someone else for you to consult.

On the subject of fees, you will definitely get what you pay for. Solid advice and expert planning are not available at cut-rates. If you know that you have a specific interest or problem, then you ought to look for the best help to meet your needs. Furthermore, beware of situations where the consultant may have a distinct conflict of interest. In other words, you cannot be sure that you are getting independent tax advice from a person who is also trying to sell you a tax shelter in which he has a personal financial interest.

Finally, you should also expect that the person with whom you are dealing should take enough interest in your circumstances to look beyond your immediate questions and make more far-ranging suggestions if they are warranted. Even if you only use an accountant to prepare your tax return, you should make sure that he feels a responsibility for pointing out some of the more obvious ways in which you could be saving tax dollars. For example, if the same accountant prepares tax returns for a married couple and he notices that the husband has $2,000 of interest income while the wife has nothing, it appears only reasonable for the accountant to explain the advantages of having both the husband and wife earn $1,000 a year. This would lead to an explanation of the rules covering loans between husbands and wives (see pages 50 to 52). This may not amount to a full-scale personal evaluation, but the accountant should certainly be prepared to tell you that you can benefit from making a bit of an effort. You may not want to authorize a complex tax check-up, but at least, you should have the satisfaction of knowing that someone is interested in your financial affairs and is willing to extend some information to you.

What Not to Expect

Simply put, it is not always possible for an adviser to tell the client what he wants to hear. Sometimes, there is no way to alter or improve the present position and in certain cases large amounts of income taxes are just not avoidable. This, in itself, however, can be valuable information because it will give you a basic understanding from which you can go on to make further personal decisions.

Do not expect any responsible professional to give you specific advice on tax evasion. Many times, a client will create his own problems by not seeking tax advice at the proper time and when he finds out just how heavily his actions are going to cost him, he looks for any alternative. However, falsifying documentation or altering records is clearly a criminal offense and these are not the types of suggestions that you should be expecting from your adviser. In some cases, an accountant or lawyer can only help you try to make the best of an already bad situation.

Along these lines, something should be mentioned about confidentiality. Lawyers have a privileged relationship with their clients so that what is explained to them in confidence may not generally be demanded as evidence in court. However, the accountant and his client do not enjoy this same privilege of association. Thus you must understand that whatever information you give your accountant, be it verbal or written, is open to subpoena. Naturally, any accountant is reluctant to provide information, and most certainly he would not voluntarily disclose personal information about you to third parties. However, your accountant should not be used as your confidant if there is any likelihood that the information would reveal that you are not following perfectly legitimate practices.

How to Stay in Control

Many times an adviser's reputation or the size of his fees will so intimidate the client that he does not feel confident in asking all questions in sufficient detail. If anything, expensive fees should entitle you to get every bit and piece of information necessary to understand your situation fully. No matter how large the reputation of the professional or how lavish his office, remember that he is still just a person who has been hired by you to perform a service. See to it that you get it.

Be sure that you understand completely the planning or advice which is being given to you. Don't allow your ego to prevent you from asking necessary questions even if you think they are basic or simple. If the adviser uses a term with which you are unfamiliar, don't hesitate to ask for a definition. Make the adviser repeat the same information several times or commit it to writing if necessary, so that in the final analysis you feel comfortable. If you are not receiving the type of advice you are looking for, or if you are unhappy with the level of service you are receiving, then the first thing to do is to communicate your dissatisfaction to the accountant or lawyer whom you are using. That person should be interested enough to try to straighten out the matter with you. However, if he does not or if you are still dissatisfied, then simply fire him. Some small extra expense may be necessary to acquaint your new adviser with your situation and your personal interests. However, in the long run, you will be better served.

There are many instances when it is advisable for two people involved in the same business or investment transaction *not* to use the same tax adviser or lawyer. Certainly, business partners should use the same accountant to prepare financial statements. However, independently, they could have concerns which produce conflicts of interest. For example, where there are majority and minority shareholders, it may be difficult for the person in the minority position to be sure that he is getting legal and accounting advice best suited to his personal interest if he is using the same adviser as his majority partners. The same consideration applies to other circumstances, such as where a husband and wife carry on business together or, where a partner's other business interests may prevent a specific professional from giving unbiased professional service.

Interestingly enough, the problem of conflicts of interest is one that must be recognized where major corporate executives receive personal tax advice from the same firm that does the audit of their company. Remember that the audit client represents the bread-and-butter income to the accounting firm and the executive may therefore find that he is receiving overly conservative advice. Frequently, aggressive advice has a certain degree of risk built into it and an executive who finds himself in an argument with Revenue Canada could take out his frustrations by opposing the reappointment of the accounting firm as auditors for his company. As a general rule, therefore, we recommend that executives should forgo the benefits of having their company's accountants give personal advice. It is often true that the cost of such personal advice, when provided by the company's accountant, is simply buried as part of the audit fee. In other words, it is not reflected on the executive's personal T-4 slip as a taxable benefit. On the other hand, if the company pays the costs of an independent adviser who renders services on behalf of the executive, such amounts may be more easily assessed as taxable benefits. This increases the cost of such a service to the executive. However, again consider that you only get what you pay for.

How to Minimize Fees

Every client has to be concerned about how much he pays his adviser and he should make sure that he is receiving a commensurate level of service. You can minimize your costs by being thoroughly prepared before you go to the first meeting. First, have in mind your specific goals. Know what you want to accomplish and have some questions which are geared towards that end. Second, organize your information early and bring in as many documents as are available and pertinent to the situation. These would include your income tax return for the previous year, a personal statement of net worth and any financial statements or legal documents that are relevant. Then, be candid about your family situation, your personal interests, and the objectives that you have in mind. Be explicit about how aggressive you are willing to be in your planning. Don't wait until the last minute before seeking the professional advice that you require. Work that must be done quickly and under pressure can lead not only to premium billings, but may be sloppy or slipshod in the final analysis. Be concise and direct in your requests. Numerous useless phone calls can get to be very expensive. If you are on friendly terms with your adviser, you may find that a comfortable lunch may very well get you a little bit of free advice. However, don't expect to get extensive or sophisticated counsel at no cost.

How to Hire a Professional

There is no easy way to locate the right person for you to deal with. In all cases, it becomes a matter of trial and error. If there are substantial amounts of money involved or if you are looking for either a tax adviser or a lawyer to work with on an ongoing basis, then you may be able to do a little comparison shopping. Talk to, say, three different accountants who have been recommended to you and try to determine whether any of them suit your requirements and share your personal attitudes. If not, then keep looking. If you have a long-standing relationship with a particular professional or firm and you have become seriously dissatisfied, then try to resolve the matter before going elsewhere. However, if this is not possible then try to interview a few people who have been recommended by close personal friends. The disadvantage to this is that it is not a normal practice and many professionals may be reluctant to spend considerable amounts of time with you on a no-fee basis. However, if they recognize that you could be an important long-term client, they ought to be willing to set aside a half-hour to discuss your general situation. Even if you encounter one or two professionals who are unwilling to have an exploratory meeting, keep in mind that it is your money and you are entitled to the best that it will buy.

If you have a large tax reassessment or a serious argument with the tax department, you may find that one of the big national accounting firms will provide you with the best support. While there are several excellent independent tax practitioners across the country, the name and reputation of a big firm does tend to carry extra weight in special circumstances.

Do not necessarily rely on finding people who are involved in your neighbourhood, church, or social groups. While a true professional will not discuss your personal affairs with friends and neighbours, there is still the possibility of conflicts of interest. What happens, for example, if you try to negotiate to buy or sell a business to someone who, by coincidence, also happens to be a member of your church organization and that other person is also represented by the same accountants or lawyers?

Women who seek specialized tax or legal advice will often feel more comfortable and have a better rapport with a female professional. However, in all instances, you should seek the best advice tempered by personal confidence and not necessarily look for a representative of any particular interest group.

Summary

Before you seek the advice of a professional, you should be thoroughly prepared to present your problem completely and succinctly as well as being able to provide all of the necessary details. In this way, not only will you minimize the costs of these services, but you will also clear away a lot of the confusion and be able to deal with your advisers in an intelligent and straightforward manner.

If you decide that you are not satisfied with the service you are receiving—either because there is a marked degree of disinterest, or because you do not have sufficient rapport, or feel that you are being condescended to—then make it clear that you will seek better service elsewhere. When you are dealing with large amounts, perhaps the cost of a second opinion is warranted. Always remember that professionals, whether individuals or firms, are hired by you to perform specific services. Since you are the one who is paying, remember that a hired man can be fired if the "employer" does not get what he pays for.

If you have realistic expectations and a willingness to act upon sound advice, you can get a great deal from any professional relationship. Most important, be aware of those instances in which you do need access to top-quality professional advice. Do not wait until you have already committed yourself to a particular transaction or until the tax authorities are knocking on your door. Once you have made a commitment to do something, it is generally too late to change things around. At that point, the accountant or lawyer simply has no choice but to serve to help you record the transaction and to comply with the law. It is your money. Plan to get the most for it.

CHAPTER FIFTEEN

The Investment Clime for 1983

"I am relying primarily on the dynamism and creativity of the private sector to bring about durable recovery." So said the Honourable Marc Lalonde, Minister of Finance, as he tabled his first major federal Budget in the House of Commons on the evening of April 19, 1983. While staunchly maintaining that economic recovery has already begun, Mr. Lalonde nevertheless predicted that unemployment would average 12.4% in 1983 and not less than 11.4% in 1984. According to government estimates, inflation is expected to average 6.3% this year and 5% in 1984.

From the government's fiscal standpoint, there was good news and bad news. The deficit for 1982/83 ended up at "only" $25.3-billion, some $2-billion less than forecast in February 1983. On the other hand, the 1983/84 budgetary deficit is forecast to rise to $31.3-billion, of which Mr. Lalonde attributes just under $2-billion dollars to "stimulative measures" contained in his Budget.

From an investor's standpoint, Mr. Lalonde proposed significant changes in two specific areas. The first is the Registered Home Ownership Savings Plan (RHOSP) which we discussed briefly in Chapter Six. The second is the Indexed Security Investment Plan (ISIP), which for many Canadians, may become a very appropriate method for investing in the Canadian stock market. Both of these programs will be dealt with in detail later in this chapter.

Unfortunately, in our opinion, Mr. Lalonde had very little room to manoeuvre. We feel that there are two missing factors without which it is impossible to spark a sustained economic recovery. The first is the expectation of at least *modest inflation*. Think back to the late 1970s. If you walked into a store and you were undecided whether to buy something, the salesman made his sale by simply telling you about the 10% price increase slated for the following month. In other words, the expectation of higher prices *forced* you to *buy now* and, possibly, *pay later*. Today, the psychology is somewhat different. If you don't buy today, you say to yourself, perhaps the price will be *cheaper* tomorrow. In fact, if the merchant can't sell his product and goes bankrupt, you can count on getting a real bargain.

A healthy economy needs at least some expectation of inflation in the minds of consumers. Unfortunately, governments in North America have done *too* good a job in solving the inflation problem. There is no longer a rush to spend money.

A second major stumbling block impeding recovery is the lack of a fixed interest rate. You are no doubt familiar with the old cliché, "Once bitten, twice shy." Few people are willing to risk substantial debt commitments as long as future interest rates are, at best, uncertain. How can the construction industry recover if developers are afraid to borrow for long-term projects? How can even a small business commit itself to a plant expansion or the acquisition of inventory if the owner can't budget his interest costs within a range any narrower than perhaps five or six percentage points?

The government refuses to give us any assurances whatsoever. In his Budget Papers, Mr. Lalonde projects an average interest expense over the next three years of *$20-billion a year*. However, his "fiscal plan" states the following: "As interest rate movements are extremely difficult to predict, the level of public debt charges in the planning period should be viewed as a highly tentative projection." If the Canadian government, which has the largest interest expense of anyone, doesn't know how to forecast *its* expenditures, how can private businesses handle theirs?

You might ask why Mr. Lalonde is so powerless. The answer is simply that Ronald Reagan hasn't told him what the interest rate will be this year, next year, or the year after. And this is probably because Ronald Reagan *himself* doesn't know. It depends who his advisers are at any particular time and what they think. If there is one thing that we have learned in the last two years, it is that, economically speaking, Canada has virtually no independence whatsoever.

In a nutshell, then, the two missing ingredients for economic recovery are the expectation of at least modest inflation and a stable interest rate. If even one of these two factors comes into play, we may see a much more vibrant investment climate in the future.

Two Important Changes—RHOSPs and ISIPs

In contrast to the now infamous Budget of November 1981, which was brought down by Mr. Lalonde's predecessor, the Honourable Allan J. MacEachen, the spring 1983 Budget contains nothing that is particularly offensive to any group. However, despite the fact that the government has stopped clobbering the business and investment communities with tax changes for the moment, this is not a recovery budget. How can unemployment be reduced while government policies continue to curtail inflation? And yet, we must have some sympathy for Mr. Lalonde. He certainly has his hands tied as a result of the large deficits which he has inherited. Measured in hundred-dollar bills, a deficit of $30-billion represents a pile *over five times the height of Mount Everest*.

While the Budget may not produce any economic miracles, it has proposed important changes in two popular areas of investment—home ownership and stocks. The following sections will explore the latest opportunities presented by the Registered Home Ownership Plan and the new Indexed Security Investment Plan.

Changes in the Registered Home Ownership Savings Plan

In order to encourage people who don't already own residential real estate to acquire homes quickly, Mr. Lalonde made special concessions to individuals who buy newly constructed homes between April 20, 1983 and December 31, 1984. These individuals will be able to claim a one-time special deduction from income of $10,000 less all tax-deductible RHOSP contributions made in previous years. So, an individual who has contributed $4,000 prior to 1983 will now be able to claim an additional lump sum $6,000 deduction if he buys a new home within the specified period. Technically, an individual who has not made any contributions in the past, but is otherwise eligible, can obtain a full deduction of $10,000 in one year. The deduction will apply not only to the purchase of a home, but also to the furniture you buy to put in it. Such furniture will include normal household furniture and appliances, curtains, drapes, rugs and carpeting, but not home entertainment equipment, computers or outdoor appliances and furniture.

There are, however, a few catches. First, if an individual or his spouse owned a dwelling anytime after 1981, they are ineligible to make the lump sum contribution. Second, if a dwelling is eligible for *either* the grant *or* the special RHOSP contribution, but not both. Finally, in a case of a married couple or any other joint purchasers, only one person will be able to make use of the special contribution. Occupancy of the home must take place no later than February 28, 1985 although anyone who has signed a purchase agreement prior to April 20, 1983, will be eligible as long as the date of closing was not before that day.

Home Furnishings

Because the government wants to encourage consumer spending, individuals who have RHOSPs will also be able to withdraw all or part of their accumulated savings to buy new home furnishings and appliances before January 1, 1984, even if they do not purchase a new home. You will not be required to close your plan for such withdrawals and any amounts taken out will not affect your eligibility to make tax-deductible contributions in the future. However, anyone withdrawing funds in order to buy furnishings in 1983 will not be able to claim an RHOSP deduction for contributions made after April 19, 1983 and before December 31, 1983. Qualifying furnishings must be delivered no later than February 29, 1984 and any taxpayer taking advantage of these rules will be required to include sales receipts along with his 1983 tax forms. Any RHOSP withdrawals not spent on household furniture and appliances (or the other furnishings described in the previous section) will be subject to tax.

The Indexed Security Investment Plan (ISIP)

To fully benefit from Chapter Eight, Investing in the Stock Market, you should review it in light of the new Indexed Security Investment Plan which was also unveiled by Finance Minister Lalonde as part of his spring federal Budget.

The ISIP program is due to take effect on October 1, 1983. It appears that if this plan is introduced, it will become the most effective way for many individuals to invest in Canadian publicly-traded common stocks.

The basic mechanics are straightforward. Say an investor buys $1,000 of securities at the beginning of the year and these securities increase in value to $1,100 by year end. If the securities were purchased in an ISIP and inflation were 6% over the year, the cost of these securities would be adjusted upwards to $1,060 and the capital gain recognized for tax purposes would become $40 instead of the actual gain of $100.

Under the ISIP proposals, an investor will be permitted to spread his tax on his net gain over several years. Using the numbers in our previous example, the investor, even if he doesn't sell his investment, would be required at the end of the first year to take into account one-quarter of his "real" inflation-adjusted capital gain, or $10. Of course, only one-half of the $10 would be a taxable capital gain. The $30 balance of the real capital gain would then be deferred for tax purposes to later years. As long as the ISIP program is maintained, individuals would generally be required to report only one-quarter of their cumulative inflation-adjusted gains each year.

One-half of any plan administration fees will serve to reduce gains or increase losses. In the same way as the inflation adjustment in an ISIP would reduce a capital gain, it will increase the amount of a capital loss. There will be, however, no restriction on the amount of ISIP losses that can be deducted against income from other sources. This is in contrast to the normal capital loss rules which limit the deductibility of net capital losses to $2,000 of other income.

There are, however, some very important restrictions. First, only individuals and trusts for individuals will be permitted to participate in this program. In other words, corporations that have available investment capital are excluded. Second, although dividends on securities in an ISIP will be eligible on an ongoing basis for the dividend tax credit, they will not be eligible for the annual $1,000 investment income deduction. Thus, an ISIP becomes less attractive for anyone who does not already earn up to $1,000 of Canadian investment income.

HOW THE ISIP WORKS

Purchase of stock	$1,000
Assumed appreciation rate	10%
Assumed inflation rate	6%
After one year	
Value of stock (110% × $1,000)	$1,100
Cost for tax purposes (106% × $1,000)	1,060
"Real" capital gain	$ 40
Gain reportable for tax purposes (25%)	$ 10
Taxable capital gain (50%)	$ 5
Deferred gain ($40 − $10)	$ 30

More importantly, interest on money borrowed for ISIP investments will *not* be tax deductible. This means that you would not ordinarily want to borrow money in order to participate in such a program. However, it appears that the proposed legislation will allow investors to use ISIP assets as collateral for other loans. This could lead to some interesting planning.

Let's say you have $100,000 in Canada Savings Bonds and would now like to move into the Canadian stock market. You could sell your bonds, contribute the cash to an ISIP program out of which qualifying securities would be purchased, and then borrow funds against your ISIP assets to repurchase your bonds. In this manner, it appears that your interest *will become tax deductible*.

The biggest problem, however, is that the proposed legislation does not accommodate situations where the stock market is falling and it then becomes expedient to sell short. Even if you feel this technique is too risky for your own taste, you should still consider selling off your investments if you believe that their values will decline. If the investments in an ISIP are sold off, to the extent that the assets are less than the deferred gain, the difference will then be reportable for tax purposes. This means that gains would be recognized for tax purposes much quicker than at the 25% a year level that the government anticipates.

Moreover, at this point, there is some question as to what the various institutions will charge for administration. If the annual fee is, say, two or three per cent of investment capital, this can be a substantial amount. Even after considering that a portion of the fee would reduce taxes payable, the advantage of the ISIP can easily be dissipated. Whether, in real life, this will occur, only time will tell.

We caution you, however, that although the draft legislation has in fact been released, there can be changes before the plan is eventually implemented in October 1983. So try to keep abreast with changes that are made and attempt to evaluate these before deciding whether or not the ISIP program appeals to you.

CHAPTER SIXTEEN

Awareness and Discipline — The Keys To a Successful Investment Strategy

Most of us are now painfully aware that the Canadian investor today is in a significantly different position than he was in the 1970s. Although the investment climate is fraught with uncertainty, anyone who permits himself to be immobilized by insecurity will be unable to take advantage of the many varying opportunities to capitalize on especially difficult situations. The recent recession should have taught all of us to put our financial houses in order and to be prepared to alter our investment strategies as necessary over the rest of the decade.

In troubled times such as these, where do you begin to construct an investment strategy? Because the investment climate and the economy are subject to rapid and drastic change, your strategy must of necessity be short-term, flexible and well-timed. The only long-term investments we have dealt with in this book are real estate and collectibles — and then only if they suit the specific objectives of the investor. While gold and silver can be held as long-term investments, they also present opportunities for substantial profit from short-term fluctuations. Similarly, the stock market, bonds, commodities and options lend themselves to profit-making both in good times and in bad. Even the investments within an RRSP can be changed as investment conditions fluctuate. The advantage of any short-term program is that if your assumptions about the investment are incorrect, you are able to quickly liquidate and re-establish yourself in a more profitable position. Time and time again, we have stressed the necessity of being willing to accept small losses *before* they become large ones.

Of first importance in the creation or reshaping of an investment strategy is the requirement that you carefully examine your present situation. We have strongly encouraged you to use excess income or investment gains to pay off personal mortgages. This is essential in order to provide basic security as well as to eliminate very expensive non-deductible interest and to free-up an asset which has tremendous equity potential. We have also encouraged you to expand your range of choices when you come to think about making investments. We have tried to highlight the fact that many investments which in the past have been considered extremely risky can, in some instances, be made less so.

A successful investor must be flexible and be prepared to alternate between suitable strategies which apply to various economic conditions and trends. The solution to the investment dilemma of the 1980s is certainly *not* to simply maintain interest-bearing investments only. As a matter of fact, as we have demonstrated in Chapter Four, this not only can be extremely expensive from a tax point of view, but it can also cause you to lose most of your money over the long-term.

Of course, there are times such as those which we have recently experienced, where the only immediately correct investment conclusion is to keep cash. Maintaining a "cash only" investment policy is a temporary strategy through which the investor accepts a short-term loss in real purchasing power as insurance against losing even more. However, as soon as the investment climate moves in one direction or another, either for better or worse, the astute investor must recognize the beginning of a change from a period of stagnation to one in which he can then invest in various ways to produce a profitable return.

As we have repeatedly stressed, there is no single investment strategy which is appropriate for all investors, even within a specific investment climate. However, it should be some relief to know that there is no single right answer which we all must desperately seek. Rather, it is a matter of individual attitude and personalized planning. Given the changing times, you must explore areas of investment which you have perhaps not experienced before to determine which of these areas will be profitable to you. Then, we encourage you to be as active as is comfortable for you. Considering new areas need not imply increasingly greater and greater risks. Rather, the idea is to spread your risks over a wide-ranging portfolio of investments, which is designed for balance during the changes in our business cycles. To maintain financial stability, it is no longer possible to simply rely on inflation to produce wealth. What goes up often comes back down again!

In order to move with the times, you must first develop a perspective on what *you* believe is happening in the economy and what is likely to transpire in the reasonably near future. This can be extremely difficult when people all around you are in a state of confusion and doubt. However, we believe that your own instincts are your best starting point and that, from there, you can become educated to make better — although not necessarily more risky — investment decisions.

There is a limit to what any book can do for you. After reading this, it is necessary that you develop the personal experience which will help you decide what type of strategy you are willing and able to live with. Nothing tells you more about yourself than an active involvement in your own investments. Remember that you have the capacity to develop a portfolio which meets your requirements and over which you are still capable of maintaining control without sacrificing either large amounts of time or precious sleep. With this in mind, we encourage you to start by looking at the investment patterns which you have set for yourself over the last ten years or so and review them to see whether they have really suited you in the accomplishment of your objectives. Perhaps they were overly conservative. Consider the possibility that *you* may have changed while your investment strategies have remained fixed. If so, a readjustment may be required to accommodate your current thinking and circumstances. Above all, be flexible and develop your sense of timing. There is an investment strategy for every one of us in the 1980s and we hope that this book has been of some help to you in constructing yours.

Glossary

ADJUSTED COST BASE: The cost of property for tax purposes. This may be either the cost to the taxpayer or the value as of December 31, 1971, subject to any adjustments required by the Income Tax Act.

AMORTIZATION: The allocation of an expense or debt over a period of time.

ANNUITY: A series of regular payments (usually equal) consisting of interest and principal.

APPRECIATION: An increase in the *fair market value* of a property. Compare *capital cost allowance*.

ARM'S LENGTH: Where the parties to a transaction are unrelated by blood, marriage or adoption.

ASSET: A property which is owned and has value.

ATTRIBUTION RULES: A series of tax provisions whereby income generated from property transferred by a husband to his wife (or vice versa) will be reallocated for tax purposes to the person who made the transfer. Similar provisions also apply for transfers to minors.

BENEFICIARY: A person who receives (or is named to receive) money or property from an insurance policy or *will*. A person for whose benefit a *trust* exists.

BOND DISCOUNT: The difference between the face value of a bond and its selling price on the bond market. A bond whose stated annual interest rate is much lower than the prevailing rate is called a "deep discount bond."

BUTTERFLY SPREAD: The use of four separate options to reduce the risk for an investor in the options market. See pages 168–70.

CALL OPTION: The right to buy a stock or commodity at a particular price within a certain time period. Compare *put option*.

CANADIAN-CONTROLLED PRIVATE CORPORATION (CCPC): A company incorporated in Canada where the majority of the shares are not held by non-residents or public companies or by any combination of non-residents and public companies.

CAPITAL COST ALLOWANCE: A provision for depreciation as permitted under the Income Tax Act to recognize wear, tear and obsolescence and to allocate the cost of an asset over the period for which it is useful to generate revenue.

CAPITAL GAINS: The profit realized when certain assets such as real estate and shares of a public or private company are sold for proceeds in excess of cost. A taxpayer's capital gain is measured as the difference between the selling price of property and its *adjusted cost base*. One-half of a capital gain is taken into income when proceeds are received. This is called a taxable capital gain.

CARRYING CHARGES: The costs (such as interest, storage and insurance fees) incurred in maintaining an investment.

CASH SURRENDER VALUE: The amount payable on an insurance policy if the policy is cancelled.

CLASSES OF ASSETS: For tax depreciation *(capital cost allowance)* purposes, assets are divided into pools or groups. Each pool has its own depreciation rate, which is usually related to the useful life of the assets which it contains.

CLOSING: The time that a real estate transaction is concluded legally in a registry office.

COLLATERAL: Stocks, bonds, or other property pledged as security for a loan. A lender has the right to sell collateral in the event of a borrower's default.

COMBINED INDIVIDUAL TAX RATES: Rates (usually expressed in percentages) which take into account the effect of both federal and provincial taxes.

COMMODITY STRADDLE: The purchase of offsetting contracts to shelter the *capital gain* on a particular commodity. See pages 163-65.

CONSIDERATION: Compensation, in the form of gift or payment, for something of value.

CONVERTIBLE BONDS: This type of bond can be exchanged for common stock of the issuing corporation, at a fixed price.

DEEMED DISPOSITION: An event such as death, departure from Canada or the making of a gift, where an individual is considered for tax purposes to have sold his property for *consideration* (generally) equal to its *fair market value*.

DEFERRED ANNUITY: An *annuity* under which payments of principal and interest will only begin some time after the annuity is acquired.

DEFERRED PROFIT-SHARING PLAN (DPSP): An employer-sponsored fringe-benefit program under which up to $3,500 per participating employee may be set aside out of profits in order to provide a *deferred annuity* subsequent to the employee's retirement.

DEPRECIATION: See *capital cost allowance*.

DIVIDEND: A distribution out of after-tax earnings or profits which a corporation pays to its shareholders.

DIVIDEND TAX CREDIT: A reduction from taxes otherwise payable by an individual who receives a dividend from a Canadian corporation. The tax credit takes into account the fact that a dividend is a distribution by a corporation out of previously taxed profits.

EARNED INCOME: The sum of incomes from employment, self-employment, rentals, pensions and alimony minus losses from self-employment and/or rentals. Up to 20% of earned income qualifies for an annual investment into an individual's *registered retirement savings plan* (maximum $5,500).

EFFECTIVE TAXES: Combined federal and provincial taxes as a percentage of total income. (Compare *marginal rate of tax*.)

ELASTICITY: A term which indicates how responsive the demand or supply of a good is to changes in its price. Demand or supply which is responsive to price changes is called "elastic"; if there is little change the demand or supply is considered "inelastic".

EQUITY: The *fair market value* of a property less any financial encumbrances such as *mortgages*.

EQUITY CAPITAL: The funds in a business which have been invested by the owners and not loaned by others.

ESTATE FREEZING: An exchange of assets whereby properties with growth potential are exchanged for properties whose value remains constant from time to time.

ESTATE PLANNING: The orderly arrangement of one's financial

affairs so that assets may be transferred on death to persons designated by the deceased, with a minimum loss of value due to taxes and forced liquidations.

EXECUTOR: A person named in a *will* to carry out the provisions of that will.

FAIR MARKET VALUE: The price for property that a willing buyer would pay to a willing seller on the open market in circumstances where both parties deal at *arm's length* and neither is compelled to transact.

FEE SIMPLE: Absolute ownership of property. Compare *right-to-use* timeshare.

FIRST MORTGAGE: The senior *mortgage*, as established by date and time of registration. It takes precedence over any other in the event of foreclosure.

FRONT-END LOAD: An administration charge for handling investment capital which is levied against the initial contribution(s) to a savings plan, such as an RRSP.

FUNDAMENTAL ANALYSIS: A long-term investment technique used to determine the value of the corporation whose stock is traded (as described on pp. 141–42). Compare to *technical analysis*.

GIFT TAX: A tax imposed on the donor of property where the value of a gift exceeds certain maximum allowable deductions. In Canada, at the present time, only the province of Quebec levies a gift tax.

GROSSED-UP DIVIDEND: When an individual resident in Canada receives a dividend from a Canadian corporation, the amount which is taxable is one and one-half times the actual payment received. The individual is then allowed a *dividend tax credit* approximately equal to the 50% gross-up.

GUARANTEED TERM: A minimum term under which annuity payments are guaranteed. In the case of a life annuity with a guaranteed term, the payments will continue through the guarantee period even if the recipient of the annuity dies before the end of that period.

INCOME-AVERAGING ANNUITY: A special type of annuity designed to spread the impact of Canadian taxation on certain (generally non-recurring) types of lump sum receipts. The

1981 tax changes eliminated the use of such annuities for 1982 and subsequent years.

INDEXED SECURITY INVESTMENT PLAN (ISIP): A new program which will allow investors in Canadian publicly traded common stocks to adjust the value of capital gains and losses to reflect the rate of inflation.

INVESTMENT DEDUCTION: A provision under which the first $1,000 of *arm's length* interest, grossed-up dividends and taxable capital gains received by an individual from Canadian sources is deductible annually in arriving at taxable income.

INVESTMENT PORTFOLIO: All investments that are held by an investor or an investment fund. Taken as a whole, these investments reflect the investment strategy of the individual or group.

KARAT: A measure used to indicate the purity of gold jewellery. Each karat represents a 1/24 portion of pure gold.

LIQUIDITY: Refers to the ease with which an *asset* can be converted into cash without a significant loss.

MARGINAL RATE OF TAX: The combined federal and provincial tax rate that would apply to the next dollar of taxable income earned by a taxpayer in a given year. Compare *effective taxes*.

MORTGAGE: A transfer of property from borrower to lender as security for a loan.

MORTGAGE TERM: The period of time given a borrower before the lender can demand repayment of the *principal balance* still owing on the loan. Compare to *amortization*.

NET INCOME: Gross income from all sources less expenses to earn this income, but before personal exemptions and taxes.

NON-RESIDENT WITHHOLDING TAX: A flat rate of tax imposed on investment income such as interest, rents, dividends and annuities paid to a non-resident recipient. In Canada, the rate of withholding tax is 25% unless reduced by a tax treaty with the country in which the non-resident lives.

PARTICIPATING SHARES: Shares in a corporation which participate in the growth of a business and its assets and on which (theoretically) unlimited dividends may be paid.

PENSION INCOME DEDUCTION: A provision under which the first $1,000 of annual pension income (other than the Canada/

Quebec Pension or the Old Age Pension) is deductible from an individual's income for tax purposes. The pension deduction applies to a pension received after retirement, while amounts received from an RRSP qualify if the recipient is at least sixty-five.

PERSONAL EXEMPTIONS: An automatic deduction permitted to any individual in arriving at taxable income. For 1983, the basic personal exemption is $3,770. There are additional personal exemptions available to individuals who support other dependants, such as a spouse or children.

PERSONAL PROPERTY: Property such as art, jewellery and coin collections, which has been purchased by an individual primarily for his own, or his family's use and pleasure. See also *principal residence*.

PREPAYMENT CLAUSE: Gives the borrower the right to pay additional amounts off the *principal balance* of a loan or *mortgage*.

PRESENT VALUE: A tool used in the analysis of investments to discount future inflows or outflows of money to reflect their value in today's dollars.

PRINCIPAL BALANCE: The outstanding dollar amount owing on a debt.

PRINCIPAL RESIDENCE: A housing unit ordinarily occupied by an individual during a given year and designated as being his (or her) principal residence. Only one such residence may be designated for each year. Where an accommodation which was a principal residence throughout the period of its ownership is subsequently sold, the *capital gain* thereon is exempt from tax. Pursuant to the 1981 tax changes, a family unit of husband and wife can designate only one property at a time as a principal residence.

PUT OPTION: The right to sell a stock or commodity at a particular price within a certain time period. Compare *call option*.

REGISTERED HOME OWNERSHIP SAVINGS PLAN (RHOSP): A savings program whereby qualified individuals may contribute up to $1,000 a year on a tax-deductible basis towards the purchase of a home. A one-time special deduction has been introduced for 1983–84. See Chapter Fifteen.

REGISTERED RETIREMENT INCOME FUND (RRIF): One of the settlement options available to taxpayers over age sixty who wish to draw an annuity from their registered retirement savings plans. Under this option, payments received increase annually until the recipient is ninety.

REGISTERED RETIREMENT SAVINGS PLAN (RRSP): A government-approved program whereby individuals may make annual, tax deductible contributions of up to 20% of their *earned income* to a maximum of $5,500 as a savings towards retirement.

RECAPTURED DEPRECIATION: *Capital cost allowances* previously claimed which are determined (in the year that depreciable property is sold) to be in excess of the actual amount by which the property in question has depreciated.

REFUNDABLE TAX: A portion of corporate taxes previously paid by a private corporation on its investment income. Initially, the investment income is subject to a 50% tax rate although an amount equal to 16% of the investment income is refundable back to the corporation upon payment of dividends to shareholders. The net corporate tax on investment income is thus reduced to 33%.

REPLACEMENT PROPERTY: In certain circumstances, gains on the disposition of property may be deferred for tax purposes if other property (i.e., replacement property) is acquired. The tax cost of the replacement property is reduced by an amount equal to the deferred gain.

RETIREMENT ALLOWANCE: A payment made by a former employer to an employee in recognition of long service or for loss of employment. In some cases retirement allowances may be transferred to *registered retirement savings plans*.

RETRACTABLE PREFERRED SHARES: A holder of a preferred share will receive dividends before the common shareholders receive any return on their investment. The holder of a retractable preferred can redeem it for cash at the end of a stipulated time.

RETURN ON INVESTMENT: The percentage of the original investment cost represented by the after-tax profits earned on that investment.

RIGHT-TO-USE TIMESHARE: Represents ownership for a specific time period, usually fifteen to fifty years. Compare *fee simple*.

ROLLOVER: A transfer of property from one person to another where the tax rules permit a deferral of gains at the time the transfer is made.

SELLING SHORT: The sale of a stock or commodity which the investor does not own, but has "borrowed", in the hope that he can purchase it later at a lower cost.

SMALL BUSINESS TAX RATES: A special incentive available to *Canadian-controlled private corporations* earning *active business income*. The first $200,000 of annual profits is taxed at a 15%–25% rate (the rate varies from province to province), until $1-million is earned cumulatively. (Before 1982, the limits were $150,000 and $750,000 respectively.)

SOFT COSTS: Various specific components of a construction project which may be deducted for tax purposes during a construction period instead of being subject to a long-term write-off through depreciation *(capital cost allowance)*. Soft costs include landscaping, interest on money borrowed during the construction period and certain administrative expenditures.

Only corporations whose principal business activities involve real estate may deduct soft costs for projects initiated after 1981.

SPOUSAL RRSP: An option available under a *registered retirement savings plan* whereby a taxpayer may earmark all or a portion of his annual contributions into a program for his (or her) spouse. This option is designed to ensure future *annuity* benefits for that spouse.

STOP-LOSS ORDER: An order that you place with your broker instructing him to sell an investment for you if the price moves too far in the opposite direction from your projections.

TAX CREDITS: A direct deduction against taxes otherwise payable. Among others, tax credits are available to individuals with respect to Canadian dividends received and to all taxpayers with respect to foreign taxes previously paid on foreign source income.

TAX DEDUCTIBLE: Amounts which may be subtracted in arriving at one's income for tax purposes.

TAX DEPRECIATION: See *capital cost allowance*.

TAX DEFERRED: This refers to opportunities whereby taxes on

income or benefits may be postponed until some future date.

TAX HAVEN: A country which does not impose personal or corporate taxes.

TAX LOSS VS. TAX SHELTER: A tax loss is a loss from business or property which is deductible in arriving at income for tax purposes. A tax loss becomes a tax *shelter* in circumstances where it is created by claiming *capital cost allowances* and does *not* involve an actual outflow of cash or a reduction in the value of one's investment. As a result of recent Budget amendments, the use of tax shelters has been severely restricted.

TAX SHELTERED: Income which is not taxable currently but will be taxed at some future time.

TAXABLE BENEFIT: A benefit provided by an employer to an employee where the value is taxed in the hands of the employee as additional remuneration received.

TAXABLE INCOME: Net income from all sources minus personal exemptions, the investment and pension deductions, a provision for medical expenses and donations, and miscellaneous other deductions. For Canadian corporations, taxable income is computed after deducting dividends received from other Canadian corporations. Taxable income is the base on which income taxes are levied.

TECHNICAL ANALYSIS: A short-term investment technique used to determine the trend of stock prices at a certain time and their current position within that trend (as described on pp. 142–43). Compare *fundamental analysis*.

TERM INSURANCE: Life insurance which only pays if death occurs within a specific time period. There is usually no cash value under such a policy. Compare *whole life*.

TESTATOR: A person who makes a *will*.

TRACKING: Earmarking the flow of borrowed funds to clearly indicate the purpose for which these funds have been used.

TRANSFEREE: A person to whom a transfer of title, rights or property is made.

TRANSFEROR: A person who makes a transfer of title, rights or property.

TREASURY SHARES: Shares which a corporation has the authority to issue but which are still unissued.

TRUST: An arrangement made in a person's lifetime or effective upon death whereby legal title and control of property is placed in the hands of a custodian *(trustee)* for the benefit of another person or group of persons who are known as *beneficiaries* of the trust.

TRUSTEE: A person who acts as custodian and administrator of property held in *trust* for someone else.

UNDEPRECIATED CAPITAL COST: The cost of depreciable assets minus accumulated *capital cost allowances* previously claimed.

VESTING: The process whereby a right to property passes unconditionally to a particular person.

WILL: A legal statement of a person's wishes about what shall be done with his property after he is dead.

WHOLE LIFE: Life insurance which remains in force until the insured dies, irrespective of when this occurs. Whole life insurance policies usually have cash values which increase over time and which may be borrowed against, or for which the policy may be surrendered.

YEAR END: The end of the business cycle each year. For tax purposes, a business must file an annual report disclosing its profits. Initially, the year end may be selected to fall on any date. However, no change in the year end may be made subsequently except with the permission of the Revenue authorities.

YIELD: Return on investment, usually computed as the percentage of the anticipated (or realized) annual income relative to the capital invested.